Watershed

Also by John F. Stacks

TO SET THE RECORD STRAIGHT
(with Judge John J. Sirica)

STRIPPING, THE SURFACE MINING OF AMERICA

WATERSHED

The Campaign for the Presidency, 1980

JOHN F. STACKS

Times
BOOKS

Published by TIMES BOOKS, a division of
Quadrangle/The New York Times Book Co., Inc.
Three Park Avenue, New York, N.Y. 10016

Published simultaneously in Canada by
Fitzhenry & Whiteside, Ltd., Toronto

Library of Congress Cataloging in Publication Data

Stacks, John F.
    Watershed, the campaign for the presidency,
1980.

    Includes index.
    1. Presidents—United States—Election—1980.
2. United States—Politics and government—1977-
1981. I. Title.
E875.S73   1981   324.973'0926   81-50093
ISBN 0-8129-1001-X   AACR2

Manufactured in the United States of America

For Dory, John Jr., and Ben

Acknowledgments

To attempt to make some sense of an American presidential election, it is necessary to actually see the process unfold and to have access to the key people who shape and react to the hundreds of small events that make up the complicated process by which this country chooses its most important leader. For the chance to be present and to record the 1980 presidential campaign, I am deeply indebted to the editors of *Time* magazine who trusted me with the title of national political correspondent and whose guidance, patience, and good sense thus made this book possible.

I am especially grateful to Richard L. Duncan, who as *Time* magazine's chief of correspondents, directly supervised my travels and contributions during the political year. Ray Cave, managing editor of *Time,* and Otto Friedrich, editor of the magazine's "Nation" section during the election year, provided the editorial judgment that shaped the way I covered the presidential campaign. Henry Grunwald, editor-in-chief of Time, Inc. and one of the country's wisest judges of political ideas and personalities, was

ACKNOWLEDGMENTS

generous in approving the rendering of my journalistic endeavors in book form.

No reporter can be present at every event of importance in a political campaign. No one charged with providing an overview of the entire process, as I was, can know each player as well as the specialists assigned to each campaign. My colleagues at *Time,* each of whom covered one candidate or another in great depth over many months, were generous with their own impressions and recollections, both during the campaign itself and afterward as this book was written. My thanks to Chris Ogden, Doug Brew, Johanna McGeary, Walter Isaacson, Eileen Shields, and Laurence I. Barrett. My thanks too to Katharine McNevin, Pam Thompson, and Rudolph Rauch, of Time-Life News Service, for their assistance throughout the campaign and the conventions. And to Jane Keyser, who typed my manuscript, my thanks for her skill and good humor when confronted with impossible deadlines.

Ned Chase, my editor at Times Books, is himself a keen and informed student of American politics. He has, from the beginning, guided and shaped this book with his sound and valuable political and editorial judgment.

When I started out years ago to make a living as a journalist and writer, I served an apprenticeship on the Lancaster *Intelligencer-Journal,* the newspaper my father Harry F. Stacks edited. He was thus my first boss and first editor. For this project he returned to his duties as an editor and, despite his chagrin that his son still lacks any talent for spelling English words, has helped me enormously in the final shaping of this book. And for all that went before, I thank him and my mother, Helena.

J.F.S.
Chevy Chase,
Maryland

Contents

CONTENTS

Foreword

No campaign for the presidency of the United States is quite like those that have preceded it; the characters in the drama are different, the historical setting is, of course, much different, and the format of the whole production is always changing. Yet, there are some things that remain relatively constant. Some voting patterns have a long history of consistency, by both demography and geography. There usually have been certain advantages attached to being an incumbent president and clear disadvantages associated with being the challenger. Organizing the candidate's supporters into a coherent campaign is important, and advertising the candidate's record and positions is thought to be a key element in any campaign. The quality of staff work and harmony within that staff usually is helpful in building a winning effort.

For a journalist attempting to keep up with the candidates, their positions, their staff operations, the changing attitudes and preferences of the American voters, and the changing rules under which campaigns are run, the problem is always to sort out what is important in *that* campaign. There is a huge temptation, as my friend and colleague Richard Reeves once put it, to cover the last campaign, not the one at hand.

In the 1980 election standard truths of American politics were once again shattered. Most important, the notion that the incumbent enjoyed a decided advantage was proven at least a questionable nostrum about American politics. Other patterns too gave way, like the size and dependability of the Democratic vote from the Jewish electorate. Conventional wisdom held, however, in other areas. That the strength of independent and third-party candidates usually fades in the fall was again proved true. That the American people usually vote their pocketbook was still self-evident, meaning in the election that the candidate saddled with the blame for high inflation and rising unemployment had only the slimmest chance of victory.

American presidential campaigns are an endless affair, beginning years before the event and totally preoccupying much of the country's political elite for at least eighteen months before the votes are counted. For all the marathon quality to this process, it seems, in memory, to have been quick and sudden and more like a rapidly rotated kaleidoscope than an interminable, slow-motion film. Events tumble upon each other and each twist of political fortune influences the next turn of political events. Primary results influence subsequent primaries. Misstatements by the candidates reverberate and alter their standing and those of their opponents. Especially in 1980, events external to the campaign—and indeed beyond our shores—played major, perhaps determinate, roles in the outcome of our presidential selection process.

The point of this book then is to try to sort out which patterns of American politics held to form and which changed and why during the 1980 process. Unlike the clamor, speed, and disorder of political journalism, which is plagued by deadlines, by the lack of perspective necessarily attached to analyzing an event before its real impact is clear, by the fatigue of travel and the sheer tedium of watching the same men say the same thing hundreds of times, I hope here to slow down the story so that it makes more sense. I also hope that with this longer look we may know more about the very process we Americans use to choose a president and how that process helps determine the outcome.

Most important, however, is a longer look at the men (there were still no women in serious contention for the presidency) who subject themselves to the process, who have ambition enough to undergo the ordeal of a presidential candidacy, who have hubris enough to think they, above all the rest, deserve to be president of the United States.

I should announce here that I am hopelessly ambivalent about presidential politicians. On the one hand, I admire their pluck, their energy, their determination, the sheer size and heft of their aspiration. On the other hand, I am, like many Americans, suspicious of their motives, doubtful of their capacity to lead, at times appalled by their tactics, their facile misuse of the language, and their gross insincerity. These mixed feelings obviously vary according to the particular candidate, and the exact mix will be clear as these men move through the pages of this book. In the end, however, I can make a kind of generalization about my feelings toward these main characters: They are what this system produces. There are surely better men and women to lead America, but in 1980 the men who thrust themselves forward are the ones the voters—and the journalists—had to listen to, decide among, and try to live with once elected.

In the past much of political journalism has tended either to lionize or to totally discredit our politicians. Not just journalists but our country as a whole tends to swing between poles of contempt and adoration for our politicians. I don't agree with Mencken's rule that the only way to look at a politician is down. I think they have to be looked straight in the eye, seen for what they are and for what they are not nor could ever be. A bit steadier treatment of our politicians may produce less euphoria about their successes but also less disappointment in their performance once in office. I do not believe that winning the presidency is any longer —if it ever was—a sign of particular political and personal virtue. The American system of political selection is too complicated, too unsteady; the level of voter participation is too low, the quality of information about the candidates too poor, to make a hero out of the winner. I believe elections these days are lost more often than won, and that fluke and luck and accident are as important as the great tides of history in deciding their outcome. That Ronald Reagan ascended to the presidency had as much to do with the weaknesses and failures of his opponents as with his own strengths and virtues.

Which brings me back to the first problem the journalist faces: to sort things out. I trust when the reader has finished this book, the 1980 campaign for the presidency will seem a bit clearer than before.

Watershed

Introduction

It was Monday, March 30, 1981. The President of the United States, in office only two months after a triumphant landslide victory in the November election, strode happily out of a Washington hotel. He had just given a speech to a labor group and was moving, smiling and waving, toward the bulletproof limousine in which he would be whisked back to the White House. As he stood poised to enter the car, shots rang out. Ronald Wilson Reagan, the nation's fortieth president, was struck in the chest by a .22 caliber "devastator" bullet. The projectile pierced his lung and lodged a few precious inches from his heart.

It had become so depressingly familiar in America. A political leader rises up, ignites the hope of the nation, and is then felled by a bullet, fired from a cheap gun, held by a young psychopath who has been wandering the country in a fog of loneliness and lunacy, possessed by the need to kill in order to exorcise the demons that possess him.

On that March afternoon the country reacted with practiced

grief. The television networks cleared their airwaves for nonstop, slow-motion replays of the event, a ritual now so necessary to the assimilation of the event. Reagan walking and smiling. The shots. Confusion. White House aide Mike Deaver wincing and ducking for cover. The President shoved into his car by a Secret Service guard. Another Secret Service man struck by a bullet and falling. The gang tackling of the assailant. His arrest. Guns drawn. And on the ground a Washington cop and White House press secretary Jim Brady. Sweet, funny, professional Jim Brady. The press loved the guy. We remembered him from the Hill, from other administrations, from the Connally campaign where he was a counterweight to the candidate's distaste for the press. We knew him from the later stages of the Reagan campaign. We laughed when he could make fun of his own boss. "Killer trees, killer trees," Brady had shouted as the campaign plane flew over a forest fire, mocking Reagan's silly assertion that trees and plants were responsible for most of the nation's air pollution. There was blood on Jim Brady's forehead. There was going to be so much to absorb. The loss of Brady's friendship. The starting over with a new president. The anger at having the tedious and interminable process of selecting a president overruled by a bullet from a cheap gun from a pawn shop in Texas.

But the story quickly veered from its expected, awful path. The wounded President actually got out of his car and walked into the hospital. He cracked movieland jokes on his way to the operating room. "All in all, I'd rather be in Philadelphia," he said, stealing from W. C. Fields. He was out of surgery. The next day he signed official papers. In two weeks he was back in the White House. And Brady too. Against the odds, he progressed, talked, smiled at his wife.

Someone had written a different ending to this script. It was like a Western movie. The hero was "just creased." It was as if this old man was somehow invulnerable to the pattern of tragedy in political life established over the past two decades. It was conceivable that the national run of bad luck had lifted as he came to office. The day he was sworn in, the hostages were released from Iran after fourteen months of captivity. The country was off again on another fresh start.

At the helm was the most improbable president of the twentieth century, a movie actor and a political hoofer, an old man in a nation that revered youth, an innocent in the age of skepticism and cynicism. He arrived in Washington in the twilight of his years, but with boyish good humor and optimism. He took the capital by storm and built a booming popularity despite earlier doubts and reservations about his competence. He replaced the prevailing pessimism with his own pleasant optimism. He seemed an antidote to the times in which he came to power.

The pattern of American politics usually produces a cycle of euphoria around the arrival of a new president. That the spendid glow of his early months couldn't last did not matter so much. That his early appointments were an odd mix of competent conservatives and pious zealots didn't matter. That his understanding of foreign affairs was dangerously simpleminded didn't matter either. Not at first, anyway.

Reagan had come to Washington. And while he was there he would try to fundamentally redirect the role of the federal government. His election was a critical event in American politics, a watershed from which great changes would flow. He would produce, either by design or by inadvertence (for his failures, too, will determine a new direction in American politics), a profound change in the way America is governed. The question is, Just how did this man ascend to the presidency of the United States of America?

SUMMER
1979

1

Malaise

On an enervatingly humid Wednesday, which happened to be the two hundred-third birthday of the nation, the President of the United States virtually disappeared from public view. He had hurried back from a summit meeting in Japan, canceling a vacation stop in Hawaii, to prepare for a major speech on energy policy. He had gone to his mountain retreat at Camp David with his wife, Rosalynn, to review the draft of the message prepared by his speech writers. The two worked together on the speech, as they had on so many projects crucial to Jimmy's career over the years. The pair were truly inseparable. She had bent her entire life to serve his goals. What he wanted, she wanted; what he did, she did, whether taking lessons in Spanish or learning to appreciate classical music. They had sought political office together. Indeed, they governed together.

Rosalynn felt that the speech was adequate, but questioned whether anyone in the country would pay much attention to what it said. He had been over the same ground several times before,

9

to little effect. His program to deal with the crisis was being battered in Congress. The country knew there was a problem with energy supplies and prices. Plagued by long lines at gasoline service stations, the American people were in a sour mood about the whole difficult and complicated situation.

After the Carters talked together about the speech, the President picked up the phone and was connected through the White House switchboard to Vice-President Walter Mondale and to a few of his most trusted aides. Abruptly, he canceled the speech, which had already been scheduled for prime-time network television the next night. He offered no explanation and ordered that no rationale for the change in plans be given to the public. His aides followed his directions, and only the decision to cancel the speech was announced. With that, the most public man in the country, the person around whom all public attention to government and, indeed, around whom the collective life of the nation centered, vanished from view, leaving only the memory of his toothy grin as evidence that the country had a president at all.

During the next several days, military helicopters ferried the top leaders of the Carter government in and out of the Catoctin Mountain presidential resort. There, the Carters questioned their visitors together, scribbled notes on yellow legal pads, and mulled and discussed the plight of the nation and the plight of the nation's president. Locked in the secrecy and luxury of Camp David, Jimmy Carter was attempting, without really knowing it, and certainly without acknowledging it, to salvage his presidency. In the rustic comfort of the retreat, the President and the First Lady were searching for the bit of advice, the idea, the inspiration that could be translated into a speech that somehow would lift the sinking chief executive above the morass of national problems by which he seemed engulfed. It was as if Carter felt that if he could just *say* the right thing, the political problems that had been plaguing him would be eased.

The stream of officials and advisers built to a torrent over the next few days. Leaders from outside the government were soon included. An invitation to one produced the need to invite another, so that feelings and political sensitivities would not be offended. Soon, the process itself was out of Carter's own control, like the real world outside on which he was trying to impose his leadership. Prominent Americans from business, labor, the civil rights movement, and religious institutions were choppered into Camp David to give their thoughts to the President. Even as Carter was trying in this unprecedented way to find the means for restoring confidence in his presidency, the very mysteriousness of his series of encounter groups was causing a near panic in the world outside. The value of the dollar plummeted on world markets. In the incestuous world of official Washington, rumors of presidential disability swirled and were denied.

More than a week later, Carter ended his retreat by flying off to meet with some "average Americans," citizens chosen by the White House staff to discuss the country's problems with the President of the United States. This was a characteristic Carter device, one invented during his long march to the presidency. It allowed the then-candidate to demonstrate his humility and his reverent regard for the common wisdom of free citizens by visiting with just plain folks, staying the night in their homes, making his own bed, and acting for all the world like just any ordinary person. Although Carter seemed to believe strongly in the wisdom and efficacy of these little meetings, they had also been contrived to make clear, back then in 1976, that this was a man, unlike the corrupt Nixon, who wanted to remain close to the people, not insulated by power and its trappings.

But now, with the President in deep political trouble, the meetings with citizens had the air of desperation, not only of a man looking everywhere for help, but also of a politician looking anywhere for the key to the great problem that plagued him: just how to seize control of the country and its problems.

Indeed, the entire Camp David exercise had overtones of some strange religious act of self-flagellation. For the President of the United States was quick to solicit and almost too eager to receive the candid criticisms of all those invited to the summit sessions. Meeting with a select group of journalists the night before he planned to speak to the nation, Carter was unrelenting in criticizing his own handling of the presidency. He took the blame for having a poorly organized cabinet and White House staff, for not making it plain what were the most important items in the laundry list of reforms he sought. He confessed to having not stayed "close to the American people." Carter held fast to the notion that the

11

collective wisdom of the American people could make him a good president, if only he could gather that wisdom to himself.

And so, on July 15, Carter addressed the nation on television. And the nation, ever more curious about just what its president had been doing up there in the mountains, was ready to pay close attention for a change.

"This is a special night for me," he began. "Exactly three years ago on July 15, 1976, I accepted the nomination of my party to run for president of the United States. I promised you a president who is not isolated from the people, who feels your pain, who shares your dreams, and who draws his strength and his wisdom from you.

"During the past three years," he continued, "I have spoken to you on many occasions about national concerns. . . . But over those years the subjects of the speeches, the talks, and the press conferences have become increasingly narrow, focused more on what the isolated world of Washington thinks is important. Gradually you have heard more and more about what the government thinks or what the government should be doing, and less and less about our nation's hopes, our dreams, and our vision of the future."

As a spectacle, the speech was riveting, not so much for what Carter said, but for what he was trying to do. The President, at that moment, was in a situation similar to that faced by Richard Nixon when he gave his famous "Checkers" speech, invoking his dog and his wife's cloth coats to save himself a place on the Republican ticket in 1956 after it was discovered that he controlled a political slush fund. Carter's situation was like the series of Watergate "explanations" Nixon had offered on his way out of the White House in 1974. Nixon, of course, had been attempting, by the force of words, to stave off disgrace. Carter, only five years later and president almost as a direct result of Nixon's failure to hold on to his office, was not fending off moral disgrace, but he was doing battle to prevent failure—failure of his presidency, failure to measure up to the very standards of excellence in public office he himself had set, failure of the most massive and public sort: the political failure in the coming year to gain a second term as president. In his own terms, Carter was playing for very large stakes indeed. For a politician who had had the cheek to name his campaign biography *Why Not the Best?*, for a man who had made self-improvement an obsession, for a president who had worked harder than any underling and who would later that year press himself to exhaustion in a public footrace, the prospect of political failure was as threatening as disgrace had been for the prim and unctuous Nixon. And while Nixon had fought for his office by announcing his innocence, Carter fought for his place in history by confessing his failures. Before millions of his compatriots, he read aloud the criticisms he had accepted during his retreat:

"This from a southern governor: 'Mr. President, you are not leading this nation—you're just managing the government.'

" 'You don't see the people enough anymore. . . .'

" 'Don't talk to us about politics or the mechanics of government, but about an understanding of our common good. . . .'

" 'If you lead, Mr. President, we will follow.' "

And referring to his very first energy speech, in which he had overblown his rhetoric by calling his program "the moral equivalent of war," someone told Carter: "When we enter the moral equivalent of war, Mr. President, don't issue us BB guns."

It was an odd tactic, but one true to the Carter notion of the origins of political power. That the president of the United States should submit himself to the kind of criticism he had endured at Camp David and then to read them to the country over national television was, on the face of it, an act of self-diminution. It would have been wiser to have listened patiently in private, to incorporate the best of the advice, and then to have acted. Carter sought instead the sympathy that exists for someone who admits error and promises to mend his ways. It is not common for American politicians to admit even that they have been wrong on specific policies or issues; it was unprecedented for one to admit he had totally failed in the presidency itself. But Carter, operating in the wake of the Johnson-Nixon era, had tried to substitute humility for their arrogance. It had won him the office, but had not helped him govern.

His campaign humility was reassuring to a nation concerned about presidential excess. It was a useful campaign device. But once in office, Carter failed to respond to the different demands on him as president. He failed to project the sense of sureness, of direction, of certainty that is required of any president. The irony

13

was that as a campaigner, Carter often seemed to me an arrogant man decked out to seem humble. As a president, he seemed a humble man pretending to power and decisiveness. The truth was that Carter was neither of the things he pretended to be. Too full of self-doubt to be a certain leader, he was at the same time too proud to admit his real shortcomings. There was something about him that was more than a bit reminiscent of Nixon—an odious comparison to be sure and not intended to impugn Carter's integrity—in that both men needed the presidency and the power to fill some emptiness in themselves. Neither the humble Carter nor the proud Carter was ever a sure leader of the nation. And that failure was especially damaging during the times in which Carter governed. He provided his own description of those times in his July speech. He said it was a time in which "a fundamental threat to American democracy" had arisen. The threat was "a crisis of confidence. It is a crisis," he said, "that strikes at the very heart and soul and spirit of our national will. We can see this crisis in the growing doubt about the meaning of our own lives and in the loss of a unity of purpose for our nation. The erosion of our confidence is threatening to destroy the social and political fabric of America.

"We have always believed in something called progress," Carter continued. "We've always had a faith that the days of our children would be better than our own. Our people are losing that faith, not only in government itself, but in the ability as citizens to serve as the ultimate rulers and shapers of our democracy. . . . In a nation that was once proud of hard work, strong families, close-knit communities, and our faith in God, too many of us now tend to worship self-indulgence and consumption. Human identity is no longer defined by what one does, but by what one owns. But we've discovered that owning things and consuming things does not satisfy our longing for meaning. We've learned that piling up goods cannot fill the emptiness of lives which have no confidence or purpose.

"The symptoms of this crisis of the American spirit are all around us. For the first time in the history of our country the majority of our people believe that the next five years will be worse than the past five years. Two-thirds of our people do not even vote. The productivity of American workers is actually dropping and the willingness of Americans to save for the future has fallen below that of all other people in the Western world.

"As you know, there is a growing disrespect for the government, . . . the churches, . . . the schools, the news media, and other institutions. This is not a message of happiness or reassurance, but it is the truth and it is a warning.

"These changes did not happen overnight. They've come upon us gradually over the last generation, years that were filled with shocks and tragedy.

"We were sure that ours was a nation of the ballot and not the bullet, until the murders of John Kennedy and Robert Kennedy and Martin Luther King, Jr. We were taught that our armies were always invincible and our causes were always just, only to suffer the agony of Vietnam. We respected the presidency as a place of honor, until the shock of Watergate.

"We remember when the phrase 'sound as a dollar' was an expression of absolute dependability, until ten years of inflation began to shrink our dollars and our savings. We believed that our nation's resources were limitless, until 1973 when we had to face a growing dependence on foreign oil.

"These wounds are still very deep. They have never been healed."

The President went on then to urge a renewal of faith "in each other, in our ability to govern ourselves," and in "the future of this nation. The strength we need will not come from the White House but from every house in America."

After describing yet another energy program, Carter concluded: "Whenever you have a chance, say something good about our country. With God's help and for the sake of our nation, it is time for us to join hands in America. Let us commit ourselves together to a rebirth of the American spirit. Working together with our common faith, we cannot fail."

As a political device the speech was a modest success, at least temporarily. Public opinion surveys taken a few days after the performance showed as much as a nine-point rise in Carter's meager popularity, although the increase likely derived mostly from the fact that Carter had finally said something, anything at all, about his political troubles. But that improvement was quickly dissipated when the President, a few days later on July 17, asked for the written resignations of his entire Cabinet and White House staff. The Cabinet balked at the request, arguing that it was too reminiscent of Nixon's mass shakeup in 1972. But Carter went ahead and fired some of his most able Cabinet secretaries. HEW chief Joseph Califano was first to go, since he had long irritated the President's closest White House aides, like Hamilton Jordan. Treasury Secretary Blumenthal was also fired. Energy Secretary Schlesinger and Transportation Secretary Adams quit as the axes began to swing. Griffin Bell, who was an old associate of Carter's from Georgia, used the opportunity to execute a planned escape from his job as Attorney General. Having touched something of a nerve in the American psyche with the "crisis of confidence" theme, Carter destroyed any struggling new confidence in his own leadership by this wholesale scrambling of his top echelon of advisers. The episode yielded the sense of a man not wholly confident of his own abilities. It also yielded speculation in Washington over Carter's mental stability, so clumsily had the episode been handled.

The brief lift Carter received from his speech came from the public sense that he was at least trying to come to grips with his political failure. But as a view of the particular historical circumstances of the United States the speech was somewhat askew. Surely, Carter was right in sensing that the United States was in a period of drift; after all he had begun his speech by admitting his failure to lead. And certainly he was right in noting that the country was ill-at-ease with changing world circumstances, with its dependence on foreign oil, and with its confusion over the social upheaval of the late 1960s and early 1970s. But this was hardly a threat to the very fabric of our national life. It was surely not a worse time than the despairing days of the Civil War period. The mood was surely not darker than during the worst days of the Great Depression. It could not have been the first time in the history of America that the nation believed the next half decade would be worse than the preceding five years. In 1860, in 1918, in 1931, and in 1941, with wars looming and economic ruin unchecked, America was darkly pessimistic. The President had confused his own desperation with the national state of mind. The country was confused and uncertain but by and large it was not seized by panic.

For Carter himself the speech was an unusual departure from form. His previous speeches had been of two sorts: those packed with little encouraging homilies that stressed the basic goodness of America (and the ways in which he, Carter, reflected that goodness) and brittle lectures on the mechanics of curing this problem or that. It was a new venture for him to suggest that the American people were filled not with compassion but with self-interest, not with generosity but with greed, not with wisdom but with confusion. No one asked at the time just how it was that he as president could draw his strength and his guidance from such befuddled and misguided people as the self-doubting American public.

The origin of the speech was, of course, Carter's own frustration with his ineffectual presidency. But the formative notions came largely from the President's pollster, Patrick Caddell, a bright, slightly overweight prodigy who had done his first presidential campaign polling during the 1972 McGovern campaign while still an undergraduate at Harvard. Since those days, he had grown a full beard that featured a patch of gray on his chin that seemed to add some seniority. It was the public opinion surveys done for the White House by Caddell and his Cambridge Survey Research Organization that convinced the President that there was a national "malaise" (the term coined later to describe the Carter vision). And it was Caddell's data that underlay Carter's assertion of the loss of optimism by the American people. But other public opinion experts argued immediately that Caddell had misunderstood his own findings and that, in fact, there was no new crisis of confidence, only short-term and understandable loss of spirit because of Carter's own mishandling of the economy and a growing partisan opposition to Carter himself.

Caddell defended himself in an issue of *Public Opinion,* a journal devoted to digesting the findings of the national polls. He claimed to have found a decided shift toward a pervasive pessimism early in 1979, when a large number of people rated the current situation as worse than that which prevailed five years earlier (a time, incidentally, that directly followed Nixon's resig-

17

nation and the Arab oil embargo). At the same time those he surveyed felt that the next five years would be even worse than the present. But even Caddell had to admit that while attitudes about the nation's welfare and the government's effectiveness had declined, people still felt, although less dramatically than was once the case, that their own personal lives were better in the present than in the past and would get better still five years into the future. Caddell's survey also showed that a plurality of those questioned said it would make no difference who was elected president.

Dissenting from the Caddell-Carter vision of the despondent American, Warren Miller of the University of Michigan's Center for Political Studies said his polling research showed that although people's confidence in government was indeed low, overall it had changed little since 1976. Miller did find a dramatic decline in the public confidence in government, however, among Republicans and independents. Miller, in the same issue of *Public Opinion* that carried Caddell's statements, argued that what Carter had called a "crisis" had in fact predated his administration and was one that he had not managed to solve, despite his campaign promises of restoring trust in government. And indeed, he had a point. Various indices of public mood supplied by other pollsters showed a sour, even cynical, attitude toward government and political leaders. But then, why shouldn't that have been the public's opinion? Watergate, Vietnam, assassinations, the sudden and threatening fact of a foreign oil cartel replacing the old American oil cartel, inflation, and meager economic growth—could this chain of events have been expected to produce an era of rosy American optimism?

Everyone conceded that public attitudes toward the government, its leaders, and its institutions, and toward the future they would help shape, was grim—and that it had been grim for some time. What no one argued was that the attitude was perfectly rational, given what had gone before and the problems the country was facing. What then was the point of the Carter speech? What the President seemed to be doing was subconsciously pinning much of the blame for his own political travail on the good and decent people of the nation. Hard on the heels of his public apologia for having failed to be an effective president, Jimmy Carter was saying, in effect, that it was the country's fault that he was unpopular and that his energy program was being shredded by Congress. He was saying that he was trapped in a vicious circle: He could not lead because the nation was too self-absorbed and too paralyzed by its own depression to follow him. His critics were saying that the President couldn't lead because he was too full of self-pity and too busy blaming the mood of the nation for his failures. Vice-President Walter Mondale, for one, disagreed with Caddell's analysis and argued from inside the Carter administration that the problem was much more specific—jobs, inflation, and the like—and less one of the national psyche. He argued to no avail that the government needed to solve the problems and the national mood would take care of itself.

As part of his intensive self-analysis at Camp David, Carter had read, among other dire tomes, Christopher Lasch's *The Culture of Narcissism,* which asserted, in an excessively elaborate argument, that the American people were so busy tending and mending their egos, through materialism and psychotherapy, that they no longer had time or interest in the public good. He also read Richard Sennett's *The Fall of Public Man.* Sennett found America a society inflicted with the barbarism of intimacy. Sennett contended that in the pursuit of an idealized notion of personal relationships Americans had lost their sense of community. Dissatisfied with their own lives and even more disillusioned with public life, the Americans depicted in the President's reading matter were no longer the happy, confident, hard-working, purposeful, patriotic Americans of historic myth. They had more—more money, televisions, cars, houses, clothes, food processors, geegaws, and gadgets—than any people in the history of mankind. Yet, they were unhappy with themselves, not placated by their wealth and their possessions. Their spiritual strength, their faith in God, their faith in themselves as a people had declined dramatically.

There was, of course, a certain truth to this that the President recognized. But the question that went begging was, again, Just how serious was this depression? If the life of a nation is something like the life of an individual, was America's problem simply a postadolescent depression, born of a series of failures in a tough world? Or was the depression of a more serious sort, an adult depression born of too much failure, lost self-esteem? Was it a paralyzing depression that leads to confusion, inaction, disgust, and self-destruction? In a very real sense America had lost its way. But was the loss permanent? Was the malaise so profound as to mean the beginning of the decline and fall of the American Republic? What Carter lacked, and what his speech had proved he lacked, was his own balanced vision of America entering the 1980s. Carter simply did not understand the country he was trying to govern.

Even as Carter was digesting these diagnoses of doom, another pollster on the other edge of the country was asking his own questions of the American people, also searching for clues to their state of mind. Richard Wirthlin, a quiet, controlled man of a little less than average height, and with a gray complexion from too much time spent in offices and not enough in the California sun, was at work for Republican Ronald Reagan, then a sixty-eight-year-old former governor of the state, a defeated candidate for his party's presidential nomination in 1976, and a man who had one more chance to become president.

Wirthlin and his staff interviewed 250 people, each for six hours. They probed political and personal attitudes and then ran the results through their elaborate computer system. They later tested the results from that intensive study with a cross-sectional poll of many more Americans and produced a document they called the "Values and Aspirations Study," which was their interpretation of the collective state of mind of America in the summer of 1979.

Like Caddell, they found a dyspeptic American citizen, fed up with government, taxes, and inflation, discouraged by the defeat in Vietnam, the corruption of the Nixon government, and all the rest. Everyone felt that it was not a happy-go-lucky America. Seven out of ten Americans, Wirthlin found, agreed with the statement that America was "off on the wrong track." He also found numbers that seemed to confirm Lasch's elaborate description of what writer Tom Wolfe had called the "me decade" of the 1970s. Considerably more than half those questioned agreed with the proposition that "an individual should not depend on other persons or things and that the center of one's life should be found inside oneself." Whether this was a profound turning inward, and thus away from community and country, was at least questionable, however. Those questioned may as well have been voicing their belief in self-reliance, an old American trait.

But the most important difference in Wirthlin's interpretation as compared to Caddell's was that Americans still felt that they and their country had a bright future and that they still, to some extent, had a hand in controlling their destiny. The Wirthlin researchers asked their subjects whether or not it mattered who was elected president in 1980. Seventy-six percent felt that it did indeed make a difference, an opinion directly contrary to Caddell's findings on that question. Wirthlin's conclusion, which formed one of the basic assumptions of the coming Reagan candidacy, was that the morale of the American people was low but that it was rooted in a loss of confidence in the country's leadership, not in the country or in the citizens themselves. The Reagan campaign looked at Carter's July speech as a kind of abdication of his leadership duties. And they felt that by blaming the public mood for his political difficulties he was setting the stage for just the kind of campaign they wanted to wage—a campaign that made America feel hopeful again. That goal, no matter how unrealistic, was in stark contrast to the Carter analysis in the summer of 1979, which said, in effect, that no president could do much about the nation's problems at that particular historical juncture. The Reagan forces, out of office and out of the line of direct responsibility for solving the problems that Carter found too large, believed, as Carter himself had believed five years earlier, that they could change America.

That Carter was in political trouble was, in many respects, not much of a surprise, given the circumstances he faced. Throughout his presidency, and well before it had begun, it was hard to find the sort of good news or examples of great national and collective success that breed confidence and unity in a nation. No matter how many times the great crises of the last two decades are recalled, it is nonetheless amazing to consider the passage the nation has made from the election and then assassination of John Kennedy in the early 1960s to the end of the decade of the 1970s.

America's bright hopes have been systematically smashed and dashed for two decades. Myths were destroyed when the great ghetto uprisings of the sixties reminded the nation that its school-book democracy was unequal and unjust. The burst of guilt and energy that brought forth the last great spate of liberal programs —the war on poverty, Head Start, the Jobs Corps, urban redevelopment, the civil rights acts opening public facilities, housing, and jobs to the minorities, the Peace Corps and so on, a program for every problem—was then replaced by the inflation-bred anxiety they helped produce. That we could control the spread of communism by fighting counterinsurgency wars in jungles also proved illusory. But then, in the 1970s, the resulting urge to control military spending and to disengage American power from its outposts around the world left us in the uncomfortable position of watching Soviet strength grow and of seeing our economic power eroded both by competition from Japan and Europe and by the cartelization of world oil supplies by otherwise weak and often chaotic nations in the Middle East and the Third World.

The nation watched as its rules of personal conduct were changed dramatically in the waves of political unrest. Sex became a public commodity to be hawked at newstands, featured in movie theaters, and exploited in silly and tasteless television comedies. But at the same time the old fears surrounding sex were removed (mercifully), new fears about personal responsibility sprang up (justifiably). Women's roles were redefined to include access on a more equal footing to the labor market, to schools, to sports, and to other areas once reserved for men only. This too was for the good (although in part the result of economic necessity fostered by the pressure of inflation). But the revolution in behavior gave rise to new stress as well. Child-rearing patterns began to change and many Americans worried about leaving their children at home unsupervised while both parents worked. Television became a full-time child custodian in many homes.

Across the nation Americans flocked to social workers, psychotherapists, and psychologists to cure the confusion that resulted from all this sudden change and counterchange, from the lack of clear expectations about how they should behave in given situations. Psychological counseling became middle-class America's pastime in the 1970s and, predictably, it, in turn, created its own problems. The search for answers led many people to charlatans and fakes, to swamis and gurus and cultists, to highly commercial and nonsensical group exercises that produced an impenetrable jargon and a compulsive need to discuss "feelings," without yielding much in the way of personal change or happiness. It led, too, to the burgeoning of fundamentalist religious groups that supply pat moral certainties to ward off the moral confusion of the times. The search for self dissolved the bonds of marriage, and in the late 1970s one marriage in three ended in divorce.

America had lived with the belief that it could do anything, could fix anything, could build anything, could cure almost any ailment, be it social, cultural, or personal. As Daniel Patrick Moynihan put it, America lived with the "therapeutic ethic," the notion that everything and everybody—even hardened criminals —could be made well.

But as the 1970s wore on, the therapeutic ethic began to die. Among intellectuals it led to some despair. Their ideas for change and prescriptions for a better society no longer commanded respect and attention. In many areas of concern there was no longer even intellectual agreement about what these prescriptions should be. The glorious days of self-assuredness in academe had passed. The liberal intellectuals fell to arguing and some transmogrified into "neoconservatives" ("neo" because they hadn't been), and those like Irving Kristol, Norman Podhoretz, and Midge Decter began counseling a whole new set of answers to social problems, which consisted largely of shutting down the social programs they had argued for in the 1960s and letting the invisible hand of the free market guide the American nation on its way. Many of the neoconservatives also left behind the dreamy sense of cooperation with the Soviets and became advocates of a tougher American foreign policy that, as it had in the 1950s, saw the world as a largely bipolar arrangement.

Domestic economic ailments and a decline in U.S. power abroad, both caused to some extent by the failure of the liberal nostrums of the 1960s and by perverse historical trends, denied the nation a chance to lapse into a kind of benign befuddlement to match the easy prosperity of the 1950s. Rather, the problems the nation faced heightened uncertainty into a profound confusion. The nation welcomed many of the changes in values and attitudes brought on in the 1960s but was ambivalent about the consequences. It was glad to be rid of the old strictures but uncomfortable about what the new limits were—if there were any.

Fifty years after the 1980 election, when the decades of the 1960s and 1970s are taken apart and reassembled by historians, that period will emerge as an important and difficult period of adjustment. The analyses of the time presented by the Carter and Reagan campaign philosphers will look shallow and incomplete. Carter's July speech will look too bleak. It will stand as an example of the self-doubt of the liberals. Reagan's view, on the other hand, will appear too optimistic. While it accounted for the national distress, it invested too heavily in the bright and naive view that most of the discomfort was caused by the uncertain presidency of Jimmy Carter and the overweening power of the federal government. By implication, it banked too heavily on the California candidate's rosy personal optimism, born of his insulated and self-assured conservatism and wealthy station in life.

The year before the first presidential election of the new decade the nation was adrift—intellectually, politically, economically, and morally. It was a nation trying to come to grips with the new awareness that some problems can't be solved, that human progress is not inevitable, and that evil, something the dominant liberal ethic had begun to discount, was still a force in the world. Only the year before Carter's pronouncements on the crisis of confidence, over nine hundred poor souls living in a commune in Guyana had poisoned themselves in a mass suicide ordered by the Reverend Jim Jones, their satanic cult leader. Nothing, it seemed, was as it had been in America.

As the skirmishing for the 1980 election got under way, it was understandable that the longing for strong presidential leadership should emerge as a dominant political attitude of the moment. It was a desire diluted, however, by other national emotions, that would shape the coming political contest. In a public opinion survey by the firm of Yankelovich, Skelly and White, Inc., for *Time* magazine, the early standings of the potential candidates in September 1979, proved to be nearly an exact mirror of public perceptions of the leadership ability of those candidates. Ruth Clark, a vice-president of the Yankelovich organization, asked those surveyed to rate the candidates as either "strong leaders," "not strong," or as a middling "fairly strong." Indexing these results she found Ted Kennedy was seen as the strongest leader, Republican Ronald Reagan second, and President Carter the weakest of all the potential candidates, including relatively obscure figures like Congressman Phil Crane and Senator Bob Dole and former U.N. ambassador George Bush. Even Jerry Brown, whose 1976 success in the late primaries had elevated him to national attention, ranked ahead of the sitting president.

The rankings Mrs. Clark produced had one anomaly, however: the standing of Texan John Connally, an extremely well-known figure in national politics for decades and a man whose presence was not only powerful but often overwhelming. Only twenty-seven percent in the survey rated him "strong," while nearly as many said he was "not strong." Connally was at that moment a personification of a great contradiction that would haunt the campaign, and the country, throughout the election year. There was an apparent search for a strong leader to show the way, to take charge, to set the agenda for national action and unity. There was a profound desire to find someone to believe in, someone who would dispel the confusion. Associated with this was a continuing demand for solutions to specific social and economic problems, like inflation, unemployment, deteriorating schools, and the rest. And, as they had for decades, the American people believed that the federal government, under the leadership of a strong president, should provide those solutions.

But, at the same time, the public held a conflicting notion, one that had both long historic roots and recent reinforcement, and that was a deep distrust of politicians. In addition, there was a growing national feeling that the federal government was much too involved in the daily life of the nation, especially its business life, and that the size and reach of the Washington apparatus should be pared back.

There was, of course, a way to reconcile those opposite longings: to find a "nonpolitician" from outside the political establishment who promised that the very way to solve the country's problems was to get the government out of many areas into which it had moved too heavily. Still, the contradiction remained. Even as faith in the therapeutic society was wanning, new demands for action and solutions were being raised. More than anything else, Americans wanted the confusion to go away. They wanted direction. They wanted solutions. It was a tall order as the country began its search for a president to lead it through the first half of the 1980s.

FALL
1979

2

Ice on a Hot Stove

While the nation was in a period of perplexity, the nation's politics were in a time of turmoil. For years many of the basic institutions of the American political system had been changing dramatically, some by design, others by accident and evolution. The two-party system had been losing its power and appeal for twenty years, beginning with the decline of big-city political machines as powerful, patronage-dispensing organizations that brought both order and dishonesty to urban government. On the national level the parties lost their power as mediators between the public and individual politicians as television permitted candidates to reach past the party leadership to make direct appeals to the electorate. John F. Kennedy was really the first presidential candidate to run a modern campaign almost totally separate from his party's national organization, and he was the last Democratic president to depend on city machines, such as Richard Daley's Chicago organization, for substantial numbers of votes.

Like much of the rest of American society, politics had become atomized. Candidates for the presidency no longer depended upon the approval of the country's political elite—elected officials at all levels as well as party leaders—to launch their campaigns and to provide endorsements that could be translated into actual delegate votes at the nominating conventions. Rather, the presidential campaign had become a game of warlord politics, with the candidates forming up their armies of mercenaries and volunteers, planning long sieges in such strategically important places as Iowa and New Hampshire. No longer could a few wealthy benefactors provide the funds for a presidential campaign. New laws enacted after Watergate reduced the role of fat cats and prevented candidates from virtually extorting funds from corporate officers who needed federal approval on everything from their tax returns to their defense department contracts. Candidates were now forced to solicit money in small sums. Givers could not ante up more than $1,000 to any candidate. Federal matching funds for the primaries would only be given for donations under $250. This new rule caused fund raising to become a kind of plebiscite—with the votes being cast on bank checks—that took place months and years before the presidential primary voting ever began.

By the fall of 1979 nearly a dozen men had begun to form their armies for an assault on the presidency. In addition, the usual collection of cranks and zealots, crackbrains and publicity seekers were ready to announce their intention to become the fortieth president of the United States of America. In some respects, running for president was the best ticket to instant celebrity or notoriety the society offered, short of becoming the master of ceremonies on a television game show. By the end of the 1980 campaign, more than a score of people, including the President, his chief challengers, freshman senators, ideologues of uncertain beliefs, and the usual single-issue crusaders, had actually announced their plans for the presidency.

Increasingly, politicians believe that anyone can be president, and if not president, well then, vice-president this time and president next. Even a failed campaign can make the politician better known. "Name recognition" replaced good works and a record of long service as the most important currency in American politics. The politicians were not mistaken in their sense that the presidential selection system was an open game, a role of the dice that fate and luck and accident controlled as much as any man or any idea or any political institution. The recent history of the presidency proved they were right. Begin with 1960. Jack Kennedy was too young to be president; he was also a Catholic and unknown nationally. But he not only won the nomination away from his elders like Johnson, Symington, and Stevenson, he also won the presidency over a better-known and more experienced vice-president of the United States. Then came Lyndon Johnson, elevated to office by tragedy. And there was Barry Goldwater, who ran a kind of guerrilla operation and captured his party's nomination by seizing control of his party's apparatus around the country. In 1968, Nixon, defeated in 1960, humiliated in 1962 when he ran for governor of California, won the nomination and the election. And George McGovern, planning and plotting since 1969 to become president, even when the odds favored Edmund Muskie, the 1968 vice-presidential contender, or young Ted Kennedy until his accident at Chappaquiddick. McGovern was nominated in Miami in 1972 on the strength of an antiwar revolution inside the Democratic party. And then Carter, the longest of long shots, rose up out of the South, a one-term Georgia governor whose only previous national exposure was the one-week fame of a *Time* magazine cover story on the new, progressive politicians of his region. His opponent, too, was an accidental president. Gerald R. Ford, never considered presidential material by his colleagues in the Congress or in the Republican party, became vice-president after Spiro Agnew was forced to leave office, and then president when Nixon resigned in disgrace. And he nearly beat Jimmy Carter.

It is always an amazing experience to confront a man of average years and average talents who announces, as he looks you hard in the eye, that he wants to be president and believes in his heart that he will be chosen. The urge frequently is to stifle a laugh. Sometime even a guffaw must be choked back. This is no longer appropriate behavior when meeting a presidential candidate, even one who had never been heard from previously. There are, of course, candidates whose pretensions are worthy of derision, but one must be extremely discerning in making that judgment. In America, almost anyone *can* be president.

By autumn of 1979 the very weakness that had led Carter into Camp David and then out again with his diagnosis of doom had attracted a large number of challengers. Within his own party, and despite the fact that the Democrats held the White House, a number of men toyed with the idea of challenging the incumbent. Others were beyond toying. Edmund G. (Jerry) Brown, Jr., the governor of California, the son of the former governor of California, and a man who had beaten Jimmy Carter in a string of late primaries in the 1976 race, had been talking about his own candidacy for months, and since the previous spring had been vowing that his announcement of that candidacy was imminent. Edward Moore Kennedy had been the natural heir to his brothers' political legacy ever since Robert Kennedy died of a gunshot wound on the floor of a hotel kitchen in Los Angeles. In 1968 the divided Democrats sought him out at his summer home on Cape Cod and begged him to enter the contest. In 1972 he stayed away from presidential politics to allow the memory of Chappaquiddick to blur. In 1976 many in his party had felt the nomination was his for the asking. But he didn't ask. And in 1979 the waiting was becoming tiresome for Kennedy and irritating for others in the party, many of whom believed that Jimmy Carter could not be re-elected and that his defeat would lead to a disaster for the party's other candidates. Endangered liberal senators like McGovern of South Dakota, Bayh of Indiana, and Culver of Iowa urged Ted Kennedy to run against Jimmy Carter. Still, for a man of such long association with the Democratic party, a challenge to a sitting president of that party was a big step, an act of disloyalty not to be committed lightly, or at least without good prospects of victory. By September 1979 Kennedy had every prospect of just such a victory. The Yankelovich survey, like every other major opinion poll in the country, found Kennedy an overwhelming choice over Carter. The margins were, by any standard, huge. The poll gave Kennedy sixty-two percent of the Democrats, compared to Carter's meager twenty-four percent. Jimmy Carter had offended many in the liberal wing of the party. And that was the segment most important to the nomination process, since it is organized labor and the true believers of the left who work hardest, spend most, and vote most often in the primary elections. Worse, Carter's standing against Republican presidential possibilities was weak, offering Democrats the prospect not only of having a president with whom they didn't agree but also of an incumbent seeking re-election with his chances of winning in question. The aging California conservative, Ronald Reagan, beat Carter in the same poll. Howard Baker, the minority leader of the Senate and a man of great legislative skill and intelligence but of little national reputation, ran even with Carter. John Connally, still not popular in his own party, was running only a few points behind the President. Kennedy, on the other hand, showed as an easy winner against all these Republicans.

A tide seemed to be building that threatened Carter's chances to be renominated by his own party. It has been rare that a president seeking renomination for a second term is denied that chance by his own party, although both Truman in 1952 and Lyndon Johnson in 1968 realized they had little hope of carrying their party conventions and withdrew from the race well before they had a chance to lose the nomination outright. In 1979 Jimmy Carter seemed destined to join the few presidents turned out by their own party before a second term. At least on the surface of things.

Whatever Carter's failings, he did not suffer a shortage of pluck, especially in man-to-man competition in an election battle. If he couldn't seem to grasp control of his own party, he could certainly understand the implications of a political campaign. He believed mightily in his own virtue and in his ability to defeat other politicians, especially the nearly legendary figures of his own party. In 1976, for example, he had been genuinely disappointed when Hubert Humphrey, an almost revered figure in the Democratic party, had decided to stay out of the late primaries rather than try to stop the Carter bandwagon. Carter wanted the chance to defeat Humphrey, thereby inflating his own importance. When it was suggested that Kennedy might challenge him, Carter replied, "I'll whip his ass." The White House staff quickly leaked the remark to show the President's determination.

The chances for a successful challenge from within the Democratic ranks seemed strong in the early fall of 1979, but no one had actually come forward to announce his candidacy against Carter. Ted Kennedy had been besieged with questions about his own intentions and had repeated, like a prisoner of war giving name, rank, and serial number, "I expect the President to be renominated and I expect to support him for re-election." Kennedy had walked away before from the presidential quest, but it was not clear if this time he would behave any differently. In sharp contrast to Kennedy's apparent reluctance, California's Governor Brown had never really stopped talking about his presidential plans since 1976. He said to whomever would listen that he intended to announce his candidacy, first in the spring of 1979, then in the summer, then in the late summer, then in the fall. The challenge from Brown never really concerned the Carter forces, yet a challenge from anyone meant some measure of trouble for Carter. A split in the party along ideological and personal lines could only hurt a president already in much difficulty. A challenge from Brown, say, could provide a candidacy around which anti-Carter sentiment could crystalize, opening the way to a later challenge from another Democrat in the winter and spring. As John Sears, then Reagan's campaign manager, explained to me one afternoon in the early fall, "Brown's one big advantage is that his name is not Jimmy Carter."

Jerry Brown's strength was, however, more than just not being Jimmy Carter. He twice had won the governorship of the Union's largest state and had beaten Carter in five of the six final primaries of 1976, when Carter had already assured himself of the Democratic nomination but had begun to lose his grip on the public imagination. (It could even be said that Brown was present at the start of Carter's long fall. The Georgian only barely beat incumbent Jerry Ford after leading him by thirty points in the summer of 1976, and after a postinaugural burst of popularity, declined steadily until the fall of 1979.) But more important, Jerry Brown, then barely into his forties, was in many ways the personification of his political time.

He was aging slowly, along with the rest of the post–World War II baby boom that was gradually changing the demographic face of the nation. He shared their attitudes and had shared their causes in the 1960s protests against war and racism. He was open and exploratory in finding new styles of life. He believed nothing totally and at the same time saw some truth in everything. He was spoiled and contentious and arrogant and self-confident. He was deeply suspicious and disdainful of, and in continuous revolt against, the ways of his parents.

Brown called himself a Democrat, but rejected much of what that party had advocated for generations. In an era of confusion, Brown was stunningly eclectic, picking his public philosophy from a grab bag of trendy intellectual fads. In the age of television he was more at home in front of a camera than in a face-to-face discussion with people he didn't know. In a television studio he could speak in the fragments and cryptic, semisentence symbols of the electronic medium. In person his words tumbled upon themselves; his sentences became a kind of rococo decoration for the pieces of ideas that he tried to pass off as considered opinions.

Anticipating his oft-announced intention to seek the presidency, a group of *Time* magazine editors and reporters met Brown one spring evening in the ornate Beverly Wilshire Hotel. The young governor was, as usual, elegantly tailored in blue blazer and gray slacks. His dark hair was parted on the side and a strand or two fell boyishly across his forehead. He looked like a slightly aged prep schooler, his smooth face and excessive enthusiasm belying the fact that he was in his middle years. Oddly for a governor who had already run in one presidential race and who had been interviewed for years, Brown was clearly nervous. He took up an apple from a basket of fruit and began munching noisily as he spoke. For two hours he spoke and spoke and spoke. It was a challenge to insert a question into his monologue. Jerry Brown, whether out of anxiety or out of intellectual exuberance, can hardly stop talking. Luckily for us, a tape recorder was running. We stared in amazement as the words fluttered down, piled into drifts, swirled around the room:

". . . Theorists from the academy and various think tanks are pulling for a shift from our present growing rate of consumption to a deeper commitment to investment and new technologies that will lead to greater productivity . . . those ideas I expressed in 1974, '75, and '76 and I summarized it within the last two years by saying that a recognition of limits can pave the ways for an expansion of possibilities. . . . I would say that for over a decade I have been articulating the vision that in some ways has been influenced by other thinkers, like Ivan Illich, and some ways by other thinkers writing in the more liberal magazine *Social Policy* and the more conservative quarterly *Public Interest,* but all of which have questioned some of what I would call sloppier liberal economic dogma of the recent years and the reason why people use words like *flipflop* and *opportunism* [to describe him, after he did an about-face on California's tax-and-spending-limiting Proposition 13, first opposing it, then embracing it] is that the categories of political and economic thought in the late sixties that are manifest in much political debate, I think are breaking down and are inadequate to describe the imparities of the 1980s . . . people are often prisoners of past perceptions and contemporary peer pressure. A number of the politicians and the political commentators are trying to pour the philosophy of my administration into the old wine sacks of the 1960s and this philosophy just doesn't fit. . . . I am not going to confine my analysis of the malaise in America to the conventional political categories. . . . I would like to analyze on the basis of more objective factors and longer term secular trends that are affecting not only America but the whole planet itself. . . . I see my role as interactive and as part of the messaged material that will dominate the communication processes of the 1980s. . . . I see as an emerging theme the recognition and appreciation of pattern. And pattern Gestalt quality is another order of human category [sic] or of just a category of mind and the words are difficult to find but I see in this a movement toward elegance, quality and esthetic sense over what I would call the more mundane quantitative attitude . . . my foreign policy could be described in the term *planetary realism.* . . . "

And then he was off into the night, most likely to prowl cheap restaurants with his friends, whose role it was to listen to him talk. They often moved the floating seminars to Brown's house in the Hollywood Hills. It is characteristically West Coast: an open, airy, and well-planted little hideaway. Inside, however, the house has nothing of the expected California chic. It is carelessly furnished, strewn with paperback books, poorly kept. It is graduate-student casual.

But Brown himself is anything but casual. He is intense and driven and hyperkinetic. In an interview in 1974 with Richard Duncan, now chief of the Time-Life News Service, Brown aptly compared his life as a politician to Robert Frost's description of poetry: "Like a piece of ice on a hot stove, the poem must ride on its own melting." Brown himself skitters through his days, darting unpredictably from point to point, driven by the heat of his own ideas and the sizzle of his own ambition. He is also driven by the deep need to be different from the standard run of politicians. Having arrived in the governor's office in 1975, Brown quickly and with much publicity established himself as out of the ordinary by first refusing to move into an elaborate mansion that his predecessor, Ronald Reagan, had had the state build. Instead, he took up residence in a $250-a-month apartment furnished with left-over government-issued tables and chairs and a mattress on the floor. He walked the few blocks to his office in Sacramento, and when he needed a car it was not the usual state limousine, but rather an inexpensive blue Plymouth. He arrived at work late and stayed late. On weekends in his earlier days as governor, he would visit a Zen monastery in San Francisco to meditate.

Brown was too self-absorbed to have many serious friendships, even with women, but he did strike up a courtship of sorts with rock-and-roll queen Linda Ronstadt, as friendly and fun-loving as Brown is austere and intellectual. Most of his aides were, like him, unmarried and singlemindedly devoted to the career of Jerry Brown and to their careers with him. He is a politician without the human touch, without political allies, one who avoids the back-slapping and camaraderie that often helps political leaders get their programs through legislatures.

His political philosophy is similarly unusual. His basic outlook is that of the New Deal liberal, but he had overlaid that with a streak of fiscal austerity well before that became a national trend among Democrats. As governor he imposed a limit on increases in welfare grants that infuriated the state's liberal establishment. He also endorsed a controversial proposal to enact a Constitutional amendment requiring that the federal government balance its budget. It was an idea advanced mostly by conservatives angered at the size and reach of the government in Washington. Brown's support sent a conflicting signal to those who thought him a standard liberal. "I believe," Brown had said, "that a politician can go left and right at the same time. And I think he should."

His unconventional political blends soon raised charges that he really believed in nothing and simply blew with the wind. It was true that he did not hold to any set of standard ideological beliefs. He was too bright for that, and too well aware that the answers of the past were no longer working. Brown was certainly willing to take unusual positions, to adopt ideas that were untested. No politician, of course, really adheres too firmly to any set positions forever. But the real question about Brown was just why he swung so wildly in his views, whether he was honestly and carefully working toward a new synthesis of policy positions or whether he was just showboating, tossing off ideas as a sort of political gimmick that would achieve the notice that comes with being different.

As American politics has torn free of the two-party system, attracting media attention is the first step to political success. That Brown was a national politician at all was due in large part to the fact that he was different. And that was both his strength and his weakness.

In the spring of 1979, for example, Brown dashed off to Africa, ostensibly to show some interest in lands across the seas to complement his self-interest and devotion to California and domestic politics. At his urging Linda Ronstadt went along. And so the Rock Star and the Governor barnstormed Africa. Quite predictably, the bored press corps in Africa—and their bosses in the capitals of the world—were more interested in this unusual pairing than in Jerry Brown's discussions about environmental problems in Africa. Their living arrangements were the object of high interest (in Nairobi, a shared cottage with two bedrooms, each with a double bed), and before the trip was over, Linda and Jerry were on the cover of *Newsweek*. Brown had been caught in the classic trap of political publicity. Novelty is good to attract attention, but without great skill and care, interest in the novel is quickly transformed into the kind of curiosity reserved for the simply bizarre. Brown was, through the summer of 1979, sliding into a dangerous typecast. His opponents, especially in Jimmy Carter's White House, were delighted with the African trip and the publicity it generated. Carter aides were dismissing Brown as a serious challenger and classifying him as a "kook." Brown had been highly original in his thinking, unconventional in his approach to political policy, unusual in his personal life, and with the African trip, mindless of the way his behavior was being treated on television and in the press. It could be argued that Brown's trip and his other nonconformities were really his own business and were mistreated by the leering press.

Yet Brown had a more serious problem that underlay the side-show treatment he was getting. Politicians who live only by television, flirt with destruction by television. Television is entertainment, and as such has a short attention span. Tricks and ploys get attention, but they also wear out rapidly. A politician like Brown, who uses surprise to get attention, will necessarily become boring. Continued surprise is no longer surprising. People who work in television assume that politicians plan their every act for the sake of television—not an incorrect assumption. And predictably, they get tired of the same tricks performed again and again. After getting their faces on television, after doing word tricks and behaving in entertaining ways, successful politicians need to actually *do* something in government to force the television crews to come back again and again. "Doing something" in politics means winning an election. Jerry Brown had won the attention of television viewers, but was in danger of losing the attention of voters.

He also seemed driven to be different. When he was only five years old, Jerry Brown's father, Edmund G. "Pat" Brown, was elected district attorney in San Francisco. When Jerry was twelve, his father became governor. Jerry grew up in the maelstrom of backslapping, ribbon cutting, and command performances that made up his father's political world. He hated the people who his father courted and who courted his father. He still calls them "manipulators." And he resented his father's use of his son as a kind of political prop. He still recalls bitterly riding to a baseball game with his father in a state limousine. As the big car inched through the crowds, Jerry crouched down in the back to hide, pounding his fist on the side of the door, humiliated by what he felt was ostentation. "All that pomp and circumstance," he recalls. "The isolation of politicians from the people who elected them."

Yet in the perpetual cycle of imitation-repudiation that exists between fathers and sons, Jerry used his father's name, his father's friends, and his father's money-raising ability to succeed in his father's profession. But the relationship is still uneasy. After he won his first race as governor, with his father's substantial help,

Brown accused his father of having nearly cost him the race. After he became governor he often refused to return his father's phone calls. And the younger Brown is especially annoyed when it is pointed out that he lacks his father's warmth and sense of humor. "What is this thing of giving a smile to every person you meet?" Jerry asks. "Is that a relationship? Is that honest? These politicians you think you know so well you don't know at all. You just see a face, a mask, and what does that tell you? Nothing."

Jerry Brown was determined to outdo his father, but to do so using techniques and ideas alien to his father. This may explain one element in his move away from standard New Deal liberalism as practiced by Pat Brown. Jerry once noted sourly that, yes, his father had been responsible for the state's master education plan and the huge California water project. "What do we have today?" Jerry asked. "A lot of Ph.D.'s out of work and a lot of graft and corruption in the California Water Authority." What better way, then, to supersede his father than by running not just for governor but for president of the United States? And what better way to repudiate the old politics of his father than to invent a new hip-speak political argot. But by the fall of 1979, Brown had already gone too far. He had become, in the phrase of my friend and *Time* magazine essayist Lance Morrow, "something out of the *Whole Earth Catalog.*" For months Brown had planned to announce his candidacy. He had been a potential threat to the weakened Carter. But he had waited and waited, never able to raise enough money to recruit competent workers. And as September turned to October, his problems extended beyond those he created for himself. For as Brown waited Ted Kennedy had begun to move. He was now hinting at running for president. A Kennedy challenge, in addition to being threatening to the sitting president, would obliterate Brown's chances.

In the end it was the great political vacuum created by Jimmy Carter that moved Edward Kennedy off the sidelines of presidential politics and into the action. On Labor Day, at his home on Cape Cod, Kennedy, after talking with his estranged wife, Joan, decided he would run. Kennedy then began a kind of teasing public entry into the Democratic nomination by saying he had talked with his mother, matriarch Rose Kennedy, and that she had lifted her previous objections to his running for president. Her objections were based mostly on the danger he would face being the third of the Kennedy brothers to seek the office after John and Bobby had been cut down by demented gunmen. He said he had talked to his wife, Joan, no longer living regularly with the senator and their family in Virginia, but occupying an apartment in Boston and taking courses at a local college there. She too, he announced, had no objection.

At the time, this little waltz toward a candidacy was seen as a clever political maneuver designed to buy Kennedy time to prepare his campaign and to put heat on Jimmy Carter. But in retrospect Ted Kennedy was simply being sucked into the race by forces almost beyond his control. The time had clearly come for Ted Kennedy to try to fulfill his destiny and try for the presidency. Draft movements in Iowa and Florida, the scene of early party caucuses and straw votes, had blossomed, along with draft committees in other states, and had become the de facto Kennedy campaign. These organizations were prohibited by federal election law from having any communication with the senator or his staff lest they come under the rules governing finance and fund raising. The draft movements then, while putting Ted Kennedy's name on the line in coming tests against Carter, were literally out of control, and thus represented serious risks. History had come to get Ted Kennedy. At that moment Ted Kennedy was quite apprehensive about just what history had in store for him. There was plenty of good reason for that concern.

The press and the politicians stood in line outside Kennedy's office in the Dirksen Senate Office Building in early fall. They packed his reception room, where the phones were ringing without pause and callers on hold were backed up on every extension. To get an interview with Kennedy at that time was no easy matter. He obviously wanted the big news organizations to bandy about his name, to add to the fuel of speculation about his plans and his power. But at the same time, Kennedy had grown accustomed to dealing only with selected reporters, friends from his brothers' campaigns, men and women who knew him personally and who seemed to offer little risk of the mean question or the negative story. That was an old Kennedy custom. Jack had made friends with a few of his own presidential and White House press corps.

He drew them in close, fed them the intimate details of his thinking, his plans, and his family life, and that made the reporters stars in their own journalistic worlds. The Kennedys did not invite into their glittering circle press members who seemed hostile. They dealt with other than their own favorite press people only reluctantly. As the hysteria about an imminent Kennedy announcement of his candidacy took hold in the early fall, the Kennedy staff lost control of the press. When I finally got approval to interview the senator in September, Press Secretary Tom Southwick had to explain to an obviously displeased Kennedy before the interview that an old Kennedy friend from *Time* was at the moment on vacation, thus explaining my presence.

There was, of course, always the dread that the tragic history of the Kennedy brothers would repeat itself. All over the country, the feeling was strong that in this land of cheap handguns some psychopath would surely be tempted to be the person who took the third Kennedy brother. Police from the congressional force kept careful watch on the Kennedy office. But still the deranged would stop by. As I was waiting to see Kennedy that September, a young man in white painter's pants and a baseball cap with the visor turned backward wandered into the senator's outer office. He asked to see Kennedy. He was told politely that the senator was not in the office and was quite busy. He refused to leave. The police finally escorted him out of the Senate Office Building. An older man showed up later. He had written, he said, a country and western song that should be Kennedy's campaign theme song. He stayed most of the day in the hallway. Both were apparently harmless people operating on the very fringe of mental normalcy. But the memories were always there.

In the inner sanctum of Kennedy's Senate office, the walls are filled with the framed memories of his family's glories and burdens. Jack with Bobby. Jack and Bobby with a thin, young Teddy. Old Joseph P. and Rose, the countless kids from all the families, the boats and houses. A handwritten note from the senator's mother correcting his grammar is framed and hung. Kennedy showed me the note with a restrained chuckle. He had agreed to an interview, but not to the taped question-and-answer type. This was to be more of a chat.

His official posture was that he was now actively considering whether or not to run. But he could not say what would prevent him from running. He said quietly and not altogether logically that he would be watching the state of the economy and Carter's management of economic forces to see whether or not to run. It was certain that within the few weeks or months in which he must decide to run, nothing in the economy was going to change fundamentally. It was clear that he had decided to run and was simply waiting to make a formal announcement until more pieces of the campaign were in place. He was wary about charges that he would be dividing the party—an inevitable result of his candidacy—and claimed that "the things that are troubling people are troubling them irrespective of whether I run or not." He was also defensive about his liberal record, one of the most predictable in the Senate, and was aware that the mood of the country had moved away from the "a program for every problem" formula he had stood for so long. "Labels don't mean much anymore," Kennedy said. "I introduced the airline deregulation bill with Jim Buckley [William F.'s brother and a conservative former senator from New York]. I don't disagree with Carter's spending levels. I wanted four billion dollars more for social programs and that in a budget of five hundred eighty billion dollars."

Indeed, there he was, the heir to the most popular political dynasty in twentieth-century America, having decided, after years and years of waiting and of rebuilding his reputation after the accident on Martha's Vineyard, that he was stepping into the race for president of the United States. I had expected at least relief, or perhaps a touch of the old Kennedy bravado. Instead, the senator sat stiffly in a straight-backed chair, his legs crossed carefully at the knee. He spoke so quietly it was difficult to hear him. As usual, his sentences were often incomplete. Instead, they were fragments run together to be sorted out later so they would make some sense in print. It was impossible to know whether Kennedy was uncomfortable with this conversation or uncomfortable about what lay ahead. He was ahead of Jimmy Carter by a huge margin in the polls. My colleague Hugh Sidey would soon write that Carter, facing a Kennedy challenge, was already a lame-duck president. But Kennedy had his doubts. He had been in national politics long enough and was fatalistic enough to know there is no sure thing in his business, or even in his own life. "Carter was ahead of Ford by thirty-two points after the convention in 1976," he recalled, "and it was a very close election. Nixon was once ahead of John Kennedy by twelve points. And my brother John was behind by twenty points in West Virginia and won that primary in three weeks. It will be a hotly contested challenge."

The urgings and congratulations for a decision presumably made had flooded in, and he took some notice. But he had seen that before too, when brother Robert announced his candidacy against Lyndon Johnson in 1968. "I've been heartened and encouraged by the response," he said, still very quietly, "but I'm realistic about both the burdens and challenges of a campaign. I've got a very healthy sense of realism. I've been in national campaigns." His voice then fell even more. "This is a very sober challenge," he muttered. "One that you have to approach from a very sober point of view." He paused a second and then added: "And I do."

3

The Romantic
Conservative

The oak doors to the office swung open. At the far end of the elongated office sat Ronald Wilson Reagan, then the first-term governor of California. He was leaning over his desk, pen in hand, studying some papers stacked neatly on his clean desk. His coat was buttoned, his head cocked slightly to the right. On the corner of the huge desk sat a great glass jar of jelly beans, his favorite snack. As I made the long walk across the office, the governor remained absorbed in his work. Then, as I took the last few strides toward him, the governor looked up, his face beaming with a greeting smile. He rose slowly and we shook hands, his head nodding gently.

The memory that persists through the years is the utter perfection of the way the scene was played. Every piece of the set was in place. The main character did his bit as if rehearsed a hundred times. No phones jangled. No aides clambered for one last signature, one last word with the boss. It was as if the script had read: *Entrance scene. Governor at desk, working. Rises as visitor approaches. Smiles. Shakes hands.*

It wasn't important to anyone else just how the scene was played, but the man behind the desk was a professional and it mattered to him. The impression he left was one of serenity and of a man in control, if not of the world beyond him, then at least of his own private world.

I had gone to interview Reagan about the raging protests against the war in Vietnam. Governor Reagan had achieved national attention for his harsh remarks about student protests, and I had come expecting more of the red-meat rhetoric of the reactionary right wing. Instead, the mild-mannered governor spent a friendly half hour talking quietly and rather uninterestingly about the problems of protest in the country. A hardliner in public, Reagan was the gentlest of men in private. The public anger that he could turn up to a hot flame was missing. Instead, he seemed calm and measured. The words he used with such heavy effect on the platform wouldn't come to him in the calm of his perfectly decorated office. This man who could seem so unreasonable when his words were for mass consumption, seemed the very soul of reasonableness. This man who could excoriate students for objecting to a stupid and cruel war, was, surprisingly, genuinely likeable.

Across the country, the race was on. John Connally had been raising money and traveling for more than a year. Congressman Phil Crane had been at it longer than that. Senator Robert Dole, the vice-presidential nominee on Gerald Ford's ticket in 1976, had been planning and campaigning since his defeat three years earlier. Howard Baker, John Anderson, and George Bush were in the race as well. Harold Stassen, who now always runs, said he was doing it again. An Hispanic businessman from Los Angeles, Benjamin Fernandez, was running too, to raise the cause of his people before the Republican party.

The pulse of presidential politics in America beats from election to election without pause. But in the last three months before election year that pulse quickens. There are simply too many things to do to run a successful presidential campaign through thirty-five primaries, through the caucuses in states from coast to coast, through the fund-raising events required by new federal law. An early start is a necessity.

But in October, in the sunny hillsides of the Pacific Palisades just west of Los Angeles, I sensed almost no hint of the excitement building elsewhere. Only the tense efficiency of the staff members indicated that something more than an afternoon nap was in store. The house was nestled into the luxuriant greenery of Southern California. The Pacific Ocean sparkled below the hillsides. Inside, the place was airy and open, staghorn ferns gracing the atrium by the front door. The swimming pool reflected the deep blue of the western sky. Mexican gardeners were pruning and preening the grounds. Friendly dogs wandered about.

The former governor of California, then sixty-eight years old, drifted gracefully into the room, past the piano loaded down with silver-framed pictures of the family's friends: Bob Hope, the late Edgar Bergen, Frank Sinatra. He glided through the rooms, each decorator-beautiful, past the little glass containers of jelly beans, past the Oriental artifacts and into the little library off the living room. He sat down in front of the books, all leather-bound and classic, put there for effect. It was not the grab bag of books accumulated helter-skelter in the pursuit of varied ideas over the years.

The talk of the political community at the time was that this man was too old to be president. But he looked ten years younger than his age. His cheeks had a rosy glow that suggested an almost adolescent good health. His white shirt was open at the neck. A blue cashmere V-neck sweater covered the shirt. He was wearing dark blue velvet pumps embossed with gold R's positioned back to back.

Ronald Reagan was at ease—almost. There was every appearance of a relaxed man, comfortable in his home, comfortable with himself. The lovely Nancy Davis Reagan was close by, as always. They looked moving-picture perfect. There was, however, the slightest hint of anxiety in the air. An aide shoved a microphone and a tape recorder between me and the governor to protect against the misquote. Nancy Reagan projected her usual air of alert protectiveness. Reagan himself, aware that he was about to embark on what would have to be his last attempt to win the presidency of the United States, had the look around his eyes of someone just a bit afraid he would be hurt or misunderstood, that he would falter and misstate a point and cause himself trouble. He seemed so eager to be understood, to be liked, that it was disarming. Hostility seemed out of the question in that setting, with this nice man and his nice wife in his nice house on a beautiful day beside the Pacific.

The former governor leaned forward in his seat, fingertips pressed neatly together, head tilted slightly. The campaign that stretched out ahead of him looked not much different from the life he had led for years.

"I've been making a living on the mashed potato circuit," he said smiling. "I have a feeling now that I don't get on airplanes. I get up in the morning and put them on, like a pair of pants. I wear them. In show business we used to say that if you don't sing or dance, you wind up an after-dinner speaker."

His was still the same sunny and romantic conservatism that won him raves for after-dinner speeches for so many years. It was partly the conservatism derived from wealth, prosperity, good health, a devoted wife, pleasant climate, and the applause that had rung in his ears for decades. Unlike many of those who still followed him and worked for him, his was now only rarely an angry, resentful conservatism. His brand of political philosophy was more a mildly annoyed sort of conservatism rooted in the disbelief that anyone or any government would meddle in lives that can be so perfect as his appeared. He can turn up the anger in front of a big crowd, matching his heat to their resentments, but he didn't feel it as he once did. His life was too good.

"I used to fantasize," he said, "what it would be like if everyone in government [he pronounced it "gummint"] would quietly slip away and close the doors and disappear. See how long it would take the people of this country to miss them. I think that life would go on, and the people would keep right on doing the things they are doing, and we would get along a lot better than we think." He was not serious of course. This was just another little homily to show that it is the faceless government that has led America needlessly astray. The good people of this great nation, he believed, are almost without need of a government.

"I think one of the things that has been done over the past few decades . . . was a tendency to have increasing government by an elite, and those at the government levels believing that they had to make the decisions more and more regarding how business and industry are run, interfering virtually in every one of our lives. And they are doing this to a people who for two hundred years have probably been the most independent and most individually free people in all the history of mankind. Oh, government is a legitimate function. When I talk about regulations, I always use the term 'unnecessary regulations.' I don't want medicines that could destroy our health. But then government goes beyond that protection thing, and they start trying to protect us from ourselves."

The problems of the time, Reagan asserted, are not only not being cured by government, but are actually being caused by them. "We have seen politicians in recent decades set people apart. They have helped to create special interest groups, whether on racial or religious lines or on ethnic lines, whether it's labor or management, whatever; and they have done it for selfish reasons. Then they can appeal by giving or offering a promise to one group that they'll get special treatment. They are appealing to envy and greed and pitting one group against another."

To complement his view of the unalterable goodness of the American people, Reagan still carries his dark perceptions of Soviet evil. Twenty years earlier he had written to then Vice-President Richard Nixon: "As the cold war continues, I'm sure many people lose sight of the basic conflict and begin to accept that two nations are foolishly bickering with some justice and right as well as wrong on each side. This 'tolerant' view ignores, of course, the fact that only 'communism' is dedicated to imposing its 'way and belief' on all the world." There, in the sun-drenched hills by the ocean, he believed it still. "I know this is going to be a perilous time ahead," he said. "I think the arrogance of the Soviet statements and actions reveals how far they are probably going to go to test us. I guess the biggest reaction of anything I say is to my line that maybe we should stop worrying about whether the rest of the world likes us and decide we are going to be respected in the world as we once were. I think this loss of respect is reversible, mainly because the people want it reversed.

We have backed away from our principles. We have appeased. We've certainly turned off a number of our friends."

He had said it all a thousand times before. But he did it again, on demand, and did it well. He was not mesmerizing nor powerful face to face. The lines were thoroughly rehearsed but were redelivered without any sign of boredom. His message was clear and could be taken or left, according to one's tastes. It was a mild, nearly lulling performance. "The kind of America we had," he concluded, "is still there."

This was to be Reagan's second time around the presidential track, although he had made a last-minute run on Richard Nixon in 1968, only to withdraw at the convention before the voting. In 1976 he had come within 117 delegate votes of wresting the nomination from incumbent Jerry Ford in what became a near civil war between the Reagan conservatives and the more moderate forces behind the then-President. In charge of that campaign was John Sears, a lawyer who had begun his national political work with the Nixon campaigns but who had been shoved aside by the Haldeman-Ehrlichman palace guards once Nixon was president. Sears was still at the helm of the Reagan campaign as it began in 1979. He was as intense as Reagan was relaxed. He chain smoked and interrupted his perceptive discussions of American politics with little bursts of hoarse laughter, as if to indicate how absurd much of political life is. While Reagan was relaxing at home, Sears was running a huge staff spread out across the country. He was trying to plan every last detail of the coming campaign in the hopes that their man would not make a mistake. But as the other candidates were out raising money and campaigning in the early primary states, Reagan had avoided too much exposure, too many speeches, and hadn't even made his formal announcement of candidacy. All over the country, the Reagan loyalists were getting edgy. Their candidate was ahead in the polls over all the other Republicans, but they were afraid he would be overtaken while resting in California. Sears, meanwhile, seemed to have it all figured out.

"We come into this campaign as the front-runner," he said accurately enough, "not just in the polls, but from the fact that it has been just three years since we actually ran a race. Having done it once before is a bigger advantage than popularity. Carter, at the moment, is dominating the polls by his weakness. It's like rooting for the second-string quarterback when the first-string guy is in trouble. The beneficiary is whoever is best known. About half really like you, the rest just want an alternative. Carter's weakness is irreversible. He can't be renominated, let alone re-elected. Thinking he's a good fellow doesn't mean he's got a chance to reverse that position.

"Now the tendency of front-runners is to try to protect their lead, to avoid risk, to be dead in the water. Politics is motion and excitement. On the other hand, the front-runner has more control than anyone else over the race. There cannot be a race unless and until the front-runner is ready to have one. So there has to be a careful balancing of when to get in and then running harder than if you were behind. If you're too protective and that lead starts to vanish, it looks like someone is catching you, and then he gets all the attention. Our biggest opponent is us. If we do our job right, nobody can catch us. The opponents must try to cause the front-runner to turn and fight."

Sears's understanding of the process has always been extremely astute. He knew his troops were impatient, but he was fighting against a premature announcement and a too-early campaign that would only drain money out of the Reagan treasury, a treasury limited by federal law to spending no more than seventeen million dollars through the entire nominating process. "The primary system," he observed, "is not really an elective process. Rather, it's a process for activists in each party. A very political crowd. They make their decisions in a very sophisticated way, not from your thirty-second and sixty-second TV spots. Thus, in the primaries money is not a determinate as in the general election."

The Reagan staff appeared unconcerned about their opposition. Instead, they seemed worried, as Sears put it, about "us." Underlying much of the Reagan staff activity was the usually unspoken concern that the pleasant man they represented would somehow commit some unpardonable mistake and thus make himself unelectable. He had, after all, done exactly that in 1976 when he suggested, almost offhandedly, that some ninety billion dollars in federal programs could be terminated and left to the states. The figure was so huge that it raised immediate fears of large losses in federal benefits of all sorts. Those words may well have cost him the nomination in 1976. The history of presidential elections in the television age is filled with the one-word or single-incident misstep that ends a candidacy: Romney was "brainwashed" about Vietnam, McGovern proposed giving a thousand dollars to every citizen, Edmund Muskie shed tears of anger and hurt outside the New Hampshire offices of the Manchester *Union-Leader,* which had been ridiculing his wife. None by themselves were important, except that they reverberated in the voters' heads, symbolizing some important negative impression. Romney had seemed a bit dim for the presidency; McGovern too liberal; Muskie too brittle. Reagan and his homilies had always seemed a little unsophisticated, a little too dumb, they said, to be president. The Reagan staff worried from the start that it would happen again.

Surveying the field around them, there was not much in the way of competition they thought they had to worry about. Howard Baker, they felt, could mount a terrific challenge if he ever decided to, but time was running out. They didn't bother to mention Crane, Dole, or Anderson. Nor, at the time, did they raise the name of George Bush in discussing their opponents. John Connally, who had already raised millions of dollars and had been campaigning hard all across the country, carried too many "negatives," the Reagan people said. Worse, he was a statist, not a conservative like Reagan, who wanted to reduce the role of the federal government. "He's dangerous," economics adviser Martin Anderson said. "If he's nominated I will work against him. He's got no sense of limits, no scruples about the use of the federal government. And he's smart too."

4

Big John,
Big Money

There was nothing delicate about John Bowden Connally. "Big John" the press called him. And he was big. Over six feet, a wealthy man with a huge ranch near San Antonio, a huge law practice in Houston, and a huge opinion of his own qualifications to be president of the United States. If there was a grain of humility in John Connally, he kept it well disguised. He could reel off facts and opinions with an assuredness that was awesome. He was indeed as smart as he thought he was. He had served in a series of government posts: governor of Texas (three times), treasury secretary in Richard Nixon's government, secretary of the navy in John Kennedy's government. He had been wounded when Kennedy, his seat mate in the presidential limousine, was killed in Dallas. Nearly all his adult life he had been a close friend and ally of fellow Texan Lyndon B. Johnson, for whom he had worked when Johnson first came to Congress. The two maintained a strong relationship, one filled with the bitterness common to two headstrong and mightily ambitious men who need each other's help, until Johnson's death. Although his training, alliances, and affiliation had been with the Democrats all his life, Connally had switched parties after his service with Nixon. Some said it was to take advantage of a promise Nixon had made to make him vice-president in his second term. Connally said it was because his basic conservatism was increasingly offended by liberal Democratic programs. Both explanations were accurate.

It was impossible to forget, when looking at and talking to John B. Connally, that he had been Lyndon Johnson's protégé. No matter how conservative and pro-business his politics were, the resemblance was too strong, in manner and in approach. Connally, like Johnson, believed he could understand any problem, convince any doubter, that the sheer power of his mind and his presence could bend steel. It was a damaging association for a Republican. It was impossible as well to forget that Connally had helped Richard Nixon. Connally had told Nixon, once the White House tapes were discovered, to "call in a group of witnesses, make sure it's in the open, and burn them." The advice might have saved Nixon's presidency. But it was characteristically impolitic.

Because so much of American politics is based on the perceived "character" of the candidates, that is, on the public estimate arrived at through television of the personality of the men seeking the office, each election is now, in large part, an attempt to correct the mistakes of the previous choice. Jimmy Carter rode to office on the revulsion at Nixon's smarmy illegality. His sweetness and love and smiling humility were to be the antidote to Nixonism. And in 1979 John Connally looked, in large measure, to be the antidote to the ineffectiveness, the confusion, even meekness, of the Carter presidency. Had he run in the morality play that was the 1976 campaign, Connally would have been laughed off the track. But in 1980 Connally's very size and swagger made him a factor to be taken seriously. In many ways, he was the quintessential anti-Carter. He was blunt, abrasive, experienced, cocky, and had even had a brush with the law resulting from his service in the Nixon administration.

The Watergate grand jury had indicted Connally in 1974 for

accepting ten thousand dollars from an association of dairymen, in return for his role in urging Nixon to approve higher federal price supports for milk. An associated charge of perjury also had been lodged because of allegedly false testimony before the grand jury. Connally went to trial on both charges and hired himself the best criminal lawyer in Washington, Edward Bennett Williams, for a reported fee of a quarter million dollars. Williams battered the prosecution's chief witness (who allegedly had paid Connally the money) until he was no longer convincing to the jury. A parade of character witnesses then appeared, including the Reverend Billy Graham. Connally was acquitted of the bribery charge. The perjury charge, on the other hand, had been separated from the payoff charge during a conference in the judge's chambers. The charges and the trial were, of course, weapons with which to assault Connally, mostly in private. No less a figure than Leon Jaworski, the one-time Watergate prosecutor and in 1979 a supporter of George Bush, spread the word that although the evidence was shaky on the bribery charge, a clear-cut case existed against Connally on the perjury charge. But once Connally was acquitted of bribery, the prosecutors never chose to bring the perjury matter to trial. (Jaworski himself had stayed out of the Connally case because of his Texas associations.)

As a candidate for president, Big John Connally was trying desperately to turn these weaknesses into strengths. When asked about the milk deal, as he was endlessly, Connally blustered that he was the "only certified not-guilty candidate running in either party." His image as a Texas wheeler-dealer attracted huge financial support from the captains of American industry who saw Connally as being as tough and even as reckless as they wished they could be. But for those who worried that the man was untrustworthy and would be uncontainable if he were president, Connally had a standard defense. He would stick out his jaw and say: "If you mean someone who knows how to deal with congressmen and senators, then I plead guilty. I'm a wheeler-dealer. If you're talking about someone who can negotiate with world leaders on an equal basis and not be tail-end Charlie, then I'm a wheeler-dealer. If you're talking about someone who is smart enough to go into a horse trade with a good, sound horse and not come out with one that's one-eyed and spavined, then I'm that."

When John Connally addressed a problem, he had the ability to cut through the extraneous matter and to devise a set of crisp policy recommendations. Once he had done that, he lost patience with those who questioned his decision and judgment. In early October, in a speech in Washington, Connally proposed his own solution to the thorny Middle East problems. His plan was straightforward—indeed, sensible. Israel must pull back to its pre-1967 borders, surrendering the West Bank to some sort of autonomous Palestinian state. Only moderate Palestinians who acknowledged the right of Israel to exist could be dealt with in such a process. The Arab oil states must renounce the use of oil as a political weapon and must promise fair prices. The United States should establish a serious military presence in the area to help guarantee the peace. It was not an unthinkable policy; in fact, the principles he cited were widely shared. Written by a former member of the National Security Council, the speech had even been sent to Henry Kissinger for his comments. But Connally's position was too blunt for the hypersensitive American Jewish community, which immediately interpreted his plan as asking Israel to trade its security for Western access to cheaper oil. It was an unfair interpretation, but Connally had invited it with his characteristic disregard for the sensitivities surrounding the problem.

A few days after that speech, Connally flew into Harrisburg, Pennsylvania, on his chartered Lear jet, the kind of transportation the favorite of the board rooms of corporate America should have had. In one of the tens of thousands of small motel meeting rooms in this country, all with rough-hewed, plastic timbers across the ceiling and wrought-iron chandeliers, Connally held a press conference. It was an exercise he didn't enjoy, largely because it bored him and because his basic view of the press was disdainful, the kind of disdain rich, successful people have for the poor folks who chase after them for news stories. But he reminded those of us in the press right away that he too had been poor. "I studied my last two years in high school by the light of a kerosene lamp."

"Did you also split wood?" a reporter asked laughing.

"Yes," Connally answered with a straight face, "for our wood cook stove." His pitch was that he was an underdog, a one-man campaign (he had a staff of more than one hundred) pitted against those of Baker, Dole, and Crane, who had large congressional staffs to help them with research, and up against Reagan, who "has been running for president for ten years and has nine hundred thousand names of financial contributors" (Reagan claimed 400,000). Still, he said, the race "by the end of the year would come down to two men, me and Governor Reagan."

Standing a few miles from Three Mile Island, where the nation's most frightening nuclear power plant accident had occurred only months before, Connally bulled ahead to urge that "we must build more nuclear power plants. But we must make them as safe as possible." And to make the point to the press that while he might seem overbearing, he was capable, Connally announced firmly: "What we've lacked is leadership and decisiveness."

An hour later Connally was at the West Shore Country Club, across the Susquehanna River from the state capital. He looked at home there, where he was trying to raise still more money for his campaign. A rich selection of cheese and fruit was spread across the tables. Double-tiered brass fountains with blinking red lights around their edges pumped wine up from a big bowl, discharging it in little streams back toward the base. To get a drink, one stuck one's glass into this wine-squirting machine.

"I'm not an ordinary politician," Connally told the money givers. "Running for this office is not to satisfy some deep personal yearning to be president. I could have been elected to Congress in 1948, but Nellie and I chose to seek financial security for ourselves and our family. I could have been elected governor for a fourth term. I could have been elected to the Senate. . . . I've known every leader of both houses of Congress from both parties for forty years. . . . I know how this economic system functions.

"I know something about the private sector. That's where the wealth is, that's where the jobs are, not in government. I've served on the board of directors of the New York Central Railway, Pan American Airlines, Greyhound Bus, Dr. Pepper, Texas Instruments. I'm a product of this free enterprise system. That's what I want to protect. Government is a parasite. Government is a consumer. It doesn't create wealth."

The public address system was scratchy and it annoyed Connally, used to the best of everything. At the back of the crowd, some people gathered around the wine machine fell back into their

own chatter. ". . . I'd change the whole direction of this country.
. . ." Some other guests tried to hush the cocktail chatter. ". . .
I'd accelerate all depreciation schedules for business. . . ." More
chatter. ". . . This business of having a president who is just an
average American is a nice idea, but I think we need some leadership. . . ."

If leadership were merely being able to rouse an audience, Connally would have been declared president that night in Harrisburg.
He was the featured attraction at a large fund-raising dinner that
had brought nine hundred people to the motel to eat roast beef and
to contribute to the races of other Republicans running for the
state legislature. Connally was a big drawing card, and he was not
often content simply to lend his name to other candidate's fund-
raising efforts. In some places he demanded a split of the gate.

After the band's version of the "Yellow Rose of Texas" had died
down, Connally was introduced. "With this man there is no pus-
syfooting," the master of ceremonies declared. And John B. Connally began to wind up the crowd.

His message was first one of Republican loyalty. "We need a
GOP majority in Congress," he said. "We can run a Chinese fire
drill and elect just a Republican president, but the power is in
Congress and for forty-three of the last forty-seven years the Congress has been Democratic."

As he warmed to the subject, his voice rose, but his cadences
were always perfect. His voice had power and it had authority, but
it was never out of control.

"The Democrats have said no to the future," he said. "No to
the United States' role in the world. No to the SST, no to fusion,
no to fast breeders, no to the B-1, no to the neutron bomb. The
Democrats are the party of retreat, retrenchment, and resignation.
We believe in expansion, vitality, and growth."

Connally had his program figured out. Listening to him, it
seemed to have all the answers. He would rebuild the system of
vocational education to train people for the jobs available. He
would remove the taxation burden from interest on savings accounts to encourage investment and savings. He would reduce
taxes on business. He would put "fair trade before free trade." If
the Japanese didn't begin to let some American products into their
country when he was president, Connally bellowed, "they could

sit in their Toyotas on the docks of Yokohama watching their own Sony TVs." As always, the line brought great applause and laughter. It had become a sort of campaign trademark of the big brash Texan who, by the force of his personality, would restore American prestige in the world.

"We have got to stop taking our scientific advice from Jane Fonda and Ralph Nader," he shouted, and the room went wild. He called for a tax cut of fifty billion dollars. More applause. "We must begin a moral and spiritual revival to regain leadership of the free world." Connally was hot now, his pace was quicker, the crowd was totally with him.

"This party, the GOP, stands for Growth, Opportunity, and Progress," Connally thundered. "Growth, Opportunity, Progress! The days of glory for America have not passed!"

Everyone in the room was on his feet. The applause rolled back and forth through the big motel ballroom. Connally waved and sat down.

"Wow!" said the master of ceremonies. It was Connally at his best.

The Lear jet took Connally on to Philadelphia, where, of course, he raised more money, but where he was also to speak on foreign policy before the World Affairs Council. In the previous year he had traveled the country, campaigning for other politicians, all the time thinking he was building IOUs from the Republican party all over the nation. Now he was increasing that pace, but working mostly for himself. Behind all the jetting about lay Connally's strategy. It was the notion of what he called "a national campaign." It was not in John Connally's soul to spend concentrated amounts of time in a single place, to work the town halls and meeting rooms of one or two states like Iowa or New Hampshire. Even though this sort of small-scale, focused effort had made the obscure Jimmy Carter into a president of the United States in 1976, Big John Connally would not be staying in people's homes in Iowa like Jimmy Carter had. He was not planning to do terribly well in Iowa or even New Hampshire. His hope lay in states like South Carolina and Florida and later on in Illinois.

The Connally campaign would be spread all over the nation. His plan was to raise more money than anyone else (and already he had gathered up more than two million dollars, more than any other candidate), to spend that money moving around the country, arousing big groups of Republicans like those in Harrisburg, and then to hope that his sheer presence would overcome many of the negative associations voters carried around about the Texan. Money would also be spent lavishly on national television. It was a grand strategy, an imperial campaign. Connally had decided to offer himself to the nation as a whole, take me or leave me. He would not stoop to worrying about detailed campaign organizations, even in a place like Iowa. It did not matter to him that the benefits of winning that first real contest in Iowa could be enormous. It did not matter how important organization was in Iowa, where convention delegates were picked not in the privacy of the primary ballot box, but by a complicated caucus system in which votes were cast in people's living rooms, at precinct meeting after precinct meeting, in full view of their neighbors. It was too small-scale for Connally.

It was a risky plan. The new rules of American politics made those first states, Iowa and New Hampshire, crucial to any candidate's success, simply because they generated so much television attention that the results in those states could become self-fulfilling. While the others were out speaking to ten people in a farmhouse in God-Knows-Where, Iowa, Connally was on the lecture circuit in a grand way.

At the World Affairs Council meeting in Philadelphia Connally spoke to prominent business and civic leaders who banded together to hear about foreign policy and world trade matters. His view of the world beyond the oceans was as boldly drawn and his policies as clear-cut as those he held on domestic affairs. "We are in a struggle for global leadership," Connally said. "This is not just a struggle for the world's resources, but a struggle for the minds of men.

"America has been mortgaging its future rather than investing in its future. We have failed to stem inflation and to solve our energy problems. Abroad, we are being challenged economically by friend and foe. . . .

"We have a president and an administration who cannot see or cannot understand the realities of the world. . . .

"There is no American military presence in the Middle East

worthy of the name. The nearness of the Soviet Union enhances their power to influence and subvert in the Middle East. We must achieve a rough balance of power with the Soviet Union in the Middle East. We must provide a military shield for our interests there. Our military presence will stabilize that area. . . .

"Never in history has a major power so acquiesced to such a grave shift in political power. Russia is exceeding the United States. Nuclear superiority is the queen on the diplomatic chessboard. And this administration has made a bad situation worse. . . .

"The American nuclear umbrella no longer protects Western Europe. Our strategic forces can only deter a Soviet first strike against the continental United States, and even that will soon be lost."

The problem, in Connally's view, was that America had been caught in the thrall of the "devil of defeatism" in the post-Vietnam period. To blame for this, he said, were those who were so "obsessed with Vietnam that they are more afraid of themselves than of our enemies." The real lesson of Vietnam, Connally said, is "to stand and fight only for our vital interests, but then stand and fight to win." This, he said, would replace the "so-what school of foreign policy" that had shrugged its shoulders at Soviet-sponsored inroads in Angola, South Yemen, and Afghanistan. "We must abandon tiptoe diplomacy," Connally warned, adding that military spending needed to be increased and that the American intelligence capability, reined in after the discovery of abuses of its charter, had to be rebuilt.

Although Connally said it better than any of the other candidates, his point of view on both domestic and foreign policy was nearly identical to that of the other Republicans preparing their primary races. Unlike campaigns past, the Republicans had almost no traces left of their old eastern-liberal-versus-Western-conservative split. The only dissident running in the primary contests was Congressman John B. Anderson, once as conservative in his outlook as all the other candidates, but after twenty years in Congress he had altered his positions to more closely resemble the old Rockefeller wing of the party. In the fall of 1979, Anderson promised to be no more than a sideshow to the great Republican presidential circus.

Connally perfectly articulated the Republican assault being mounted on Jimmy Carter and the Democrats. In terms of pure rhetorical style he was the best of all the GOP hopefuls. Indeed, Connally was plainly the best speaker and the best political showman in the 1980 campaign. Even the appealing Ronald Reagan paled next to Connally's ability to arouse a crowd. Connally's presence and self-confidence was perfectly matched to the party's call for a brawny foreign policy and to the party's assault on the confusion and contradiction of the Carter presidency.

But one of the persistent paradoxes of the 1980 presidential campaign was that in every instance candidates' strengths were also their weaknesses. In Connally's case his robust and self-assured rhetoric appealed to the American desire for strong presidential leadership. "Leadership for America" was the Connally campaign slogan. But at the same time his nearly arrogant approach to his campaign and to the issues aroused the lingering fears among many voters of abuses of power in the Oval Office that Johnson and his war policy and Nixon in his criminal assault on the Constitution had aroused. Connally was trapped by his own personality. And he frequently showed a blithe disregard for the truth. At a press conference after the Philadelphia speech, I asked Connally about the origins of his Middle East speech of a week before and whether Henry Kissinger had had any role in its preparation. "No," said Connally flatly and rather impatiently, directly contradicting the account of the speech's author who had told me minutes before that Kissinger had commented on the text before it was given.

Connally was raising money at an incredible rate from American big business and at the same time flaunting that money and his unalloyed defense of big business in the American economic system. Yet he was trying to deflate the popular notions that he cared little about the average man and that he was aloof and unapproachable. The previous summer Connally had invited a group of reporters and their spouses to his elegant ranch near San Antonio for a weekend of tennis and stomach-busting dining. The point seemed to be to show Connally as a nice man, a man solicitous of the views and opinions of the press. But the gesture itself smacked of a payoff: Come weekend with the Connallys and go home to write how nice he and his wife, Nellie, are. The weekend failed, partly because a number of reporters simply stayed away rather than explain on what basis they were accepting Connally's hospitality and partly because Connally, according to the stories written after the weekend, was never really comfortable with his guests. He seemed both wary of the reporters and impatient at having to contain his usual bravado.

While Connally was in Philadelphia for his foreign policy speech, Republican mayoral candidate David Marston, involved in a hopeless race against Democrat Billy Green, asked the Texan to come by his campaign headquarters so that he could have his picture taken with the presidential candidate. Connally agreed without much enthusiasm, but decided to show his Republican loyalties. When he got to Marston's office Marston announced to the Connally people that the session was canceled because he feared negative reaction from the city's Jewish community to Connally's earlier Middle East pronouncements. But Marston sought to convert an act of political fear into one of political courage. He issued a press release saying he had met with Connally to try to persuade him to change his position on the Middle East.

Connally had been stiffed. He had been used in a sneaky and useless little ploy. "A cheap political trick," Connally said with disgust later. Yet the Marston ploy had a certain irony to it. It was a case of a snake biting a snake.

From the candidates, from their professional staff members, from the academic experts, from the press and from the public, the complaint came that presidential campaigns are too long, too strung out over too many months. The complaint was more than justified, but it was mostly misdirected. It wasn't the length of the campaign per se that was troublesome. It was the cause of this attenuation that needed to be corrected.

The only way a candidate can succeed in the presidential race is by getting attention, by getting on television, by generating a kind of celebrity and a sense that his victory is, if not inevitable, then at least very likely. The expectation of victory may influence some voters, but more importantly it influences those who make the decisions about whose face will be on the magazine covers, whose speech will be covered on the evening news, and whose

63

progress will be covered on the front pages of the great newspapers.

This pressure to be seen as a winner forced the candidates into a series of apparently meaningless stunts in the fall of 1979, none of which had direct influence on the selection of delegates to the party conventions the following summer—where, after all, the actual nomination would be conferred. One of the more bizarre of these publicity tricks took place in Florida in November 1979. Both Republican and Democratic parties there decided to run a test election in which party members could vote their preference for the presidential nomination. The point was mainly to generate interest in state party affairs, and as a side benefit to attract some political tourists from the national press to sunny Florida. The results would have nothing to do with the official delegate selection process that would occur in March of the following year. But the chance to have a statewide vote, even an unofficial vote, attracted some of the candidates from both parties.

No one took the Florida exercise more seriously than John Connally. He campaigned in the state and spent more than a third of a million dollars on advertising and organizing to get out his vote. He, along with Crane, Dole, Bush, and even Reagan, who visited the Republican convention site just before the voting, was on hand for the exercise. Connally was coating his throat with honey to soothe the damage of too many speeches. He dispatched his sons to buttonhole delegates. He sent yellow roses to all the delegates' rooms. The hope was to finish ahead of Reagan, or at least a close second, and thus to generate the expectation that it was indeed a Reagan-Connally race. In the end, Connally did finish second to Reagan, with about twenty-six percent of the votes cast. But when the game is played for effect, rather than for hard results, the outcome is determined by appearances not by votes. Connally had worked hardest and finished second. Worse, he had almost been caught by George Bush, who finished third, with twenty-one percent of the vote. Connally had done adequately in Florida—at substantial cost—but not well enough to break out of the pack and generate the kind of publicity and momentum that he wanted. It was a bad omen.

———————

Every presidential campaign has its cranks and crackbrains, its candidates of the political fringe and those walking the psychological edge. The attraction to the less-than-serious candidate is naturally the publicity harvest he estimates he can reap by offering himself to lead the nation. In the more legitimate of these forlorn exercises there is at least the core of some belief, some particular issue that the candidate and his followers want to advance. In the more pitiful of these cases there are only variants of common sociopathic behavior, often elaborate versions of the craziness that causes other citizens to walk down Main Street shouting imprecations at no one in particular.

But there is another category of hopeless candidates that has neither the excuse of psychotic behavior nor the justification of true belief in a cause to explain entrance into the presidential race. Such a candidate was Senator Larry Pressler, a thirty-seven-year-old freshman from South Dakota. In September, as the field of Republicans was enlarging (it would eventually total ten) Pressler, then exactly eight months into his first year as a $57,500-a-year senator, declared that he too was running for president. From the instant of his announcement, Pressler's cause was hopeless. He was too young, too inexperienced, totally lacking in substantive accomplishment. His entrance into the race would have been a cause for laughter except that he had already been elected to a position of considerable public responsibility. His reaction to that political success was to try to reach even further, instantly. To be sure, there were other hopeless candidates in the field, some of whom held high public office, but Pressler's misuse of the process was especially egregious.

His campaign began in a committee meeting room in the Dirksen Senate Office Building, with all the trappings of an actual political event. Network camera crews were on hand, their lights overilluminating the setting. The room was packed with people sporting gaudy yellow and black lapel pins proclaiming their desire for "Pressler for President." Only a few minutes late, the candidate himself emerged from a doorway smiling an uncertain smile. At first his entrance passed unnoticed and his youthful face went blank. But soon his fans mustered the requisite applause and the smile reappeared. He adjusted the microphone, paused, grinned, and then read: "Today, I am announcing my candidacy for the presidency of the United States."

What was his candidacy about? "Let me emphasize," he explained, "the need to elect a president in the prime of his life. ... Many signers of the Declaration of Independence were my age or younger. Perhaps the difficulty and the burdens of the office is [sic] so great that we should consider electing persons in the prime of their lives rather than electing someone in the twilight of his or her career." Pressler recognized that his age and the fact that he had done nothing of national distinction, except convince the voters of South Dakota to elect him twice to the House of Representatives and once to the Senate, needed some explanation. He reached out for the Founding Fathers in their time of shorter life expectancies to justify his hubris. Like Connally, he would make his greatest liability into his campaign theme.

What did the young senator want to bring to the public debate? He promised an "idealistic campaign" based, he said, on specifics. But his only specific was to urge that the nation wean its energy appetite away from fossil fuels and toward alcohol manufactured in small, backyard stills and then mixed with gasoline. "To announce for the presidency," he said wisely, "is a very awesome thing to do at my age. The job is so big I don't think any one person can do it well."

Surely, those who knew the senator best didn't think he could do it well. His own state party chairman was phoned by a reporter for a reaction to the presidential announcement. At first the chairman thought the inquiry was a "crank call." Then, he said, "I can sum up my reaction in three words, 'Ha, ha, ha.' " Pressler's Senate colleague, George McGovern, who knew a thing or two about long-shot presidential races, called him "a political mystery." "It's all done with mirrors," McGovern said. "People will think there's something in the water out there that makes us all want to run for president all the time."

By the end of 1979 Pressler had separated $35,000 from his misguided supporters and said he had pledges of $15,000 more, well short of the $100,000 raised in twenty states necessary to receive federal matching funds for his campaign. He had displayed, during the three months of his candidacy, an eerie ability to separate himself from the unreality of his campaign. One day in December Pressler called a press conference at a tennis club on Manhattan's East Side to demonstrate his backyard alcohol still. A score or so of chairs were lined up neatly in the club. A long table held a portable public address system to carry the senator's voice. It was like thousands of other meetings between the press and politicians that year, except that in this case I was the only reporter who showed up.

The empty chairs didn't faze Larry Pressler. He launched into his pitch as if the room had been overflowing. To make his point about the utility of alcohol as a supplemental fuel, Pressler had with him an odd contraption made of galvanized buckets and tubs and funnels. The creator of this device, a bespectacled man with muttonchop whiskers and the dirty fingernails of a chronic tinkerer, poured fermented corn mash into the machine, plugged the cord into the electrical socket, and adjusted the tubes and valves. As the senator looked on hopefully, the machine produced a trickle of alcohol. The odor of the fuel mixed with the faint smell of dementia in the room. Outside, a languid game of doubles proceeded without interruption as Pressler continued to address the crowd of one inside.

To play the game of running for president to generate publicity, it is, of course, necessary for the candidate to feign total seriousness, and to express with great earnestness the conviction that despite the odds, victory is possible. The day after the one-man press conference in New York, I asked Larry Pressler just what he was up to and why it was he felt he could take time off from his new Senate duties to pursue the presidency. We were sitting in his office in Washington. His stare focused somewhere above and behind my head as he explained that running for president would make him a better senator and that, after all, no one had thought Jimmy Carter had a chance. He refused to admit his candidacy was a publicity stunt.

A year later Senator Pressler got some deserved attention in the press when it was revealed that he had turned down a bribe offered by an FBI agent posing as an Arab sheik in the so-called AB-SCAM affair. Pressler was being videotaped during the encounter. He turned down the money offered for his presidential campaign and explained that "I'm not going to be president. I'm running for the name recognition." He had at last told the truth.

67

Three weeks after our conversation in Washington Pressler announced that he was retiring from the presidential race, the single most rational act of his brief campaign. "I don't seem to send the blood of my countrymen rushing to their heads nor their hands rushing to their checkbooks," he explained.

WINTER
1979–80

5

A Different Kennedy

When Jimmy Carter's presidency was but two years old, the Democratic party met in a mid-term convention in Memphis, Tennessee, to hear reports on their president's progress and to debate the policies that Democrats would have to defend in the campaign of 1980. It was not a pleasant affair. Outdoors an ice storm raged. Inside the huge convention hall the activists of the Democratic party were listening uneasily to the highest ranking members of the Carter administration as they tried to explain a record that was hardly a fulfillment of the liberal dream. Carter, trapped by inflation and a weak economy, had been temporizing with federal spending, cutting here, trimming a bit there, and launching almost no new, costly efforts to help the poor. The delegates in the cavernous hall were restless and unimpressed when Jimmy Carter addressed the convention. Carter was not at his best, as he rarely ever

71

was before large, partisan gatherings of his own party. It was always as if he felt himself an interloper into their proceedings. His voice was high and reedy. His message of moderation was delivered to the full assembly more as a whine and an apology than as an inspiring call to follow a new direction.

There was, however, one fine speaker that winter weekend in December 1978. He was Senator Edward M. Kennedy, who chose to speak to a smaller conclave of the party faithful assembled in a side auditorium to hear a debate on the problems of national health insurance. Carter, concerned about the level of federal spending, had deferred any attempt to institute a national system that would have cost billions of dollars. Kennedy, on the other hand, had long persisted in urging a comprehensive program that would have covered nearly everyone in the land. Carter, feeling the political heat from Kennedy and his liberal allies, had urged instead an insurance program that would protect against the costs of catastrophic illnesses. He also had attempted to institute controls on the skyrocketing costs of hospital care. The issue was a perfect example of the different approaches of the two politicians: Kennedy the full-speed liberal; Carter the cautious moderate.

Kennedy, after sitting through the explanations offered by the Carter administration representatives in the health care meeting, tore loose from all rhetorical restraints. His voice thundering, his head nodding, the last of the Kennedy brothers delivered a moving, impassioned call for the nation to protect all its people from the financial disaster that health problems can cause. He cited his own family's huge health care problems—his broken back from an airplane crash, his father's long, terminal illness, his son's bout with cancer that ended in the amputation of his leg. He said that everyone in the nation deserved the kind of care his family could afford. It was one of the most memorable public speeches those present had ever heard. There is, of course, nothing inherently exciting about a speech explaining budget limits, the constraints of inflation, and the reasons why a particular program can't be implemented. Kennedy had the best of the situation, and he used it to maximum effect. "We must sail against the wind," Kennedy concluded, and the applause rang in his ears for long minutes after he finished.

There was, however, something curious about Ted Kennedy's

performance. He projected a sense of detachment, the feeling that he was watching someone else stir the passions of his audience. It was as if one Ted Kennedy had told another Ted Kennedy to give it his best performance, and as if the first Ted then stood back, enjoying immensely the theatricality of the more public Ted. The performance was nonetheless exciting, but the detachment of the performer robbed the speech of the kind of raw intensity that his brother Robert had been able to muster, full of the kind of emotion that could bring tears or cries of joy. John Kennedy had that same kind of distance from himself, but his speeches were cooler and more polished. It was as if Ted Kennedy could imitate both. But he could equal neither.

Nearly a year after that speech, as autumn turned to winter, the situation in the Democratic party was quite without precedent. The incumbent president had dropped so low in the public opinion polls, and inflation had climbed so high, that the bitter joke in Washington had Carter becoming the first president with poll ratings lower than the prime interest rate. It was not new that a sitting president should be unpopular. Herbert Hoover, Harry Truman, Lyndon Johnson, Richard Nixon, all had managed to sink low in the esteem of the electorate. But at no time in modern political history had a president's low standing coincided with the apparently overwhelming approval of a challenger from within his own party. Every respectable measure of public opinion showed that Ted Kennedy was preferred by Democrats as the next presidential nominee by more than a two-to-one margin. Carter, through the first three years of his presidency, had managed somehow to disappoint every major constituency that had voted him into office. Blacks, whose votes in the southern states had helped return that region to the Democratic column in 1976, were unenthused about Carter and wild about Kennedy, just as they had been for his brothers. The working-class voters—labor, urban, ethnic, and the very backbone of the Democratic Party since FDR —were likewise cool, if not hostile, to Carter. They were ready to invest their hopes in Ted Kennedy. They were ready to believe that once again things could be as they had been with the Kennedys, full of hope and promise, with an activist federal government intent upon righting the wrongs and lifting the working and lower classes up. That the problems were not the same as they had been and that the world had changed dramatically since the last Kennedy had run for president twelve years before didn't initially detract from Ted Kennedy's enormous popularity. Indeed, it seemed to help him. Looking at the apparent demise of Jimmy Carter, Senator Gary Hart of Colorado, who had once managed the sorry presidential campaign of George McGovern but whose own political skill was enormous, observed: "The American people are looking for a politician of *stature,* perhaps as a substitute for solutions."

Stature. Ted Kennedy had that. Or it seemed at the time that he did. Most of the sophisticated political community shared the view held that autumn by Mervin Field, the California pollster who is among the most astute in his profession. Field noted that Kennedy's popularity "is an accumulated, generational perception. He is part of the American culture. His popularity is like a great reservoir that is filled to the brim. He can't use much more support. It would just slop over." The question about Ted Kennedy's presidential campaign was, Field continued, "how much of that reservoir will he have to draw down?"

Not many people involved in the political profession figured at that time that he would have to draw down much. Kennedy had become a truly mythic figure. The nostalgic popularity of his slain brothers had transferred to him. He had never lost an election in his life, save for a nasty little internal fight over the position of whip in the Senate, where, shortly after his accident at Chappaquiddick, Senator Robert Byrd out-organized Kennedy and took the job away. His liberal credentials were impeccable, having received the highest rating for his voting record from the Americans for Democratic Action year after year. All the auguries looked good. The mantle of his brothers would now fall on his shoulders. He had waited and had worked hard in the Senate. His adolescent behavior seemed to be behind him. The cheating at Harvard, the accident that killed Mary Jo Kopechne more than a decade before, the stories of womanizing, these would all be pushed into the shadows of his great sweep toward the presidency.

In Florida the Draft Kennedy movement was being run by two young and enthusiastic political organizers, Sergio Bendixon and Mike Abrams. They were running hard to pack the state Democratic caucuses for the symbolic statewide vote and thus to give a psychological victory to the Kennedy campaign, even though that campaign had not formally begun. The pair had recruited one state government official to their cause, despite the fact that the governor of Florida, Robert Graham, was a staunch Carter supporter. That official, State Controller Gerald Lewis, represented perfectly the kind of uncritical enthusiasm only a Kennedy could elicit among Democrats. One afternoon that fall, I spoke with Lewis at the Draft Kennedy headquarters in Miami. He began a nearly euphoric account of Ted Kennedy's qualities. Soon, however, it was clear he was not talking just about Ted Kennedy. Rather, he was talking about John Kennedy and Bob Kennedy, about Camelot, about the moral certainties of the fight against the war in Vietnam, about the civil rights crusades, and the countless other great but half-remembered moments of recent liberal Democratic causes and struggles. He was talking about a dream he and others had once had, about the kind of political movement that was no longer part of the Democratic party or of its candidates. He was hoping, like so many others who were saying they were for Ted Kennedy, that he could carry them back to times gone by. "Had he ever met Ted Kennedy?" I asked Lewis. "No," he said, astonished at the question. It had not occurred to him that this was a different Kennedy.

All the Kennedy boys seemed destined for their places in American history. Rose and Joseph P. Kennedy had raised them that way, with money and access to the powerful, with ideas and discipline, and an instilled need to excell. Their father had pointed them toward the highest office in the land, and when young Joe died in a World War II bomber, Jack stepped in to fill the ranks. He had made it to the top, only to be martyred in Dallas. That his presidency lacked much in the way of real accomplishment, that it had set the course toward Vietnam, would not matter years later when the young president and his stylish wife would be remembered only for the tone and enthusiasm, the humor and grace they brought to the nation's capital. Then came Robert in 1968. Lyndon Johnson, successor to John, was in trouble for having expanded the Asian war he inherited. But Bob Kennedy held back from challenging Lyndon Johnson, held back until the maverick liberal Eugene McCarthy had damaged Johnson enough to force the incumbent's renunciation of a second term. Only then did Bob Kennedy jump into the race. He was on his way, perhaps, to winning his party's nomination when he too was shot down.

And now it was Ted Kennedy, the kid brother. It was an enormous legacy to carry around, that burden of the Kennedy myth. And Ted Kennedy had held back, first in 1968, then in 1972, when he had no choice because of Chappaquiddick, and again in 1976, when he could have run against Carter. But now, he said, he was ready to be president.

If there were two dozen politically savvy people unattached to any campaign in the United States and willing to bet large amounts of their own cash on Jimmy Carter's chances of retaining his party's nomination against Ted Kennedy, they stayed well hidden in the fall of 1979. Even inside the Republican party the expectation built that it would be Ted Kennedy the party's nominee would face in the fall of 1980. John Connally allowed as how he always heard destiny calling him to square off against the last of the Kennedys, just as it had put him in the car to be wounded when President Kennedy was shot. The Reagan camp also worried about Kennedy. They liked the idea of launching their ideological assaults against a certified liberal, but they were concerned about Kennedy's youth, energy, and vigor (how that word echoes back from the earlier years!) in comparison to the elderly Ronald Reagan.

A few politicians, however, were neither surprised by the Kennedy challenge nor daunted by the prospect. The Carter campaign's chief political strategist, Hamilton Jordan, had felt since the Kennedy assault on the President at the Memphis mid-term convention that the senator would definitely run in the 1980 Democratic primaries. Moreover, he felt that Carter would beat Kennedy badly, largely because Kennedy himself would be the main issue. The Carter aides also believed that Kennedy's liberalism would hurt him eventually. Carter himself had waffled back and forth trying both to move the Democratic party away from Great Society liberalism and to avoid offending the constituencies that the large federal programs had created. Kennedy, the Carter strategists felt, would prove too liberal for the conservative mood of the country.

But beyond the sense that Kennedy's political stance was out of tune with the country, a few others wondered about Ted

Kennedy himself. Winning the presidency requires a variety of qualities and characteristics, most of which have very little to do with the skills necessary for governing the nation once elected. The successful candidate must be driven to achieve the presidency; he cannot merely want the office. He must be at once acutely sensitive to the nuances of each constituency's desires and thoroughly thick-skinned about the abuses he will suffer from the press, from his opponents, and from the constituencies he chooses to ignore. He must, in most cases, be extraordinarily energetic, capable of surviving on minimum sleep, able to tolerate jet lag, motel beds, and the plastic food served by nearly every hotel restaurant, from the humblest Iowa motel to the plusher hundred-dollar-a-night high rises in the big cities. He must want the presidency more than anything else—more than his family, his friends, more than wealth, more than time to think, to read, to relax, to be alone. It must be a consuming desire, a monomania of epic size.

The question raised by those who doubted whether the youngest Kennedy brother was as bright, as tough, and as driven as his brothers was whether Kennedy really wanted the job. Was he, they asked, just performing a rite of passage required by his family's history? Had it become psychologically necessary, in that family, to run for president to become a full adult? Had he not, they asked, tried to disqualify himself from the presidency, or at least from competing with his brothers, with periodic acts of self-destruction? There was the unexplained failure to report the Chappaquiddick accident until the following day, even though his young female companion had drowned in the sunken car. There was his broken marriage, with Joan living alone in Boston and Ted at home in McLean, Virginia. There were the persistent rumors of his goings-on with other women. Would he not, sometime during the endless presidential campaign, find some way again to take himself out of the race? It was not an empty question, for there seemed to be a flaw at the center of Ted Kennedy, a flaw at least in comparison to the myth of Kennedy invincibility, of their power and political savvy, their blinding intelligence, their wit and good humor. To those who saw Ted Kennedy up close, he was certainly less than all that. But then no one could be what the myth required. And there were the polls, and Carter's weak hold on the popular imagination. Kennedy might be less than many wanted to think he was, but he still seemed more than Jimmy Carter. The questions, however, persisted. Greg Schneiders, a Carter campaign staff member and an instinctively good judge of political matters, wondered whether, despite the great lead in the polls, Ted Kennedy had the grit for the presidential race. Schneiders had traveled hundreds of thousands of miles as a personal aide to Jimmy Carter in 1976. By the fall of 1979 he was working with Carter's television advertising expert Gerald Rafshoon. "Teddy is more like Nelson Rockefeller than John Kennedy," Schneiders observed that fall. "JFK scrambled up the ladder. The House. The Senate. He lost the vice-presidential nomination in 1956, and then barely won in 1960. Teddy wants to be and feels qualified to be president, but like Rocky he wants the country to turn to him. Does he have the stomach to go through the humiliating, deflating experience of actually fighting for it? We want to fight him at every turn to see if he has the guts, to see whether he will withdraw or panic."

Carter himself would later use that word, *panic.* He would say that he had kept a steady hand on the helm and had "not panicked in a crisis." The reference was, of course, to Kennedy's conduct after the Chappaquiddick accident. The Carter forces would follow Hamilton Jordan's earlier premonition. Ted Kennedy would be the issue in the Kennedy-Carter race, and the Carter campaign would make sure he was the issue.

From other quarters there were also quiet doubts about the Kennedy candidacy, even if there was little expectation that he would lose to Jimmy Carter. In the Congress, despite the summertime pleas of endangered Democrats who felt they needed help at the top of the party ticket if they were to hold on to their seats in the face of a determined assault by right-wing candidates and activist groups, there were many others who had spent years carving out their own identities back home. The politics of the late twentieth century does not encourage party loyalty, but rather rewards a kind of go-it-alone tendency of every politician to paint himself as a fiercely independent maverick interested only in Right and Truth (and, of course, his own re-election). The prospect of a Kennedy nomination made many of these Democrats realize that they would have to refashion that independence, disavowing Kennedy (carefully, so as not to offend his constituents) just as they had separated themselves from Carter. Colorado's Gary Hart, facing a tougher re-election fight than even he then knew, summed up the Kennedy candidacy this way: "It doesn't do me much good." Maine's Edmund Muskie was equally cool. "I know of at least a dozen Democrats who are less than enthusiastic about Kennedy." Some resented his liberal policy notions. Others just resented him. "This administration," Muskie told me, "is the responsibility not just of the President but also of the whole Democratic party. This early challenge will only lead to his [Carter's] earlier collapse. And if I wanted to run, I'd feel that responsibility very heavily, heavily enough to do nothing until next year. Obviously Kennedy doesn't feel any such restraint."

In early October I was listening to another of Jerry Brown's interminable monologues, this one at his home in the Hollywood Hills. The announcement of Kennedy's candicacy was imminent, and Brown vowed that he would announce his plans to run for the presidency after Kennedy, apparently to show that he was not about to be run off by Kennedy. Brown turned his attention to Kennedy. His own unorthodox view of American politics gave him a clearer perspective on Kennedy than many, especially those in Washington who had simply been awaiting and assuming an eventual Kennedy presidency. "Why is Kennedy running?" Brown asked, not at all disingenuously. "Just what is his debate with Carter? The only issue is that he thinks Carter can't win. If the only issue is career advancement, you can't run a campaign that way. That's why people aren't interested in this process. I think there'll have to be some kind of political realignment. The nation is not governable without new ideas." It was, despite the self-promotion inherent in the analysis, the wisest thing Jerry Brown said that fall.

For so long as he was only a prospective candidate, Ted Kennedy's lead over Carter was massive. But as the days ticked away and Kennedy's formal announcement came closer, attitudes began to change. Kennedy was being compared to the myth that both propelled his candidacy and, by necessity, reduced the stature of the real man. A poll by the Yankelovich organization in late October, only a week before the expected formal Kennedy declaration, showed Kennedy's lead over Carter had already shrunk to only ten percentage points from the thirty or more points he had enjoyed in late summer. The change in public perception of the two men was hardly based on a resurgence of Carter popularity. No more than seventeen percent of those polled said they had much confidence in Carter's handling of the economy, energy problems, or foreign affairs. Kennedy, on the other hand, had three times higher ratings in these areas. But in the age of personality politics, with decisions made by voters more on the basis of perceived character traits than on policy positions, Kennedy was suffering from the fact that more people expressed doubts about his character than said they fully trusted him. Carter, on the other hand, had about half those polled saying they fully trusted him and half saying they had their doubts. In a series of direct comparisons, Kennedy rated higher than Carter in knowing how to get things done, as being more experienced, more dynamic, more attractive looking, and as having a better personality. At the same time, he was rated less trustworthy, less honest and forthright, less morally upright, and not as good a family man as was the President. The sense that Kennedy was too liberal had grown over the months too, with almost half of those polled in late October agreeing that he was too far left.

A year earlier, a poll by the same organization had registered massive approval of the idea that "it is time to forget Chappaquiddick and judge Kennedy by what he has done since then." That opinion still held on the eve of the Kennedy candidacy. But attitudes about politicians and about events like Chappaquiddick, scandalous, unexplained happenings in which the virtue and character of public figures are involved, are complicated indeed. There is always the public feeling that perhaps these personal matters shouldn't enter into the rational process of picking a leader. Polls pick up this sense of propriety, as people vow that only issues and policies should be judged. But beneath the surface, events like Chappaquiddick bother voters intensely. They worry about the implications of the conduct of a public figure once he attains office. They worry about what the incidents might predict in terms of future incidents and embarrassments. Given half a chance, voters will try to forget the personal failings of a candidate. But, on the other hand, given even the smallest reminder of that sort of behavior once a campaign is under way, the bad memories flood back and become crippling. After asking voters about the importance of Chappaquiddick politically, the Yankelovich organization asked them how they felt personally about the incident and Kennedy's explanations later. Almost half, forty-four percent, said that they were still bothered by Kennedy's part in the accident. Among those saying they were Carter supporters and among those registered as political independents, the figure went up over half, to fifty-five percent. It had been exactly ten years since the senator had driven off the Dyke Bridge. His car had plunged beneath the waters of a pond and his companion had died. And as he began his campaign to inherit the political place his brothers had left him, the incident on Martha's Vineyard remained a submerged and dangerous impediment to his ambitions.

A few days before his formal announcement, CBS news televised a special report on Ted Kennedy written and narrated by the network's Capitol Hill correspondent Roger Mudd. The program was rushed on the air before the expected announcement to avoid federal equal time rules that would have required the network to cover other candidates just as extensively as they were showing Kennedy. The piece was a well-assembled combination of film of Ted Kennedy past and present, Ted in political settings, and Ted in family settings (including a section showing Ted taking a load of Kennedy kids on a camping trip). Much of the work on the piece had been done in advance, but Mudd requested an interview with the senator specially for the show. Kennedy, although he knew Mudd well and liked him, resisted. His young press secretary, Tom Southwick, strongly urged him to give the time to Mudd, feeling that such unmatched national exposure just before his announcement would provide a big and valuable boost to the campaign. Southwick had only been with Kennedy for a few years and had had no other experience in national politics. He knew Kennedy's strengths, but he did not seem to understand Kennedy's weaknesses and vulnerabilities.

The show that Mudd put together was, in a word, devastating. Next to all the wonderful shots of Ted Kennedy booming out a speech in Boston, of him with the matriarch Rose and all the kids, there was also Ted Kennedy trying once again to explain Chappaquiddick. Only this time, incredibly enough, he was even less at ease, less assured, than he had been a decade earlier when, after careful coaching by some of his brothers' most powerful advisers, he had condemned his own behavior but apologized effectively to the people of Massachusetts.

Why, Mudd asked pointedly, had he turned right, off the paved road, onto the dirt road leading not toward the ferry back to Edgartown, where he claimed he was heading, but away from the ferry and toward the bridge?

"Well," said Kennedy slowly, "first of all, it isn't as described, as all the signs led to the . . . different way. I was on my way back to what I thought would be the ferry and back to . . . back to Edgartown. And, the difference between paved and unpaved, for anyone that lives on the Cape Cod or visits the islands, the roads are indistinguishable, in most parts of the islands, and many of the areas still . . . the areas of Cape Cod . . ."

Mudd interrupted to point out that the road "is like a washboard."

"Oh," said Kennedy, "if you've traveled on either Cape Cod or in the islands of Martha's Vineyard, Nantucket, you go from paved to unpaved really without interruption."

It went on like that, and then Mudd asked: "Do you think, Senator, that anybody really will ever fully believe your explanation of Chappaquiddick?"

Said Kennedy: "Oh, there's—the problem is—for that night— I, I found the conduct, the behavior, almost beyond belief myself. I mean that's why it's been—but I think that that's . . . that's . . . that's the way it was. That . . . that happens to be the way it was. Now, I find it as I have stated that I have found that the conduct that in . . . in that evening and in . . . in the—as a result of the impact of the accident of—and the sense of loss, the sense of hope, and the . . . and the sense of tragedy, and the whole set of—circumstances, that the behavior was inexplicable. So I find that those . . . those . . . those types of questions as they apply to that . . . questions of my own soul, as well. But, that . . . that happens to be the way it was."

The Chappaquiddick discussion was very damaging for Kennedy, but it was not the only damage he sustained during the one-hour show.

"What is the present state of your marriage, Senator?" Mudd asked.

"Well, I think that it's a . . . it's had some difficult time," Kennedy stammered, "but I think we have . . . we, I think, have been able to make some very good progress and it's . . . I would say that it's . . . it's . . . it's delightful that we're able to . . . to share the time and the relationship that we . . . that we do share."

"Are you separated or what? How do you describe the situation?" Mudd asked.

"Well, I don't know whether there is a single word that should have for a description of it. Joan's involved in a continuing program to deal with the problem of alcoholism and she's doing magnificently well, and I am immensely proud of the fact that she's faced up to it, and made the progress that she's made. And that process continues and that it's the type of disease that one had to continue to work on, and she continues to work on it. And the program that has been devised is in Boston."

To end the show, Mudd asked what should have been a great, big, slow-pitch, softball question: "Why do you want to be president?" At the sound of those words from an inquisitor most politicians salivate with eagerness. They pump themselves up and describe how the great tides of history have intersected with their own destiny, how they (modestly) hope to lead the nation in new directions, toward new greatness, toward new self-confidence and power and prosperity. They further draw unfavorable (but always charitable) comparisons with their hapless opponents and suggest pointedly (but with good humor) just how sad will be the condition of the United States of America should the voters make the wrong choice. If a presidential politician cannot club this question into the second deck in center field, he should change sports. Edward Moore Kennedy had this to say:

"Well, I'm . . . were I to make the announcement and to run, the reasons that I would run is because I have a great belief in this country, that it is . . . there's more natural resources than any nation of the world; there's the greatest educated population in the world; greatest technology of any country in the world, and the greatest political system in the world. And yet I see at the current time that most of the industrial nations of the world are exceeding us in terms of productivity, are doing better than us in terms of meeting the problems of inflation; that they're dealing with their problems of energy and their problems of unemployment. It just seems to me that this nation can cope and deal with its problems in a way that it has in the past. We're facing complex issues and in this nation at this time but we have faced similar challenges at other times. And the energies and the resourcefulness of this nation, I think, should be focused on these problems in a way that brings a sense of restoration in this country by its people to . . . in dealing with the problems that we face. Primarily the issues on the economy, the problems of inflation, and the problems of energy. And, I would basically feel that . . . that it's imperative for this country to either move forward; that it can't stand still or otherwise it moves backward."

"What would you do different from Carter?" Mudd asked.

"Well, in which particular areas?" answered Kennedy.

"Well, just take the . . . the, the question of leadership."

"Well," said Kennedy, "it's, um, you know, you have to come to grips with the different issues that, ah . . . that, ah, we're facing. I mean we have . . . we have to deal with each of the various questions that we're talking about whether it's a question of the economy, whether it's in the area of energy."

It was not a particularly large television audience that saw this rambling, babbling performance by the most popular politician in America. Other network shows appearing at the same time swamped the Mudd show in the ratings. Yet the effect was widespread, largely because the political reporters and editors who had seen it were stunned by how ineffective Kennedy had been. The mythology about Ted Kennedy—that he was a direct political descendent of the smooth and powerful and articulate brothers who came before—was beginning to shatter. Looking back, it is a wonder that it had taken so long. But for years in the Senate Kennedy had been protected by carefully choosing the reporters to whom he would talk at length about personal matters, and they, by and large, had protected him by rendering his meandering, inarticulate sentences into English. I had done so myself. It was often difficult in those years to decide whether the stumbling, almost shy, Kennedy being interviewed lacked intellectual power or was simply uncomfortable with the situation, with the probing and prying. On the stump Kennedy was almost always powerful, in control, working his crowds superbly, joking, often in the disarmingly self-deprecating way that endeared his brothers to the voters. On the Senate floor he was usually so well prepared that there was rarely a sign of discomfort or intellectual inferiority. If he was often less than brilliantly articulate in face-to-face interviews, his other performances were so polished as to make the interview failings seem unimportant. And they would have been still, even in a presidential race, if, as has always been the case, his other public performances were powerful and impressive. Certainly that would have been the case against Jimmy Carter, whose personal interviews were direct, confident, packed with information, but whose public appearance usually lacked spark and the ability to inspire. The Mudd interview had damaged Kennedy, but it had not crippled his campaign. It was a setback that could be offset later as the campaign unfolded and if the power of Kennedy's public persona took effect.

On November 4, 1979, precisely one year before the presidential election of 1980, a horde of ragtag revolutionaries who had supported the overthrow of the Shah of Iran and the ascension to power of the Ayatollah Ruhollah Khomeini, overpowered the marine guards at the American embassy in Tehran and took the occupants of that compound hostage. The seizure followed a decision by the Carter administration (urged on them by important Republicans like Henry Kissinger and David Rockefeller, to whom Carter paid great attention) to admit the deposed Shah to the United States for treatment of cancer and other ailments. The possibility of a seizure had been threatened by militants in Iran before the Shah was admitted. In fact, the embassy had been stormed before and the number of embassy personnel had been reduced dramatically because of that danger.

The seizure of the embassy produced a huge emotional outburst in the United States, emotional and complicated. Across the country college students burned Iranian flags just as the militants in Tehran were burning American flags. Thousands of Iranian students in the United States on student visas had been demonstrating against the Shah for years. When they took to the streets after the Americans were seized, they were assaulted and taunted. Persian rug dealers were boycotted and harassed. Posters were printed in high-school print shops across the nation showing a raised middle finger forming the I in Iran. It was the largest outpouring of national hate for another nation since the Germans and the Japanese were the targets of American anger in World War II. Beneath the pure outrage—which in some ways felt luxurious in its purity and righteousness, especially after the guilty years of Vietnam—there was also a feeling that had become uncomfortably familiar in America in the late twentieth century. It was the frustration of powerlessness on the international stage. Together with the futility of the Vietnamese experience and the new economic position imposed on the West by the oil producers in 1973, the outrageously criminal act of taking hostages represented a fundamental and traumatic repudiation of the myth of American hegemony. America was being forced to adjust its sense of itself in the world. It was not an easy process.

In the first flush of rage against the Iranian action, a wave of patriotic fervor swept through the country. Recruiting stations for the armed forces had to extend hours to process the angry young men who were signing up with the avowed hope of being sent to avenge the kidnapping of American diplomats. On the political level this wave of patriotism could only help the man who was the nation's highest official. And so President Jimmy Carter began quickly to enjoy a new popularity. The fact that the incident had happened on his watch, so to speak, was secondary to the fact that the nation was rallying around the flag, and Carter was the man holding that flag.

No event during the campaign for the presidency had more importance than the hostage crisis. It was often remarked during the campaign that the results of the American election had more to do with events abroad than at home. In large measure that was true. Once the hostage crisis began, Carter became almost invulnerable to political assault, especially from Ted Kennedy, who, unlike the Republicans who had their own internecine struggle to fight, needed to assault Carter. And, in a sense, with an international crisis going full tilt, the question of replacing Carter became, for critical months, irrelevant.

In 1976 Carter had lost the huge lead he enjoyed over Jerry Ford, and then only narrowly beat the incumbent president. But the Carter forces believed, nonetheless, that Ford had not been very clever in the uses of incumbency to wage his campaign. They had vowed that in 1979 and 1980 the Carter presidency would become their most potent political weapon. And once the hostage crisis began, Carter used his office and his responsibilities as president to campaign for president. He did this by simply refusing to campaign in the conventional sense. A promised debate with Ted Kennedy in Iowa was canceled quickly because Carter vowed not to leave the White House for political travel until the hostages were home. At the time the strategy looked supremely hypocritical. He was moving up in the polls and Ted Kennedy was moving down and Carter simply insisted that he couldn't do anything but work on the hostage crisis.

In fact, the tactic was not only hypocritical, it was also wrongheaded in terms of attaining the release of the hostages. Carter became obsessed with the hostages. He took their captivity as a personal affront. He thus gave the Iranian crazies more power, both within their own country and over the United States. The crisis paralyzed the United States government and it paralyzed Jimmy Carter. The short-term result was politically helpful to Carter, but in the longer run it no doubt prolonged the crisis itself. Perhaps, however, Carter understood that, Ted Kennedy and the nomination battle aside, he would eventually be judged by his handling of the crisis. There can be no doubt that he wanted the hostages home. In fact, he wanted them home too much. He personalized the crisis and became deeply and emotionally involved in a problem that would likely have responded more rapidly to a more clinical treatment. In the end he would be haunted by these events outside our borders.

The hostage crisis and Carter's immunity to conventional political attack frustrated Ted Kennedy enormously. By December Kennedy had generated a pack of his own problems, with the Mudd interview and with a meaningless but nonetheless embarrassing loss in the carnival caucuses in Florida, where the enthusiastic Draft Kennedy campaign was outspent and out-organized by Carter's professional forces.

The frustration of this situation soon began to wear on Ted Kennedy. Early in the month, after another in the endless string of fourteen-hour days that make up presidential campaigning, Kennedy was dodging questions in yet another local television interview. This one was being done by San Francisco station KRON. With campaign spending limited by federal law, presiden-

87

tial candidates had come to rely more heavily on free television time gained by granting "exclusive" interviews to local electronic reporters. It was an effective technique in that it virtually guaranteed an appearance on local television, since no station would decline to run an interview by their own local reporter with such a prominent national celebrity. The risks, at the same time, were minimal, since the local questioning was rarely as sharp or as probing as that from the hardened national press corps that traipsed around the country with the candidate, growing surly and often disrespectful as they became as fatigued as the candidate himself.

Asked in San Francisco whether the United States didn't owe the Shah of Iran permanent sanctuary in the United States in return for his friendship over the years, Kennedy blurted out that to the contrary, the Shah had presided over "one of the most violent regimes in the history of mankind" and had stolen "umteen billion dollars" from his own people. When the interview was actually shown on television, those particular remarks were edited out. But as protection against getting scooped, one reporter from the traveling press corps always sat in on the local interviews. In this case, United Press International's reporter Dean Reynolds, son of ABC's Frank Reynolds, had drawn the watch and he filed the comment about the Shah. His editors in New York played the line heavily on their wire and a sensation was born.

In the superheated atmosphere following the hostage seizure, criticism of the Shah was seen, wrongly of course, as support for Khomeini. The Iranians called Kennedy "an American prophet," deepening the problem, and the irresponsible and sleazy *New York Post* bannered the headline: "Teddy is the Toast of Teheran."

By mid-December, one and a half months into his presidential campaign, Ted Kennedy was in deep political trouble. Mervin Field, watching the debacle from California, began, like other political professionals across the country, to change his mind about the Kennedy power. Field said that he had thought the American people knew Ted Kennedy. "Quite obviously, they don't," Field said. "Until he declared, there was an illusion about the man. Now, he is found wanting. Now, it's a whole new ball game." Field thought a bit more about it and then concluded, prophetically, "He's not going to make it."

6

Cornfield
Confrontations

What was important about George Herbert Walker Bush, at least
in his own view, was what he had been and where he had come
from. His origins and his accomplishments were impressive
enough. He had been a member of Congress for two terms. He had
been the director of the Central Intelligence Agency. He had
served as ambassador to the United Nations and as special envoy
to China. He had been the chairman of the Republican National
Committee during the party's mortal embarrassment over President Richard Nixon's conduct in office. He had been an independent oilman and had made a million dollars in that business. And
he was the scion of a rich, eastern Republican family. His father,
Prescott Bush, also a businessman and politician, had been a pillar
of the progressive and aristocratic wing of his party.

Believing that his preparation for the highest office in the land was complete, Bush, in December 1976, first broached the subject of organizing his own campaign for the presidency. Although he realized that the defeated Governor Reagan would still be a political force in 1980, and that the defeated President Ford might want badly to avenge his loss to Carter, he also estimated that both Reagan and Ford were now damaged goods. Ford was only an accidental president and one who could not cling to the office even with the power of incumbency behind his candidacy. Reagan, aging and a two-time loser in presidential politics, would stand to inherit the party's nomination, but he seemed to some too worn and too familiar for the glitzy, trendy, fadishness of politics in the media age. Bush, faced with four years and nothing much to do with his life, began then to contemplate his own future. He went so far, only a month after the 1976 elections, as to approach James A. Baker, III, a wealthy Houston lawyer who had just managed Ford's presidential campaign. Bush asked Baker to run his own 1980 campaign. They were natural allies: Bush, a Yale man to the tip of his rep ties; Baker, a Princetonian with a Texas accent. Baker said he would sign on, but only if Ford chose not to run again. Later, after getting Ford's approval and his promise that he would not run in the primaries, Baker agreed. He gave Bush the literature of the 1976 campaign that explained Jimmy Carter's victory. Carter's had been a simple strategy: travel, travel, travel. Give speeches everywhere in every primary and state caucus. But above all, focus on the early states, Iowa and New Hampshire. For the obscure candidate—and Bush, despite his experience in public life, still easily qualified as obscure—victories in the early tests were not only important, they were vital. Victory in the early primaries begets victory later. Almost as much as it is a war of words, ideas, policies, and personalities, presidential politics is a war of perceptions. And building the perception of being able to win, of being popular, especially of being a dark horse closing on the front-runner, can be everything in presidential politics. Bush read the books and understood the problem. He would follow the Carter strategy while campaigning not so much against his Republican brethren, but rather against the failed presidency of Jimmy Carter.

For all the GOP candidates behind Reagan, the goal was the same: to pierce the armor of the front-runner. For those candidates back in the pack, just about any sort of victory would do. In the fall of 1979, for example, all the major contenders poured money and organizing effort into stacking a fund-raising dinner in Iowa. At such dinners it had become popular to have straw votes during the festivities so that the diners could express their preference for their party's presidential nomination. It did not take fund-raising chairmen around the country long to realize that such events would attract the attention of the presidential candidates and their field organizations, that the candidates themselves would then drum up business for the fifty-dollar-a-plate chicken dinners, that the television cameras would show up to see who won the straw vote, and that, in the end, more money would be raised than had just a single presidential hopeful been prevailed upon to give the after-dinner speech.

The Bush people had spent thousands of their campaign dollars to get their supporters to the Iowa dinner. They did a mailing to their friends urging their attendance. They phoned all over the state. They rented a hot-air balloon, a band, and buses. Senator Robert Dole proceeded more directly by buying up seats and then filling them with volunteers whom he thought would vote for him (most didn't). The candidates themselves flew in to be on hand for the evening's fun. It was one more media event in the electronic campaign for the presidency. "It's part of the great circus that goes on," the dour and intellectual John Anderson told a *Washington Post* reporter. "I enjoy circuses. I take my children to them all the time."

But in Iowa a pattern had started to emerge from the foolishness of straw votes and chicken dinners. George Bush had been winning, or coming close to winning, time after time. It meant simply that Bush was becoming known and that he had put in place an organization that could produce people on command. Producing bodies was, in Iowa, the point of the exercise. Iowa, like a number of other states, picked its convention delegates by holding caucuses all across the state, precinct by precinct in 2,531 living rooms, church basements, and firehouses. The caucuses were simply little meetings, open to anyone who was not a member of any other party, at which preferences for a presidential nominee were expressed. There was no secret ballot. Instead, there was a division of the room, with, say, Bush people gathering in one corner,

Reaganites in another, Connally people clustered somewhere else. Friends and neighbors had to divide and show their preferences. It is hard enough in the American election system to get people out to vote in the usual manner. It is doubly difficult to get them to spend an entire evening at a meeting and to risk friendships in the open expression of political choice. From the results of these little caucuses, representatives to congressional district meetings are chosen in proportion to the strength each candidate shows. And from the congressional district another proportional delegation is sent to a state party convention. From that convention, finally, the delegates to the national nominating convention are chosen, still in proportion to the strengths shown by each candidate that first night of the precinct caucuses. Iowa Republicans and Democrats sent only a small delegation to each of the national conventions. But, of course, the real prize was the national attention the winner would get.

The caucus system is not usually susceptible to the common manipulations of electoral politics. Television advertising, for example, is nearly useless, except to impress party pros with a campaign's commitment of resources to the state. Large meetings, rallies, and the like—even the local television interview—are not suitable to produce a caucus win. It is instead the hardest kind of political work to win a statewide caucus. It means organizing cadres of supporters into committed units, who, come snow or sleet, wind or rain, will trudge to the meeting place to stand up and be counted.

The Bush campaign people understood that simple fact better than other Republicans, just as Jimmy Carter's people had understood it four years earlier. James Baker and Bush's political director, David Keene, who had been a Reagan operative in 1976, found a bright, young political organizer from New York named Rich Bond and dispatched him to Des Moines months before the caucuses were to be held. Bush himself had tapped friends he had made in the Iowa Republican party when he was chairman of the Republican National Committee. With those party leaders as a nucleus, Bond built the networks of people who would, on the twenty-first of January, appear at the caucuses. Bond was one of those rarities in the ranks of political organizers. He could smile. He could laugh at himself and at his candidate. But he could wring every last ounce of work and effort out of himself and out of others. He could be tough and no-nonsense and severe without being nasty or arrogant.

Presidential candidates usually pick staffs that reflect their own strengths and weaknesses, and often their own personalities. Bond was typical of the Bush operation. From Jim Baker on down, Bush's people were urbane and good humored, professional and dedicated. They did not fear the press, but rather courted it, helped it, and thus helped their candidate. In addition, they had a healthy realization that there was more in their lives than the future of George Bush. At a dinner with a few reporters one night at the Petroleum Club in Houston, for example, Baker and the campaign's chief fund raiser, Robert Mosbacher, an independent oilman, brother of the former America's Cup sailor Emil "Bus" Mosbacher, and a world-class competitive sailor himself, spent as much time talking boats as talking politics. And as much worry was expressed about an oil well being drilled on Baker's land by Mosbacher as about whether George Bush would become president. They were realistic in their expectations about their candidate. They understood his weaknesses and political problems. Many felt privately that Bush's best chance in 1980 would be to become the vice-presidential choice, not the presidential nominee. Baker's well in Texas was a failure, except as a tax shelter. But the Bush campaign in Iowa was about to strike paydirt.

By the time the first snow fell in Iowa in the presidential season of 1979–80, George Bush had already spent nearly a month of campaign days in the state in the year gone by. When his chartered two-engine plane flew in over the whitened cornfields around Spencer, Iowa (population twelve thousand) in December, he was reminded that a year earlier, when he had come to speak to the chamber of commerce, that too had been the day of the first snow of winter. Bush bounded out of the airplane, to be greeted not by a throng of eager supporters, but by a little knot of people huddled against the wind at the tiny airport terminal. Bush grinned happily, shook hands, and climbed into a huge black Cadillac owned and driven by Lee Holt, a big, friendly man with a round face and a thin-lipped smile. He was Spencer's leading car dealer. The two men cruised off into the failing winter light, down arrow-straight roads, past stubbled cornfields, toward a modest country club, where, overlooking the wintry fairways, George Bush yet again gave his pitch.

Sipping beer from a tall pilsner glass, the gangly Bush mixed easily with the folks from Spencer who had contributed little bits of money to his campaign. Finally, he set the glass aside and launched into the litany of his accomplishments. It was his résumé he recited, both by way of introduction and by way of explanation of the gall it takes to seek the presidency. "I have done everything else," he seemed to be saying, "and now I'm ready." The rambling life history had another, sharper point to it as well. Bush was saying, indirectly, that he was a man of the world, a man with Washington experience, with experience in international affairs, with connections to his party's apparatus across the nation. Unlike Jimmy Carter, Bush could be, in the words of his advertising campaign, a "president we won't have to train."

Although he was not uncomfortable in this little town, and his well-bred manners and natural pleasantness made him easy to be around, there was an almost adolescent earnestness about his speech. There was not the depth of self-assurance of John Connally, nor the easy congeniality of Reagan, nor the cool reasonableness of Howard Baker. Bush was intense, too intense, trying too hard to present himself as worthy of the highest office in the land. Bush was then fifty-five years old, but this boyishness, this awful earnestness had not been worn away by the years. Standing there in Spencer, Iowa, I wondered why. Had he been too successful, too rich? Had it all been too easy? It made me think of the prep schools he had attended and then look around the little room in the country club and count the number of young men in Weejuns and young women in Shetland sweaters listening bright-eyed to this candidate. He was dressed in a gray Brooks Brothers suit, a subdued foulard four-in-hand knotted thinly, and a straight-collared shirt with blue pin stripes. It was a grown-up's outfit that was a sign of his origins. There were no broad-shouldered jackets like those of Reagan, no wide Windsor knots on colorful ties like Connally's. Bush was indisputably from the East, from boarding schools and Yale. But he was in the heartland trying to put himself across. And he was worried about his roots and how they would be judged by the farmers and small businessmen across America, by the Rotarians, the Kiwanians, the Lions, the Moose, the Eagles, and the smalltown Jaycees. And in spite of himself, he could not ignore the preppy problem. "They say I'm a patrician," Bush told the group assembled. "I don't even know what the word means. I'll have to look it up." The remark was supposed to be self-deprecating. Instead, it was patronizing.

As always, Bush's standard stump speech was first the résumé and then a discussion of the political chances he saw for himself. Bush wanted to lead the country, but first he had to convince others—and perhaps himself—that he wasn't acting the fool chasing after front-runner Ronald Reagan, when the polls only showed Bush as an asterisk after "don't know." He talked strategy. He would do "better than expected" in Iowa. He would be strong in his native New England. He would run respectably in the southern primaries that followed. And then it would be a two-man race with Reagan through Illinois and Wisconsin and the industrial states. He never mentioned Texas, his adopted home, because his chances there were slim, with Reagan's conservative constituency and Connally's decades-old popularity as a native son. And he didn't mention California, the last of the big-state primaries and a deep well of Reagan support. In campaign speech after campaign speech Bush sounded like the steam engine in the children's story, puffing and huffing, "I think I can. I think I can."

After the country club performance Bush was driven in Lee Holt's Cadillac to the bank in the center of Spencer. There a crowd of about 150 people sipped coffee, munched on cookies and cakes, and waited to hear George Bush. In a way, the setting was ludicrous. Here was a man who was seeking to be president standing before a little audience in the basement of a bank in a tiny town in rural northwest Iowa. Off to the side of the room a huge glass case contained a stuffed polar bear, preserved forever standing up on its hind legs, reaching eight or nine feet into the air. The polar bear's mouth was open as if to gobble up some prey, or perhaps to give a speech. In a second case were the mounted heads of two Dahl sheep and those of a grizzly and a brown bear. The president of the bank was a hunter, and had helped himself to some of Alaska's specimens. The candidate, already exhausted after a long day of airplane travel and speeches, stood there with the bears, reading his résumé, enunciating foggy positions designed to appeal to his party's preferences, knocking himself out when he should have been having a dry martini with friends in his club, discussing puts and calls.

Looked at another way, however, it was a reassuring scene. If the presidency had once been imperial, certainly campaigning for the presidency was now an antidote for arrogance. If a politician wanted the most powerful job in the nation, first he had to submit himself to the powerless, and submit not just his name on a ballot or his face on a television screen but himself—his body, his energy, his ideas, his person. Anthropologist Elias Canetti reports a ritual followed a hundred years ago by an African tribe before they crowned a new king:

> As he [the soon-to-be king] was walking on the shore . . . he was suddenly set upon by the entire populace, who proceeded to a ceremony which is preliminary to the crowning, and which must deter any but the most ambitious men from aspiring to the crown. They surrounded him in a dense crowd, and then began to heap upon him every manner of abuse that the worst of mobs could imagine. Some spat in his face; some beat him with their fists; some kicked him; others threw disgusting objects at him; while those unlucky ones who stood on the outside, and could reach the poor fellow only with their voices, assiduously cursed him, his father, his mother, his sisters and brothers, and all his ancestors to the remotest generation.*

The point, of course, was to remind the future king of his humanity and vulnerability before he assumed absolute authority over the villagers' lives. An American presidential campaign is only slightly less primitive in what it requires of its candidates. But the effect is roughly the same: to expose those who would lead our democracy to the ideas, feelings, needs, hopes, and fears of the people who will pay their salaries. That George Herbert Walker Bush, aristocrat, patrician, son of privilege, ambassador to the powerful, leader of the largest intelligence force in the free world, had to parade with the polar bear in that Iowa bank was not altogether a bad thing.

The first question Bush was asked that night was about the

*Elias Canetti, *Crowds and Power* (New York: The Seabury Press, 1978), p. 412.

hostage crisis in Iran. Like Ted Kennedy the Republicans too had been frustrated by the hostage situation. They too wished to attack Carter, largely because it was easier and less divisive than attacking their Republican competitors. They preferred to jump on Jimmy, but it was getting more difficult with the President solely in charge of the crisis in Iran. The backlash against Kennedy's criticism of the Shah had further frozen the Republicans and they were reduced to merely announcing that they supported the President in whatever he did. Only around the edges could they imply that Carter had been responsible, in part, for the crisis. "I'm just so outraged by the humiliation of our country," Bush said, his fist clenched for emphasis. "I just hope he does have a plan, and I mean an action plan." It was only a pale version of what Bush really thought about Carter, which he had expressed privately as we flew into Spencer. Without the crowds to hear, Bush had said: "Carter just has no class, and I don't mean in a social sense. It's a shame for the presidency to have that little guy in there."

After Spencer it was Omaha for the night and an early-morning fund-raising breakfast. Bush, bleary-eyed, his gray flannel suit wrinkled, spoke that morning with a fervor that was out of keeping with the hour and his physical state. He clenched his fists and worked the muscles in his jaw. The veins in his neck popped out as he again recited his résumé. "I make no apology for having a good education. I believe in excellence. One of Carter's many failures has been the lack of excellent people around him," he shouted as his listeners gulped coffee and gobbled scrambled eggs. His speech was sprinkled with the keys to his background. He was given to overuse superlatives. Events were "faaantastic" or "amazing." But his talk was also littered with Texasisms, as in "I'm fixin' to surprise a lot of people." But it was the intensity of this man, usually relaxed and pleasant in private, that was striking. For months his stump speech had been derided as flat and boring. And he had, after the criticism, turned up the heat of his presentation. Yet, it was more than an act, for George Bush wanted the presidency. He had proved that with his commitment to nonstop travel and speaking, handshaking and money raising that had already consumed two years of his life. The drive seemed to come from his father, "a *faaantastic* man," who had taught him honor and the obligation of public service as repayment for his wealth and privilege. And Bush had passed it on to his children, all of whom were busy in one primary state or another, working for their father. Presidential candidates are all driven by some need, and George Bush needed to serve. He had early on sold out his shares in the independent oil drilling company he had started in Texas. He had sold them before they would have blossomed into a huge fortune, as they did for those who stayed behind in the company. Bush had about a million dollars to his name, enough, certainly, to live comfortably. But he needed public service to satisfy the memory of his father.

At the end of that long day that began in Omaha, Bush was standing on the tarmac at yet another Iowa airport. He spoke of his days in China and drifted into a reverie about the beautiful art he and his wife, Barbara, had seen there. He remembered that the cashmere overcoat he was wearing had been made in China and he joked a bit self-consciously about its third-rate tailoring. The flight on the tiny chartered plane had been delayed while county police checked out security arrangements. A pair of local fellows had been stopped near the airport with two high-powered hunting rifles in their car. Bush grinned at his curly-headed press secretary, Peter Teeley, as capable and pleasant a press handler as there is in politics. Teeley saw the jibe coming and began to smile.

"Teeley," Bush asked, "Would you throw your body in front of the candidate to save this country?"

Teeley flashed an even larger smile. "Hell no, George," he answered, truthfully.

They folded themselves into the plane and flew off into the cold and crystal clear Iowa night.

While Bush was laying siege to Iowa, his competitors were not. Reagan, following the advice of John Sears, was campaigning only lightly across the nation, and almost not at all in Iowa. Through the whole year preceding the caucuses, Reagan had been in Iowa only ten hours. The state's newspaper polls, however, showed Reagan with a comfortable lead over Bush and over the rest of the field, and the Reagan strategists believed that with a massive telephone canvas just before the caucuses they could turn that popularity into votes. Howard Baker, realizing late that his organization in Iowa was nearly nonexistent, flew in and out of Iowa in the final days, but he had reacted too late. Dole, hoping for heavy support in the farm belt because he was from Kansas, could afford neither the time away from the Senate nor the money it took to build an organization. Connally staged a forty-eight-hour marathon bus tour of rural Iowa to show his stamina and his interest. Anderson talked waspishly to campus groups and tried to distance himself from the conservative Republican pack. Crane, who had campaigned longest, continued to be hidden under the long shadow of his ideological twin, Ronald Reagan.

It was Bush who was working in the way it counts in Iowa. At a chili feed for two hundred Bush's volunteers showed up with leaflets and sign-up sheets. Back at headquarters, those who had given their names as Bush supporters were blitzed with mail and phone calls, given precise locations of their precinct caucuses, told who their precinct leader was, and had their names forwarded to local volunteers who kept account of the Bush support. Politics, John Sears had pointed out in the fall, is motion and excitement, and the problem for a campaign is to generate and maintain that motion and excitement and to time it so that its crest hits on Election Day. Only Bush was attempting that sort of effort in Iowa with any competence. Reagan was hanging back, not wanting to give the others a target, not wanting to spend too much money too soon and in the wrong place. It was a serious mistake.

The major event of the Iowa campaign for the Republicans was a debate sponsored by the Des Moines *Register.* Six of the seven major GOP contenders appeared; Ronald Reagan, known as "Dutch" when he was a sports announcer for a Des Moines radio station, stayed away. Sears explained that Reagan didn't want to draw attention to the others by lending his front-runner's presence. That was only partially true. The fear of a Reagan blunder, brought on by the pressure of such an encounter, was the controlling reason to keep Reagan away. And Reagan himself agreed. That too was a serious mistake.

On display at the debate was an impressive Republican field. The lingering impression after the questions had been asked and answered was that the party, without Ronald Reagan, had produced a crop of attractive and competent candidates. They, of course, all had their weaknesses: Connally, his arrogance; Dole, his cutting and often bitter humor; Baker, his inability to mount an effective organization in the state; Crane, his patent copying of Reagan's positions; Anderson, his schoolmarmishness and his positions too liberal for his own party; and Bush, his sometimes giddy boyishness.

A panel of reporters politely inquired about Iran that night, and each Republican in turn ducked away from the question, wanting to avoid seeming selfish and self-aggrandizing in the face of the threat to the hostages' lives. They inquired next about another foreign policy crisis that had brewed up in the winter. In December, after two years of edging closer and closer to a takeover, the Soviet Union had marched into Afghanistan and seized control of that godforsaken land, unimportant in itself but dangerously close to the oil supply routes in the Persian Gulf. Carter had responded quickly by announcing an embargo on further U.S. grain shipments to the Soviet Union, shipments desperately needed by the Russians, since her agricultural system again had failed to produce enough food for her people and her livestock. The action had been unpopular throughout the grain belt, where the bounty of the plains nearly always threatened to overrun U.S. markets and where the export outlet was needed to make grain farming reliably profitable.

The Republicans had found a stick with which to beat Carter and they joined in with relish. "I do not support an embargo of foodstuffs to the Soviet Union. I think we almost always starve the wrong people. I doubt that we will ever even inconvenience the leaders of the Soviet Union in the Kremlin," said Baker. "I don't think the Iowa farmers should pay the price for the failure of the Carter foreign policy," said Connally. "He [Carter] took a poke at the Russian Bear and knocked out the American farmer," cracked Dole. "Well, in my view," said George Bush, "the President made the wrong mistake—as Yogi Berra would say." "I think the farmer has been made the scapegoat for the consistent foreign policy failures of this administration," added Crane.

John Anderson, a ten-term congressman from Illinois, with no chance of being nominated by his conservative party, took a sharply different tack. "I disagree. . . . It's not easy sitting here in the heart of Iowa, in farm country, to support an embargo on the shipment of grain, but it seems to me that it is passing strange that those who are critical of our foreign policy as being deficient on the grounds that it is weak, when the first real test comes of responding to the kind of overt aggression that has just been taken by the Soviet Union in Afghanistan, are unwilling to accept any measure of sacrifice; to accept some of the cost that admittedly has to be borne if we are going to send a clear, certain signal to the Russians that we will not tolerate the kind of conduct that they have just engaged in Afghanistan." It was a surprising position, under the circumstances. The politic answer had been quickly adopted by the others, but Anderson seemed willing to offend the interests of the Iowa corn growers for the sake of principle. And the effect was powerful, not in Iowa but across the nation. Anderson had taken a chance and had followed the larger political wisdom of being, on occasion, impolitic, of saying what seemed unpopular, but true. For Anderson it was the beginning of something larger than his hopeless run for the nomination of the Republican party.

But for George Bush, the clean, handsome man his advertising expert dubbed "the American Eagle," the debate was less than a success. With the other Republicans on stage, Bush's intensity had flagged. He had been flat and uninteresting, unsure of himself in the way a schoolboy is when reciting in class. If Bush was to make something out of his long days and nights in Iowa it would have to be the result of the work he and his organization had put in. And it would have to come from Reagan's failure to take Iowa seriously.

Jimmy Carter took Iowa seriously, he always had. He had started his quest for the presidency there in 1974 and 1975, and by leading the Iowa caucuses he had put himself at the head of the Democratic pack in 1976. He and Hamilton Jordan had not forgotten how important that victory had been. Throughout his presidency Carter had been careful to keep in touch with the thousands of friends he had made in the state. Hundreds of Iowans were brought to the White House for special events and for visits by foreign leaders, and the President himself periodically phoned his supporters in the state to encourage them.

But in 1980 Carter's situation was more complicated. He was still abiding by his vow not to campaign while the hostages were held in Iran. When he made that promise Carter could not have

101

thought that sixty days later the hostages would still be captive. And as a consequence Carter was still hostage to his own words. He had moved up in the polls since the Iran crisis had struck. The very fact that it was he, Carter, who was managing the crisis had given him the aura of leadership that his muddled presidency had lacked to that point. His self-imposed absence from the campaign trail had also given him an excuse to decline to meet Kennedy in a debate in Iowa, like the one the Republicans had effectively used to command attention. The argument had raged inside the White House over whether Carter could handle Kennedy head to head in a debate, with most of Carter's advisers finally agreeing, after watching the shaky performance of Kennedy on the stump, that Carter would have bested the senator. But the President held to his word that he would not campaign.

At the same time Carter was reaping the perverse political benefits of being the commander in chief in a time of crisis, however, his absence from the campaign trail was not a help. Carter had always been an effective campaigner in the kinds of small settings that were the steady diet of the Iowa contest. His command of information, always impressive but heightened by three years in the White House, coupled with an almost overpowering sincerity, made him an unmatched performer in the fire halls and living rooms of America. To deprive himself of that tool, especially with his grain embargo on the Soviet Union unpopular in Iowa, raised the prospect that the President could be defeated in Iowa by Kennedy.

The Carter campaign organization, however, was operating at full tilt in Iowa. In fact, it had been operating since April 1979, when thirty-five-year-old political organizer Bill Romjue had been dispatched to the state full time. By summer six full-time paid operatives were at work on the caucuses; by September twenty paid workers were on board. By the time the Democrats in Ames held a Jefferson-Jackson Day dinner in October, Romjue was able to pack the house and produce a seventy-one percent to twenty-six percent win over Ted Kennedy in a straw poll. Day after day Romjue, a chunky, cautious man, with a drooping walrus mustache that filtered his words as he spoke, plugged away for Jimmy Carter. With no president to put on the campaign trail the surrogates moved into Iowa—the cabinet secretaries, the President's mother, Lillian, his son, Chip. From a rundown office above a Tasty Taco and a cheap bar in Des Moines, Romjue and the Carter machine made the phone calls, enlisted the volunteers, and hoped that Jimmy Carter could stave off Ted Kennedy.

With Carter locked into Washington much of the most important primary campaigning fell to Vice-President Walter F. Mondale. He was indefatigable in Carter's service, just as he had been in the service of the patrons who, throughout his political life, had opened the right door at the right moment for Fritz Mondale. The Vice-President had risen up through the ranks of liberal Minnesota politics serving as a campaign aide to the luminaries of the state's Democratic Farmer Labor party. In each of his major advancements, first to attorney general and then to the Senate of the United States, Mondale was first appointed by a patron and then won re-election in his own campaign. It had been the same with his ascension to the vice-presidency. Carter had chosen him, but Mondale had then more than earned the honor, outshining the often bitter Bob Dole, Gerald Ford's choice as running mate in 1976, and by some counts even adding a few percentage points to Carter's total vote.

Mondale had become, in some ways, a professional protégé. He modeled his politics and his attitude toward politics after Hubert Humphrey, whose seat he had taken in the Senate when Humphrey was tapped to serve as Lyndon Johnson's vice-president. He campaigned eagerly, almost joyfully, smiling, good humored in the face of the absurdity and exhaustion the work required. He treated the press as friends (although he and his staff were usually discreet to a fault, never breathing a word of dissent from the Carter administration's line, defending, explaining, and taking the heat for policies they were not responsible for formulating). Because of the lessons of his past patrons and by his own instinct, Mondale's politics were more liberal than Carter's, but he kept his differences on such issues as abortion to himself, never denying that differences existed but never making much of those divergences of view. Mondale was a rare politician in that he had advanced his own ambition by sublimating his own ego.

It was a bitter cold morning in Waterloo, Iowa. Another hour would go by before the sun would show itself. A light snow was falling as the early shift trooped into the Rath Company's packing plant to butcher hogs and to prepare bacon and hams. Fritz Mondale stood at the plant entrance, his face bright, scrubbed, and freshly shaven. "Good morning, good morning, good morning," the Vice-President of the United States repeated as the workers, slightly amazed that anyone not on the morning shift was standing there in the cold, snowy predawn. It was the classic plant gate campaign gesture. The point was always the same: to show enough concern to show up at the gate, to show that here was at least one politician who knew something about the lives of these voters. From Mondale there was no hard sell, not even a plea for help in the coming caucuses. Just "Good morning, good morning, good morning," in a happy, sing-song voice, with the television lights illuminating the scene and the Vice-President of the United States shivering slightly between handshakes, the snow collecting on his well-cut hair and the soft shoulders of his overcoat. For Walter Mondale, this was a small thing, one of thousands of plant gates he had stood before, on his own behalf and in the cause of the patrons he has served.

Even this little event, however, showed the practiced touch of professional politics that the Carter-Mondale team brought to their efforts. As the workers approached the gate some balked, like skittish calves refusing to enter a stockyard chute. But the Mondale forces were well deployed. A V-shaped funnel of bodies— Mondale workers, Carter volunteers, union officials—had spread out from the plant's only entrance, forcing all who wanted to work to pass in front of the smiling Vice-President. "Good morning, good morning, good morning."

And this was not just any plant. The Rath Company had almost shut down this operation because of failing profits. But a special federal grant, invented and given by the Carter administration, had helped keep it open. Mondale wanted these workers to remember. He especially wanted these labor union families to remember the Carter administration, because for months in Iowa other labor unions had been pushing hard for Ted Kennedy. In the spring and summer of 1979, when Ted Kennedy was still sailing off Cape Cod, volunteers from unions such as the United Auto Workers had been putting together their own lists of supporters. They wanted to draft Ted Kennedy and they had been laying the groundwork for a Kennedy campaign.

It was already late fall when Ted Kennedy finally announced his candidacy, but within a month there was a nearly full-blown, highly professional Kennedy campaign staff on the ground in Iowa, ready to spend the almost half a million dollars federal law permitted each candidate for the first of thirty-six state delegate selection contests around the country. The Kennedy hierarchy in Washington sent in Paul Tully, a thirty-five-year-old former Yale football player who had worked for Eugene McCarthy and then Robert Kennedy in the great antiwar candidacies of 1968. Tully, an intense, burly man, was one of the best political organizers in the country. And he was a true liberal believer. He had turned down the chance to run a Senate campaign in Pennsylvania because he figured the candidate didn't have the "fire in his belly" that would make him run the way Tully wanted him to run. Along with Tully, the Kennedy campaign recruited Robert Miller, an aide to former Iowa senator Dick Clark, who himself had resigned a State Department job with Carter to help Kennedy. Under Tully and Miller was John Sasso, a bit younger than the others, but a crack political organizer out of Boston, where election year after election year he had helped a liberal Democratic congressman run up huge margins in a bipartisan district. And these men in turn reached out to the best of their friends and professional acquaintances. Mike Ford, thirty-one, was teaching at Xavier University in Ohio when the call came. Ford dropped his teaching and before Christmas began work in his thirty-ninth major political campaign. He took over a single congressional district, covering eighteen counties and 480 precincts in central Iowa that required three hours to drive across. It was a measure of the Kennedy campaign's quality in Iowa that it had been years since Ford ran anything smaller than an entire state for a presidential candidate in an election contest. Ford flew to Des Moines, was given a tiny Chevrolet Chevette to accommodate his six-foot one-inch, 240-pound body, and sent to Waterloo. There, Ford, like the rest of the Kennedy campaign staff, had two things in his favor: valuable lists of names gathered by the Draft Kennedy volunteers and a statewide lead in the popularity polls for their candidate. "If this were a primary," Ford said at the time, "we'd be in great shape."

Iowa's disproportionate importance to the presidential selection process came from the fact that it was first, not from the fact that its delegation would, in the summer conventions, be important for its size. But Iowa wasn't just first; it was also in 1980 largely neutral territory. No candidate had a decisive advantage, such as Kennedy was presumed to have in his native New England, or as Connally would have in Texas, or Carter in the South. The state is largely rural, but sophisticated and informed. Iowans are well-educated, economically comfortable, well-traveled. It is not a backwater in any sense. Its statewide newspapers are well-written and informative. Its only regional and political bias is to worry about the economics of agriculture, but it has had, over the years, Republicans and Democrats run its government. For more than a decade leading up to 1980 it had been electing very liberal Democrats to national office. Just before the 1980 elections, however, that trend began to change, with Dick Clark booted out of his Senate seat in 1980 and John Culver, another liberal Democrat and close friend of Ted Kennedy's, in a life and death struggle to maintain his seat in the Senate. (He stayed neutral in the presidential contest and eventually lost to a very conservative Republican.) The governorship was held by a moderate Republican, Robert Ray, who similarly stayed neutral.

In many ways Iowa was as good a state to start a presidential selection process as any in the nation. And on the mild winter's night of January 21, Iowans took their role seriously. So seriously, in fact, that they reduced the plans and the strategies of most of the candidates and their organizations to empty hopes. Iowans flooded to the precinct meeting places in record numbers. The carefully identified supporters of each candidate were soon overrun by faces no one had contacted, people no one expected would show up. The precinct organizers gasped with fear and uncertainty as the unknowns crowded into the meetings. Despite the inconvenience and the necessity of spending a whole evening just to cast one vote, the Iowa caucuses became not the quiet little exercises in direct democracy that they had often been, but rather very nearly a mass process. "We planned for a caucus," said

Kennedy staffer John Sasso, "but we had a primary." On the Republican side the astonishment was just as high. "I stood there watching these people come in," said a Bush precinct worker. "I didn't know who they were."

But on the Republican side the unknowns were for Bush, and he ran comfortably ahead of the absent Reagan. Far behind Reagan was Howard Baker, whose pathetic organization hadn't been able to capitalize on the outpouring. Fourth was John Connally. Crane, Anderson, and Dole brought up the rear of the field, and for Crane and Dole the opening scene of Campaign 1980 was also the final act. They would stay around until their federal matching funds came in, pay off their debts, and then retire. Anderson, although he finished poorly, had been impressive enough in the debate to keep trying, although no one thought he would ever seriously challenge for the Republican nomination.

Iowa left George Bush the new front-runner for the Republican nomination; a tentative and untested front-runner to be sure, but, still, he had taken on Ronald Reagan and won. That night in Iowa Bush was intoxicated with his victory and acted like a Yale undergraduate after the Elis had beaten Harvard. He announced to one and all, via network television, that he now had the "big mo" on his side. By this fraternity house expression he meant, of course, that the momentum of being a winner would help his campaign. And he was right. The attention he had tried so hard to command was now all his. The number of reporters traveling with the Bush campaign tripled overnight as the entourage left for New England.

Reagan was informed of his loss in Iowa while watching a movie at the home of a friend in California. He took it easily, but inside the Reagan organization the long knives came out and they were aimed at John Sears, the mastermind strategist who had kept Reagan's profile low in the Iowa contests. Sears had been more concerned about the northeastern states where Reagan had done poorly in 1976 and where, Sears figured, any national politician would have to do well. Sears was ready for the New England primaries, but he was not ready for what would happen to him inside the Reagan camp.

The Kennedy organization, surveying the results in Iowa, figured that it had done its job. About 35,000 people had come to the caucuses and voted for delegates pledged to Ted Kennedy.

That had been their goal and that, they figured, would put them neck and neck with Jimmy Carter. But the deluge of voters had swamped Ted Kennedy. Because of Iran and Afghanistan, because of the incredible attention paid by the national press to Iowa (the local Democrats charged onlookers ten dollars a head to watch the national press cover the results in a Des Moines hotel), Iowans overran the Kennedy candidacy, voting for Carter delegates two to one. They came out, Sasso commented, "because they thought it was the patriotic thing to do, and the patriotic thing to do is to support the President in a time of national crisis."

No matter what the reason, the results in Iowa spelled enormous trouble for Ted Kennedy. He was a candidate running on the claim of his ability to win, and then to lead the nation. A loss of any sort and for any reason punctured that myth. He would have to reassess his campaign, find some new direction. Kennedy had the advantage of moving to home turf in New England after Iowa, but there he had to win or his campaign would be effectively over. Reagan too needed to win after Iowa. But his problems were somewhat smaller than Kennedy's. Reagan could concede another primary or two, especially in New England, where Bush was thought to be stronger, and then still recoup in his southern and western strongholds as the primary season wore on. And Reagan was not running, as Ted Kennedy was, against an incumbent president of the United States. Instead, he was running against an untested candidate who, by dint of hard work and excellent organization, had won a single primary. The Republican game was far from over.

7

The Politics of Resentment

Howard Henry Baker, Jr., the minority leader of the United States Senate, was walking through a crowd of his supporters in Hartford. Watching from the side of the room, I could see only a moving hole in the middle of a sea of smiling faces. Baker stood five feet seven inches tall, but he was nonetheless a pillar of the Republican Establishment in Washington. It was a distinction he richly deserved. For more than a decade Baker had worked at being a senator, worked in the classic ways of American politics. He held to his moderately conservative principles but he was too intelligent to think he had a corner on perfect truth. He was the kind of political figure who makes legislative bodies work well. He could charm, argue, trade, or, if necessary, force his way toward his policy goals, and he could do it without creating permanent enemies.

His were the consummate legislative skills, and they seemed to be inherited. Both his father and his stepmother had served in the House of Representatives. And he was married to the daughter of the late Everett Dirksen, one of the Republican giants of the Senate. The Senate seemed naturally and genetically a comfortable place for Howard Baker. So comfortable, so familiar, and in his estimation, so central to the political concerns of America that he felt he could use that institution as the platform from which to launch his presidency. He had calculated that he could build his early campaign around the fight over ratification of the SALT II Treaty, a fight he thought would be long and bitter and thus give him enormous exposure on television. He could not have known, of course, that by the winter of 1980 that treaty would be a dead letter, withdrawn by Carter as the result of political attacks by the right wing and, more importantly, a victim of the Soviet Union's invasion of Afghanistan. The entire strategy was faulty, however, not just the estimation of the progress of one piece of legislation. With perhaps the single exception of Baker's own rise to prominence during the dramatic Watergate hearings on national television, the work of the Congress simply does not penetrate the consciousness of the nation sufficiently to permit its use for long as a presidential vehicle. To have run successfully and realistically Baker would have had to abandon his role as minority leader and hit the road. That he didn't—and that he was intelligent enough to figure out just exactly what to do to gain the presidency—was a measure of what he held to be important in his life.

That is not to say that Baker didn't really want the presidency; he surely did. Four years earlier, in fact, he had desperately wanted the vice-presidency on the Ford ticket. He was approached by Ford and his hopes rose, only to have Ford pick the ascerbic Bob Dole in Baker's stead, leaving the Tennessean bitterly disappointed. What Baker didn't seem to want to do was to grub and root and chase after the presidency like a mooning high school boy pursuing the school's most beautiful and aloof young woman. In the old order of things, before the political "reforms" of the 1970s, a politician of Baker's accomplishments and stature would have had an enormous advantage when the party's top leaders began to cast about for a presidential nominee. Indeed, Baker was the one Republican candidate most feared by the

Carter White House. The operatives there and in other places in the Democratic party recognized that Baker was just the sort of moderate conservative who had the potential of demolishing Carter in the fall. Baker's southern roots could have negated Carter's advantage in that region, so important to Carter in 1976. Baker's reassuring tone, his sensible policies, his reasonableness, his intellect all would have given him excellent chances to sweep away Democratic voters in all regions of the country.

But, of course, Baker had first to be nominated by the Republican party. And for that, he would have had to travel, and to organize and to work. His standing in the national opinion polls was always respectable, even though he was not widely known by the electorate, even after his Watergate exposure. Of those who did recognize the name, the balance of favorable versus unfavorable ratings was always heavily in the senator's favor. Even the Reagan forces worried that if Baker got himself well known, if he did the hard work like that performed by Bush in Iowa, he could be a powerful threat inside the party. The level of Reagan's concern was, however, much smaller than Carter's. Baker was a more powerful general election figure than he could be in the Republican primaries, where the hard-core conservatives voted most frequently. Over the years the whole Republican minority had moved substantially toward the right. A dozen years before, Baker had been on the party's right wing. Now he stood a touch left of center in the Republican spectrum, and this added to his problems in seeking the party's nomination. Two years before, Baker had studied and reflected, questioned and discussed, and then voted for the Panama Canal treaties finally presented by the Carter administration, after steady work by three other administrations, Republican and Democratic. It was a telltale issue for the Republican right, and after he cast that vote Howard Baker never could quite satisfy the conservatives that he wasn't a raging liberal internationalist who approved the Panama Canal giveaway.

Having finished third in the Iowa caucuses, behind Bush and Reagan but ahead of Connally and all the rest, Baker moved with the pack into New England, still trying to build a legitimate campaign organization. It was something he had needed for more than a year but had failed to produce. In the fall, for example, Baker had staged what he expected would be a triumphant campaign kickoff at a party meeting in Maine. Relying on the state's popular Republican senator, William Cohen, to provide the organizational work, Baker estimated that he would win a straw vote at the meeting. Thus he invited a group of national political reporters to make the chartered airplane trip to witness his victory. Even George Bush's organization was shocked when Bush, not Baker, won the vote in full view of the Washington press corps. For Baker it was another case of not working hard enough at the details, the annoying and demeaning details of presidential electioneering.

Just before Iowa, Baker hired Douglas Bailey, an expert political consultant in Washington, who then produced the single best political advertisement of the campaign year. It featured Baker shouting down an Iranian student who questioned U.S. support of the Shah. In the ad great applause followed Baker's denunciation. But the Iranian student and others in the audience said later that the applause had actually followed the student's question, not Baker's answer, and that the film had been misleadingly spliced. After the senator's weak showing in Iowa, Bailey and other Baker advisers put the senator on the road full time, to see what could be salvaged in New Hampshire.

While Democrats frequent union halls, Head Start classrooms, and community centers during the campaign travels, the Republicans are fonder of private clubs, big fund-raising dinners in large sumptuous banquet halls and the headquarters buildings of large corporations, where the management usually seems amenable to wasting their employees' worktime to give their party favorites some exposure. In early February Howard Baker, with the press in tow, motored up to the neat colonial-style offices of the Wheelebrator-Frye Company, one of the state of New Hampshire's largest employers. Reproductions of Early American furniture were set on Oriental rugs scattered over soft wall-to-wall carpeting. It was in this refined and civilized setting that Howard Baker was at his best. And it was apparent that, like the other candidates, his strengths were synonymous with his weaknesses. In Baker's case it was his very reasonableness that was a political liability. Baker, the balanced and careful legislator, was competing not on the floor of the legislature but in the pit of presidential politics. To a large extent reasonableness, balance, and complexity are the enemies of the presidential primary aspirant. Those qualities don't produce headlines or television news spots, nor do they rouse the reluctant attention of the electorate. That this is so is both lamentable and unremarkable. Running for a presidential nomination is more a matter of attracting attention than of making detailed policy proposals or of convincing the electorate of the complexity of one's intellect. The clear-cut answer is more powerful than reasonableness, regardless of how simplistic or unrealistic the answer may be. And there was nothing clear-cut about Howard Baker's speech at Wheelebrator-Frye, nothing outrageous, nothing that snapped the audience to attention. He was just reasonable and moderate, and steeped in the understandings that come from the clash of ideas and power on the floor of the Senate.

That evening Howard Baker gave a speech as powerful as can be crafted from reasonableness. The power was in his voice, in his eyes, in his experience, and in his self-assurance. It may have persuaded half the two hundred in the audience, but it never reached the thousands who would vote, because there was nothing there for television. Every view was carefully balanced. Every thought had its qualification.

"When there's a crisis in progress, as there is in Iran, barring extraordinary circumstances, you better let the President manage it," Baker said, adding that what was called for was not opposition to the Carter policy of the moment, but rather the replacement of Carter himself. He was supporting Carter now, but sought to defeat him later. Similarly, Baker was for the use of nuclear power, but only "safe and socially acceptable" nuclear power. He was for the burning of more coal to save oil, but only burning it in a "safe and clean" way. He was for a windfall profits tax on the oil companies, but he favored a "plowback" provision, letting the companies escape the tax to the extent they reinvested their huge profits in further oil exploration. He was against excessive regulation by the federal government, but supported the Occupational Health and Safety rules. Baker was so measured, so careful, so balanced that in the end one had to wonder whether he believed strongly in anything other than being measured, careful, and balanced.

For those in New Hampshire who were mildly unhappy with things as they were, who felt things needed fixing, not replacement or radical change, Baker was perfect. But Republicans in New Hampshire were not just mildly unhappy with the state of the nation. They were angry and resentful—about taxes, about Iran, about the Soviet Union, about inflation and, most of all, about Jimmy Carter. Baker's supporters in New Hampshire had begun the tiresome work of canvassing potential voters to identify their supporters. Their phone calls found Reagan leading in the state, with Bush and Baker following. But they also found that while those voters' hearts were with Reagan (he had lost to incumbent Ford there in 1976 by less than two thousand votes), they had some questions about the Californian. They wondered about Reagan's age and his vitality. They were distressed by the imperial candidacy that had kept Reagan out of Iowa and out of the Iowa debate. They were joking in New Hampshire about the necessity of finding a good vice-president for Reagan because the actuarial tables did not favor his finishing his presidential term. "Reagan, 1980; Bush, 1981" one bumper sticker proclaimed. "This state is up for grabs," said one Baker operative a month before the primary, "and we have the potential to do well." It was both the creed and the epitaph of the Baker campaign.

The "big mo" George Bush carried out of Iowa and into New Hampshire was real enough, for a time. Within a week of the Iowa caucuses Bush led Reagan by six points in New Hampshire. Then the margin increased to nearly ten points as the hyperkinetic Bush toured the Granite State. The pressure of being the front-runner, however, seemed to be wearing on Bush. When he had been a challenger back in the pack, Bush was treated rather gently by the press. The focus was nearly always on his position in the race— that of the hopeful challenger to Reagan—and the quality of his organization. Now that he was the front-runner himself, the press and the public began to take a more critical look at Bush, and that more skeptical treatment he was receiving irritated the candidate. Up to this point Bush had avoided taking many detailed positions on the issues, preferring instead a kind of candidate shorthand, along with his eternally optimistic dissertation on his political chances. Being the front-runner brought increasing demands for more specifics from Bush. But at the heart of Bush's success lay a kind of deliberate confusion that he was trying to capitalize on.

His aristocratic origins suggested that he was part of the old Rockefeller Republican party, and he actually was somewhat less conservative than Reagan, or at least less dogmatic in his conservatism. But Bush was eager to appear almost as conservative as Reagan. Great specificity would only have diminished that appearance. If he had discussed issues the way, say, Howard Baker did, it would have quickly become clear that Bush was substantially less simplistic than Reagan, and thus he would have forfeited his ability to lure away the Reagan purists.

Bush campaigned in New Hampshire stiffly, self-consciously. His blue cashmere overcoat had been replaced by a sporty blue anorak, which looked like it was picked off the rack at L. L. Bean. It was as if he thought his new outerwear might attract a few more votes in the land where he had spent his prep school years. But rather than feeling at home, Bush tightened up. At a speech before a high school crowd in Manchester, one morning, I watched Bush indulge in a prolonged monologue about the necessity for him to ignore his new critics. It was like his days on the Yale baseball team, he told the students. When a player was easily distracted by the jibes and comments from the opponents' bench, he was said to have "rabbit ears," Bush explained. And as a candidate, he continued, he would now have to avoid being distracted by the boo birds and the dugout tormentors. His main theme was a recounting of the tactics that had got him where he was and which would carry him to victory. He conducted similar strange monologues all over New Hampshire, as if coaching himself in public. There was something missing in the Bush campaign, and there was something missing in Bush. Even after winning one of the two most important contests in the nomination fight, Bush seemed wispy and giddy. "Too lightweight," the pros kept saying, to be president. Bush did little to counter that criticism.

At the same time, the gloves had come off in the Reagan camp. Stung by their defeat in Iowa, the Reaganites were no longer content to follow John Sears's strategy designed for the Olympian front-runner. It was a decision they couldn't avoid, because Reagan, for the time being at least, was no longer the front-runner. Reagan himself abandoned his practice of jetting into the country for a few campaign stops and then jetting back across the continent for a long weekend in Los Angeles or at his ranch near Santa

Barbara. He began to campaign full time and all out. When his sixty-ninth birthday rolled around, Reagan campaigned all day and then attended a big, well-photographed party that evening in New Hampshire. The idea was not only not to ignore the age question, but to defy the very notion that he was too old to be president. Having already lost one important nomination fight in Iowa, Reagan was also freed of the burden of trying to avoid giving his challengers a target to criticize. Bush had started the fight in Iowa and the Reagan campaign came out swinging.

For the Reaganites in New Hampshire, and, indeed, for much of his organization and among his supporters all over the country, a full-scale campaign meant giving vent to the basic angers and resentments that drives the hard-line reactionary movement in this country. One of those resentments, perhaps the basic one, was directed vaguely against people with money, power, connections; people who seemed to be able to break the rules, get ahead, avoid being hurt by inflation; people whose children went easily on in life, into the best colleges, and then into the best jobs. That feeling was in some ways the oldest kind of class jealousy, and in some new and important ways it was the anger of middle-class America, caught by inflation, puzzled and confused by the whole social revolution of the 1960s and 1970s. To them Ronald Reagan was not just a nostalgic figure, he was the very embodiment of the return to the old values and rules they felt would cure their economic hardship and their moral confusion.

Months before the New Hampshire primary, James Lake, the press secretary in the Reagan campaign, had patiently explained to me over a sumptuous dinner in a swank Beverly Hills restaurant that one common denominator of many of the Reagan high command was that they were the first generation of their families to have gone to college. By this Lake meant that they were the first of their line to have driven themselves into the upper middle class and that, consequently, they were damned anxious to keep their hands on what they had. (It was not just first-generation college graduates who were worried about holding on to their wealth and achievement, of course, but Lake's point was that the Reagan forces were angry about the direction in which the country was going.) To many of the Reagan supporters, George Bush embodied that too-privileged, too-moderate, and too-liberal upper class in the Republican party against which they had fought since Goldwater rose up out of the sun belt to oppose Nelson Rockefeller's branch of the party in 1964.

In New Hampshire, itself a state of struggling middle-class workers, from shoe factory laborers to small businessmen and commuters who had fled the high taxes of neighboring Massachusetts, class resentment became a powerful tool for the local Reagan organizers. Jerald Carmen, Reagan's New England chairman, was perfectly suited to make just such an argument, and he made it at every opportunity. Carmen was a self-made businessman who operated in Manchester out of a grubby office with walls covered by fake wood paneling and insurance agency calendars on the wall. He chain-smoked, was constantly distracted by phone calls, and was busy making sure that reporters and everyone else knew that the real stakes in the Reagan-Bush struggle were to defeat the old, monied Establishment. He was especially concerned that his friends on the Manchester *Union-Leader* understood the preferred line of attack against Bush. And since the *Union-Leader* is a newspaper that every four years does for presidential politicians what the *National Enquirer* does every week for movie stars, he succeeded easily.

In early February, for example, a single issue of the *Union-Leader* had three anti-Bush articles displayed on the top of the front page of the paper. The point of two of the articles (only one of which was labeled an editorial) was that Bush was a closet liberal. One rather puerile piece began: "If you spot something which walks like a duck, quacks like a duck, swims like a duck and even looks like a duck, you would be safe to assume it is a duck. But is it? In this year's N.H. Presidential primary sweepstakes you have a 'duck' in sheep's clothing by the name of George Bush." An accompanying cartoon showed a duck labeled George Bush wearing a sheepskin, a strange, mutant creature that could only have evolved out of the *Union-Leader*'s bizarre mixing of clichés.

Below the top-of-the-page cartoon the paper's publisher, William Loeb, had placed an editorial. He praised the accompanying piece as "one of the wittiest pieces of writing as well as the most accurate that we have had the pleasure of looking over in several years." Loeb went on to say that the article had succeeded in

117

describing candidate Bush "for what he is—an out-and-out liberal trying to hide his record and his actual views and disguise himself as a conservative in order to gain New Hampshire votes. Bush is obviously the candidate of David Rockefeller and the Trilateral Commission."

It was not the first nor would it be the last time Bush would be taxed by the conservatives for having been a member of the Trilateral Commission, a well-meaning group of businessmen and political figures from the United States, Europe, and Japan who favored free trade and cooperation among the industrial nations. Bush had indeed been a member of the group, but around the paranoiac fringes of the Republican right the commission had taken on the shades of some one-world conspiracy. Bush had resigned from the commission before undertaking his campaign, knowing that the far right would criticize his membership.

Nor was it the first time that Loeb had pushed his paper to excess in order to forward Reagan's cause. Earlier in the campaign he had printed a sensational and inaccurate story accusing Phil Crane, whom Loeb felt could steal some of Reagan's thunder, of sexual promiscuity and excessive use of alcohol. To outsiders the paper seemed so ridiculously and laughably irresponsible that its impact was often discounted. But, in fact, the paper was the only one with statewide circulation, and the power of Loeb and the *Union-Leader* had ruined many state politicians and instilled fear even in former employees. I had once asked a former reporter for the paper to contribute his recollections about Loeb to *Time* magazine. He refused, saying he was frightened of Loeb and the power of the newspaper in the state. The newspaper could not, of course, ensure victory for its favorite candidates, because the paper often picked sure losers and quacks because of their apparent ideological purity. But the day-after-day beating it could administer to those it opposed was truly damaging. It was this sort of attack that George Bush was trying desperately to ignore, to avoid having, as he said, "rabbit ears."

As the battering of Bush continued, the candidate himself grew ever more tense. In the space of less than a month, Bush had moved from the back of the pack to the lead position and he was now afraid of losing that lead. Like Reagan before Iowa, he didn't want to take risks that would potentially give his opponents an advantage. "I must avoid making mistakes," he told reporters and voters alike. And so he continued to give tight little lectures on his own strategy, instead of trying to expand and solidify public understanding of his positions and the directions in which he wanted to take the country. He would repeat his cryptic positions, but his rhetoric was subdued and he remained something of a mystery to the voters in New Hampshire.

Bush could play it safe when he was campaigning alone, but when the Republicans gathered for another mass debate in Manchester a week before the primary, he could not escape being judged against the field. To most reporters and political experts, the debate seemed to help no one in particular. Bush was again tense and careful. Reagan was awkward and a bit unsure of himself in what was his first encounter with his collected opposition. But a survey done after the debate by Reagan's pollster Richard Wirthlin indicated that in fact the massive winner of the rather dull exercise had been Reagan. Wirthlin found that Reagan had managed to send enough signals to his core conservative support to shore up his lagging standing. The fact that Reagan had held his own against the new front-runner Bush especially seemed to dissipate the aura of the winner that Bush had picked up in Iowa. And what appeared to most viewers as an embarrassing moment for Reagan was seen by his pollster as a plus. At the very end of the debate a member of the audience asked Reagan whether an ethnic joke he had told a reporter earlier that month was an example of his own bias. Reagan was both angry and embarrassed by the question. He claimed lamely that he had told the joke as an example of the kind of humor that should not be used in a campaign. And he made the reporter who had printed the joke the villain by saying he had violated an understanding that the conversation was off the record. This, Wirthlin contended, allowed Reagan to share "a greater range of his emotional makeup with Republicans than he had done since the dramatic moments at the 1976 convention." In short, Reagan had showed himself to be alive and well, not the dottering sixty-nine-year-old who had been sitting back, protected by Sears and his staff, afraid to campaign. Almost immediately, Reagan's strength in the state began to build.

The turnabout was accelerated by what was planned as a Reagan-Bush debate in Nashua. The affair was sponsored by the Nashua *Telegraph,* but had been initiated by Reagan, who, after Iowa, wanted to take on the new front-runner man to man. On the Saturday before the primary voting, Reagan and Bush showed up at the Nashua High School gymnasium as planned. But without having warned Bush, Reagan had also quietly invited the other major Republican contenders to join the fray. Anderson, Dole, Crane, and Baker accepted. But the ground rules for the debate, set by the newspaper, were for a head-to-head contest, not for another multicandidate panel. And the editor of the paper, Jon Breen, held firm despite the appearance on stage of the newly invited four. Minutes before the debate was to begin, Reagan sent word that he wanted to see Bush. Instead, Bush's campaign manager, James Baker, was sent to talk to Reagan's manager, John Sears. Baker told Sears that the Bush campaign would follow whatever rules the *Telegraph* wanted to set. After that meeting Baker spotted Reagan and the other four candidates. It's gang-up time, he thought.

And so it was. Bush and Reagan and the other four trooped on stage only to have Breen announce that the rules he had made would stand and that the other candidates would not be included. Reagan grabbed his microphone and began to explain why the others should be included.

"Will you please turn off Governor Reagan's microphone," Breen said.

"I'm paying for this microphone, Mr. Green," Reagan snapped, characteristically getting one important detail wrong. Bush sat unsmiling and rigid while Reagan argued for including the others.

Reagan's temper, usually well under control, had shown itself, and he went on that night, after the other four candidates had waved good-bye, to show Bush up as an anxious and cold opponent. Not many New Hampshire voters had seen the confrontation on television, but word spread rapidly. In fact, Bush was so flabbergasted and concerned that he took out advertisements explaining that he had been the victim of a clever political ploy by Reagan. This only spread the story of his sorry performance. Reagan had laid the trap for Bush, and Bush and James Baker walked into it. They had handled the confrontation poorly. The old man in the campaign had shown himself again to be capable of anger and full of life. It was all that was really necessary to rouse his conservative constituency. On election night Bush was buried under a Reagan avalanche that gave the Californian a twenty-seven percentage-point victory. Bush's days as front-runner were over. They had lasted less than one month.

The Reagan sweep in New Hampshire was, of course, critically important. Having lost Iowa, he could not afford to lose again so quickly, for the pattern set in the early primaries is hard to break later on. It was important too because it returned the Republican race to the *status quo ante,* restoring Reagan to the front-runner's position and reducing the other contenders, including Bush, to being his challengers. With Reagan on top, the other Republicans were forced to divide up the anti-Reagan feeling in the party, and in 1980 there was not much of that to go around. But most important of all, the victory in New Hampshire set Reagan free to campaign just as he had in 1976, swinging hard from the right, expressing the resentments against government and anger over the economic problems of America that powered his candidacy before.

The successful campaign in new Hampshire also brought with it the proof, in Reagan's mind at least, that his staff had misdirected him in Iowa and that the careful planning of John Sears was getting in his way as a campaigner, not helping his quest for the presidency. Sears had insisted for nearly a year that it was necessary to retrain Reagan for his front-runner's role. It was Sears's contention that Reagan and the staff had taken too lightly the necessity for understanding the issues in depth so that the typical Reagan one-line blunder would be avoided. Sears's complaining about this problem annoyed Reagan and thus annoyed those who had been around Ronald Reagan longest. They had all been perfectly happy with Reagan all those years. They resented Sears, a relative newcomer. And over the months some of the men closest to Reagan, like Mike Deaver and Lyn Nofziger, both loyalists since Reagan's earliest days in politics, left the campaign because of Sears.

The trouble had festered for months and months. Sears never did gain full control of the campaign and this both frustrated him and produced management errors. The campaign's spending—held to a maximum of seventeen million dollars through the summer convention by federal law—was badly handled. Sears complained that two million dollars had been spent in the fall for an unproductive direct-mail fund-raising effort and for huge fund-raising concerts and a mammoth campaign kickoff dinner in New York. Sears blamed Nofziger and Deaver, then still with the campaign, for that spending. It was a classic sort of campaign disorganization. A relative newcomer is given nominal authority to run the campaign, but the candidate's loyal old pals end-run the new man and go directly to the candidate. The candidate, grateful for years of loyal service, can't say no to his old pals, and soon no one is in charge. This produces jealousy and conflict. In the Reagan campaign this appeared as ideological sniping at Sears, correctly suspected of being more interested in political operations than in ideological purity. His attempts to have Reagan present a more complex view of the issues that faced America was seen by some around Reagan as an attempt to change Reagan's ideological spots. Sears was accused of trying to move Reagan toward the political center.

The day before the voting in New Hampshire, Reagan had already been told by his pollster that he would win easily. After campaigning in Manchester, Reagan returned to his motel, invited Sears and his top two lieutenants, Jim Lake and Charles Black, to a 2:30 meeting in his room. When the three arrived, they found Reagan, Nancy, and William Casey, the newly named administrative director of the campaign, waiting. They were handed press releases saying they had resigned. Sears read the release and said coolly, "I'm not surprised." His only public statements about the firing were to defend himself against charges of mismanagement by pointing out the disorganization in the staff. And despite an offer from Howard Baker to take over his failing campaign (he had finished third again in New Hampshire) he stayed out of the Republican struggle and said he continued to believe Reagan should be president. "The country is in terrible shape. It needs to believe in somebody to be its president. And if the country can believe in someone, it can solve some of these problems," Sears said after his firing.

After New Hampshire the 1980 Republican nomination was all but Ronald Reagan's to claim. All that lay between him and the prize he had sought for so many years was, in fact, himself. He had the capacity to make foolish and frightening statements, but that was beyond the control of anyone but himself. If Reagan could avoid scaring his party to death—and that would have been almost impossible, given the conservative tenor of the Republicans who, over the years, had moved toward Reagan's own view—he would be nominated. Sears was gone and with him one of the best tactical and strategic minds in American politics. But looking back, it mattered little that Sears's particular genius was missing. Without the discomfort that Sears's presence had caused, the Reagan campaign began to function the way his campaigns always had. Reagan was given his head. He smiled and bobbed his head, making mistakes of fact and judgment, but pleasing the conservative faithful and moving steadily toward his party's nomination.

SPRING
1980

8

"The Bozo Zone"

There were moments in Ted Kennedy's campaign when it all seemed a perfect resurrection of the glories of his family's past. On the outskirts of Houston late one afternoon, Ted and Joan climbed onto a small stage in a Mexican-American community center. A crowd of several hundred people were packed shoulder to shoulder, sweltering under the television lights and giddy with excitement. Kennedy waved and then stripped off his jacket. The sight of the senator in his fitted shirt, strained by his beefy girth, sent the audience wild. They cheered and clapped, whistled and screamed. Mothers raised infants high above their heads to see the senator and his wife, knowing the sight meant nothing to the children but wanting, some day, to be able to tell them they had seen the Kennedys.

Ted stood smiling and waving from the podium on the stage. Joan crowded in behind, slightly to his right. The lights caught her blond hair for a moment. They both were smiling, he facing left, she, in profile, facing right. Frozen there, it seemed that he could

127

touch the core of the American political being, that he could bring back days gone by when the country was strong and safe and under control. Looking at the two of them, it seemed for an instant that he could win and take charge and lead a restoration of Camelot.

But then the reality of the situation took over, pushing away that nostalgic reverie. The perfect political couple bathing themselves in the wild adoration of the Hispanic crowd was not, in fact, a couple at all. They were together during the campaign, but usually they lived apart while she struggled against alcoholism and tried to get her bearings in the frantic world he had introduced her to. She campaigned with him for appearance' sake, but even there in Houston, when the speech and picture-taking were ended, he turned away from her, ignored her, stranded her in the crowd. At night they parted again, to separate rooms, separate hotels, or separate cities. This was not a triumphal campaign in which the power of the people was flowing toward this man. Rather, it had become a desperate and losing struggle, a hopeless exercise in sheer perseverance in which Kennedy made the speeches and answered the questions and seemed to be running for president, an increasingly impossible goal. Soon he was running only to prove something to himself and to his family. It was sad to know that the tableau in the community center was so hollow and so false. It was sad that he was so much less than had been thought, so much smaller than the myth, for it meant simply that neither he nor any candidate—and others were trying in different ways— could recreate the past.

Just what it was about running for president that befuddled and confused Ted Kennedy, that frequently reduced this normally able politician to a ranting, incoherent burlesque, could only be guessed at. The obvious explanation seemed that once again his behavior was destined to prevent his success. In the past it had been scandals or accidents, but as he campaigned in 1980 it was as if a cerebral short-circuit had rendered him incapable, from time to time, of logical thought and speech.

His loss in Iowa had seemed at first a tonic. A week after that defeat Kennedy appeared at Georgetown University in Washington and read a speech clearly setting himself out as a liberal Democrat, an unapologetic advocate of wage and price controls as a solution to inflation, of national health insurance, of tax reduction for the working classes, of strict environmental controls, and as an opponent of the increased use of nuclear power, of confrontation with the Soviet Union, despite their invasion of Afghanistan. It was a coherent, well-delivered speech. Kennedy had decided to stop fudging his liberalism and to find a message that he, at least, was comfortable giving. But the decision to play a straight liberal line did not improve the Kennedy performance significantly. His campaign organization, top-heavy with staff in Washington and disorganized on the road, began to crumble further as fund raising faltered in the wake of the Iowa defeat. As Kennedy campaigned in New England, he abandoned the expensive charter jet that is the most indispensable item of modern campaigning. Instead, Kennedy and the reporters trailing him lurched through New England on buses and in motorcades, chartering small planes by the handful here and there, missing meetings, arriving late for dinners, scrambling for hotel space. The logistics of the campaign, along with its central political purpose, were in utter disarray. The Kennedy band was like a routed army, its ranks broken, its spirit waning, its sense of the absurdity and futility of its endeavors building each day.

In early February the Democrats held a series of precinct caucuses in Maine to begin their delegate selection process, much in the same way Iowa had two weeks before. There, Kennedy lost to Carter again. This time the margin was smaller and the Kennedy followers took heart from the less-dramatic loss. The liberal message put forth at Georgetown did seem to energize some students and old-line Democrats to vote for Kennedy, but in Maine Jerry Brown had made his first (and last) real appearance of the campaign. While finishing last behind Kennedy, Brown had managed to attract some antinuclear activists into his column, cutting away from the Kennedy vote. The great geysers of rhetoric from Brown were all that there was to his campaign. There was no organization, no plan, no money, and no future. He had become a strange figure, arriving here and there in Maine, and later in New Hampshire, emerging from a car with one or two staff members, speaking briefly to small crowds, and then wandering off to the next little hamlet. Brown finished third again in New Hampshire, and he moved on to Wisconsin, skipping all the contests in the intervening month. There, in late March, he staged a bizarre multimedia rally that ended with a television broadcast produced by Francis Ford Coppola, the creator of the film *Apocalypse Now,* that looked more like an acid trip than a political event, and finally withdrew from the race.

After Maine Kennedy was still trailed by a large herd of reporters and by his considerable traveling staff. This band would descend on a crowd, seemingly without reason or preparation, and Kennedy would speak a shorter version of his Georgetown speech, criticizing the failures of Carter, calling for new action and new direction. And then he would take questions. It was in such situations that Kennedy was almost always bad. At one event in Laconia, New Hampshire, he was asked whether he favored gasoline rationing. In a booming monotone, Kennedy gave this answer, recorded by *Time* magazine correspondent Johanna McGeary:

"The question is on gasoline rationing and there are two ways of rationing gasoline. One is by price and one is a rationing system. I don't know what you're paying now, pretty close to two dollars . . . it varies. . . . I see a dollar twenty one day and a dollar fifty the next, but it is probably close to two dollars here, a dollar fifty by the summer, two dollars by the end of the year, probably three dollars by the end of next year. Now we're either going to have rationing by price or you're going to have a system which is going to ensure, under the system I favor, under the freeze . . . we're going to hold the price down and under my program it would be that over a three-year period the total amount of gasoline that you would reduce your consumption of then, you very much [laughs], you'll try and meet with your . . .

"This is an important question that you would reduce the consumption of gasoline by gallon of one quarter over a period of three years. Now if you're fortunate enough to be able to buy a new car over the period of not probably three years. So it's a reduction of by one quarter of the amount of gas that you use [sic]."

By the time Kennedy got this far, some of his audience had lapsed into stupor. Others were astounded by this man, about whom they had read so much, uttering such absolute nonsense and doing so at the top of his voice. Kennedy continued:

"Now there are alternatives. It's either going to be one way or it's going to be the other. There is no other easy way out. It's one way or the other. I favor the equitable, fairer system. Price down, held down, and then the distribution of gas with the reduction of a quarter . . .

"Now a final point. I'd make the allocation system different for different parts of the country. New Hampshire doesn't have a mass transit system as Massachusetts does, so that you allocate the gas based on historic use, and historic use has a component built into it about the growth patterns. New Hampshire is the second fastest-growing state in the country, and that is included in any kind of formula. So the people in the northern tier states do get more of an allocation than those that live in an urban area that has mass transit. And I do believe that this is a fairer, more equitable way of dealing with the issue [sic]."

Nor was this all the wisdom Kennedy had to share with New Hampshirites that day. A few minutes later, at a tiny local bank, he was asked about his program for wage and price controls. He replied, again in his booming voice:

"Well, on the question of prices and wages. Basically it's a program which was . . . which the U.S. had in the Korean War, World War II, and in the Nixon period. There is not really much debate or discussion about it but what you are doing with that program . . . we are establishing a moratorium or freeze for six months on all price increases, on all wage increases, dividends, profits, rents, across the board. Then, during the next period of time, I would . . . or even during that period, I would like to see achieved and accomplished the four, five major areas of economic policy that I think can make a significant difference in bringing revitalization to our economy. That is going to be in the stimulus on the supply side, stimulus, stimulating competition, deregulation, foreign trade, and I believe that those elements can be helpful and useful and valuable in breathing new life into our economy. One of the times that we have tried the freeze was during the Nixon period. They put the freeze in just before the election and then we found that Mr. Burns heated the economy with lower interest rates and you had a superheated economy coming down below and a freeze on top, and right after the election they just

131

pulled the freeze off completely and we had a bubble in the rate of inflation. I think that was very unwise [sic]." The candidate's face was now red, his words came in bursts.

"This kind of policy that I have suggested has worked in the past. . . . It is true that it has worked in times of conflict, when it worked and it worked effectively, and I think it has worked not so much because of the administration of it but because people understand that we were going to as a society . . . and a people share the belt tightening in our society and I believe now that that is one of the important factors that has to be re-established in our society. . . . I believe the alternative of inflation in the high teens or twenties is going to be devastating in human terms to people. It isn't a question of whether we have a solution that we're not sure of that may work or may not work that we ought to try; the alternative, I think, of a twenty percent inflation rate is just unacceptable. Thank you very much [sic]."

Throughout this mind-boggling performance his press corps was convulsed with laughter. They had given way to the uncontrollable hysteria that is bred of equal parts exhaustion, boredom, loneliness, and the professional frustration of chasing after a candidate who is heading toward defeat. Their antics at the back of the room further bewildered the audience, who could see Kennedy up front making a fool of himself and a group of reporters from the most powerful news organizations in the nation rolling on the floor in the back, making fools of themselves as well.

From the start of the campaign, the press corps assigned to Kennedy was enormous. Whereas most candidates begin with just a few reporters traveling along, dropping onto and then off the campaign trail to check the candidate's progress, Kennedy, even before his formal announcement, had a huge press following. On the first day of his official campaign 120 reporters covered him. His every move and every word were videotaped, recorded, and reported as if he had already won half the primaries and was on his way to the nomination and to the presidency. This led his staff, like press aide Tom Southwick, to complain that Kennedy had never had time for a trial run, for a break-in period in which to make mistakes unnoticed and unmagnified by the national press. That was, of course, true. But Kennedy was not the obscure

George Bush or Phil Crane. The very celebrity that gave him the chance to run was what attracted the press. The press attention was both the price and prize for that celebrity. That he stumbled so badly was not the fault of the press. It was his own doing. The press simply made sure every halfway alert American knew about those mistakes the instant they were made.

Inside the Kennedy operation, however, the view was more bitter. By the time Kennedy had lost Iowa and Maine and was struggling in New Hampshire, some of those closest to Kennedy blamed the press for unfairly criticizing Kennedy, especially while Carter was locked safely away in the White House. "Eighty percent of those reporters are here because of the anticipation of an assassination," Southwick observed angrily one day, as we drank coffee in a restaurant in Manchester, New Hampshire. "They want to see the . . ." He held his hand the way children do when pretending to shoot a gun. He then curled his index finger twice as if squeezing a trigger. He was right, in part. The fear that someone would try to take away the third Kennedy did cause him to be covered more tightly, watched more closely, just the way the President of the United States is never left alone by the press. "The body watch," the reporters call it, lamenting its tediousness, but living day by day with the professional fear that, surely, the moment one motorcade is missed, one speech skipped in order to drink a beer or call home, that is when the shot will be fired. There is no worse professional nightmare in political journalism than imagining talking to an editor after such an incident and having to explain just why it was that the reporter didn't see what happened. The herd of reporters was there because of that fear, no doubt. But it was not their number nor their minute inspection that caused Ted Kennedy to perform the way he did, not just that day in Laconia, but throughout his early campaign. The reporters were carrying the bad news and some in the Kennedy camp resented them for it. It wasn't, however, their reporting that was offensive, it was their behavior on the campaign that was, in many cases, truly adolescent and unprofessional. And for that, both the candidate and the staff around him seemed, strangely, to forgive the Kennedy press corps.

On any presidential campaign of the length and intensity of the one Ted Kennedy mounted in 1979 and 1980, the press corps that stays with the tour week in and week out becomes a kind of family. The closest professional friendships in the news business are formed this way, second only to those made by correspondents covering a war together. The campaign plane is home, the place they all come back to each day after a long, hard trudge through five states and six cities. It is the place where they work, eat, drink, gossip, and gather new information. But from the start there was something peculiar about the Kennedy press group. Most of the reporters were young and following their first presidential candidate. The Kennedy assignment was important, and many of the young reporters were very taken with their new prominence. Quickly the Kennedy press corps became an extremely close-knit fraternity, united in their pleasure at having been assigned to what looked like an important campaign and drawn together even more tightly by the sudden disappointment of having a sure winner turn into a bumbling failure as a candidate. They drew in on themselves and were suspicious of outsiders. Early in the campaign, for example, a reporter from *Playboy,* Peter Ross Range, appeared on the campaign plane with the intention of getting Kennedy to sit for a *Playboy* interview. That mission was doomed from the start, not just by Jimmy Carter's unhappy experience with that forum in 1976 ("I lust in my heart"), but by Kennedy's own problems with rumors of extramarital activity. *Playboy* was not the place for Ted Kennedy. But Range continued on the tour anyway. The traveling press corps began to fear that he would write about the press itself and their conduct during the campaign. During a weekend stop-over in Washington, one of the members of the Kennedy press inner circle visited a mutual friend to ask if the friend would find out just what Range was up to. The intermediary listened politely but ignored the request.

Other reporters joining the tour were either accepted reluctantly or ostracized in various ways. A woman reporter from *The New York Times* was insulted about her weight and figure. Others were simply cut out of the inner circle and not included in the vital sharing of logistical information and arrangements that the press made for itself in the absence of a campaign organization during the days after the Iowa loss.

In the past, reporters around the Kennedys often became devoted followers who admired the candidate and, especially with

Jack Kennedy, competed with one another to share his time and attention. During Ted Kennedy's presidential campaign there was not that kind of intimacy with the candidate. Kennedy himself was standoffish. Indeed, the Kennedy press clan subjected their candidate to unending ridicule and lampooning, most often in the form of a mock television reporter called Waldo McPhee, played, often hilariously, by Boston *Globe* reporter Tom Oliphant. Oliphant, with the assistance of others, like John Wolcott of *Newsweek,* frequently broadcast his derisive accounts of the candidate's day over the chartered plane's public address system. Oliphant often was showered with requests from his colleagues for a performance, as if laughing at the candidate's missteps and the inanities of campaigning, many caused by the press itself in the form of silly, unknowing questions, helped the group come to terms with the futility of the Kennedy campaign. They were all trapped on a sinking ship, but the campaign plunged on as if there was some chance of victory. This sense of unreality was soon crystalized by the press in the phrase "The Bozo Zone," a takeoff of the 1950s television show called *The Twilight Zone.* It described the clownish and surreal quality of Ted Kennedy's campaign, in which the sure winner became the loser. That Kennedy and his staff tolerated this behavior, which would have been unthinkable in the campaign of, say, John Connally, and that there was neither complaint nor retaliation in the form of reduced access, is only explained by the way Ted Kennedy himself came to regard the campaign. And that attitude seemed to change after New Hampshire.

The Granite State should have been a Kennedy stronghold. In fact, it had been when he had started his campaign in the fall. Polls showed him ahead of Carter there by two to one, just as he was nationwide. The urban parts of the state, where most of the votes are located, are heavily Catholic and working class, natural Kennedy constituencies. But the erosion of his candidacy had taken place in New Hampshire, just as it had elsewhere. Despite fielding 1,500 volunteers, many of them from across the border in his home state of Massachusetts, for a final blitz of the state, Kennedy lost to Carter by eleven percentage points. It was only the second major contest in the race for the nomination, but it was effectively the end of Ted Kennedy's chance to oust the President.

Following New Hampshire, Kennedy did manage to win in Massachusetts. But following that encounter came a series of primaries in Carter country (Georgia, Florida, and Alabama), and each was a predictable disaster for Kennedy. He campaigned only briefly in the South and was met with ugly reactions. Explaining in Birmingham that he was in favor of handgun registration because "my family has been touched by violence," hecklers clapped and jeered.

In Illinois, Kennedy and Carter both had courted Chicago's mayor, Jane Byrne. Her allegiance wavered, but ended with Kennedy. She then managed to alienate half the powerful Cook County Democratic organization, the same organization that had helped Jack Kennedy to victory in 1960 under Byrne's patron in politics, Mayor Richard Daley. The Cook County organization then gave only superficial support to Kennedy. After losing Mayor Byrne's endorsement, Carter's operatives, like Jim Johnson from the Mondale staff, descended on the state and lined up virtually every other politician of consequence, including some of the Cook County crew. On primary election day in March, Carter swamped Kennedy, beating him in black districts, Jewish districts, Irish Catholic districts, urban districts, and rural districts. The Carter vote was twice that for Kennedy, and Carter carried away 163 delegates to the convention while Kennedy collected only 16. The mathematical possibilities for a Kennedy revival were now almost zero. Kennedy was out of the race, but he was not out of the campaign.

The following week in New York and Connecticut the polls showed Carter well ahead of Kennedy. Polling in primaries, however, is notoriously difficult. Opinion tends to be volatile and voters often use the primary election as a vehicle for protest, knowing that a primary vote is not a direct vote for president. In New York especially, that was the case. The voters there looked at the Carter-Kennedy race in a different way. Kennedy had become an impossibility as the nominee. Carter, on the other hand, was sure to be defending his office against a Republican in the fall. But public patience with Carter had worn thin, especially with the unending hostage situation in Iran. With Kennedy all but technically eliminated, the voters in New York were free to send

Carter a message. And that they did. Further angered by the administration's vote for an anti-Israel resolution at the United Nations (and disbelieving an attempt the week before the election to explain the vote away as a mistake caused by a communications breakdown), New Yorkers gave Kennedy an eighteen percentage point victory. In neighboring Connecticut Kennedy won by five points. In its way, the outcome was a kind of warning about the fall campaign. And it was a warning the Carter forces took seriously.

When, in the wake of the hostage taking, Carter chose to stay captive in the White House, he, in effect, decided that his campaign for renomination would become synonymous with his conduct of the presidency. Without a separate campaign in which he explained his past performances and his future hopes, Carter chose to rise or fall with public reaction to his conduct in office. By late March the patriotic devotion that had helped him defeat Kennedy early on was replaced by a simmering sense of national embarrassment and humiliation, much of it aimed at James Earl Carter.

Carter fully understood this and had been trying for weeks to achieve some quiet diplomatic breakthroughs that would first lead to the release of the hostages and second defuse the public temper about the crisis he couldn't seem to solve. He relied ever more heavily on trusted aide Hamilton Jordan, for secret negotiations at home and abroad toward that end. It was characteristic of the Georgia siege mentality that was growing in the White House that Jordan, normally the least diplomatic of people, was used in place of career foreign service experts and even the secretary of state, Cyrus Vance, in these delicate encounters.

But Jordan had managed to procure an understanding from representatives of the Iranians that by the day before the April 1 Wisconsin primary, the hostages would be taken away from the militant "students" and transferred to governmental control in Tehran. To prepare for that move the Iranians announced that they had received a conciliatory message from Carter. Press Secretary Jody Powell denied that any message had been sent, but then Swiss authorities confirmed that there had indeed been some message sent from the White House using their embassy as intermediary.

With two striking losses to Kennedy just recorded in New York and Connecticut, Carter worried about Wisconsin. Despite polls showing a lead for the President, his strategists worried that another loss would look as if the bottom had fallen out of the Carter campaign. Moved by that anxiety, Carter shamelessly misused the office of president by summoning first reporters and then television broadcasters to the White House the night before the primary. He assured them that there were positive developments in Iran. Even more flagrantly, Carter commandeered network time the next morning at 7:00 A.M., in time for the morning television news shows, and made the same announcement to the public. By Caddell's calculations, with this maneuver the President went from a lead of about fifteen points to a winning margin of about thirty points over Kennedy. But he also paid for the victory by exposing the extent to which he would go to get re-elected, especially by using the sensitive hostage crisis. It seemed a mean and small thing to do and it presaged a major problem Carter would have in the fall.

The Pennsylvania primary, in late April, seemed to offer another chance for Kennedy to upset Carter. The large urban vote in Philadelphia and Pittsburgh, and the presence of a sizable Jewish and Catholic vote, made the state look somewhat like New York and Connecticut. To reduce this chance for defeat, media adviser Jerry Rafshoon produced a television commercial designed to remind voters of why, before New York, they had been voting against Kennedy. Citizens were shown giving their reasons: "I don't believe him," one said. "I don't trust him," said another. "You're taking a chance with Kennedy," said a third. In Pennsylvania, Carter and Kennedy split the delegates and the President's nomination was secure. Carter went on, through the month of May, to sweep primary after primary. That left only the finale, so-called Super Tuesday on the third of June, the day for the California, New Jersey, and Ohio primaries, and the day the single largest number of delegates to the convention would be selected.

On May 29 Jimmy Carter suddenly emerged from the White House for his first and only political appearance during the primary season. For all practical purposes he had already won that nomination, and it was never explained why, with the hostages still in Iran, he chose to abandon his vow of isolation, and to campaign. Doubtless he was worried that a Kennedy sweep on June 3 would, if not deny him the nomination, so tarnish the Carter victory as to give him added trouble in the fall. He chose to campaign in Ohio, the state that had sealed his 1976 nomination and where, by beating Ford, he had won the presidency.

Ten thousand people filled a public square in Columbus that day. Red, white, and blue balloons dotted the skies. A high school band marched to the site. The trappings were right, but the candidate was not. Carter, shedding his coat in the hot, early summer sun, seemed out of place and out of phase, not sure what it was he wanted to tell his first campaign audience in 1980. He had won the nomination of his party without defending or explaining himself, by profiting from foreign events, by making sure the voters knew why to vote against his opponent. By the end of May he had a lot to explain, a lot to account for. A month earlier Carter had authorized a long-rehearsed commando raid into Iran to free the hostages. The raid failed, not because it met enemy forces, but because of mechanical problems in its aircraft. After Carter approved aborting the raid, as the troops sat poised in the desert for their assault on Tehran, a helicopter crashed into a transport plane, causing a huge fire and costing the lives of eight American servicemen. There had been no immediate public reaction against Carter. "Hard luck," was the initial verdict. But below the surface Jimmy Carter was again seen as a president of growing impotence, who had led the world's most technologically advanced nation in a secret military operation that failed, like some ordinary two-car pileup on the freeway. He chose however to counterattack against all those opponents, Kennedy and the Republicans, who had been running around the United States saying things were going badly in the country: Iran, Afghanistan, inflation, rising unemployment. "I'm here to set the record straight," Jimmy Carter said in Columbus. "America has turned the tide." That was news to everyone in the crowd. Although the reception was polite, they drifted away from the only Carter campaign rally of the 1980 primary season quietly and quickly. Some left early and walked quickly six blocks uptown to where Ronald Reagan was speaking in front of the state capitol. Back in Washington, the Carter campaign quickly discarded the "tide has turned" theme and began searching for a new message.

During May, as Ted Kennedy returned to his losing ways, the news stories about him stressed his humor and his patience. He had become the gallant loser. They reported that the once terrible campaigner was now better. But campaigning through Ohio and New Jersey late that month he seemed to me to be still a meager performer. In Youngstown, where steel mills had been closing regularly and unemployment was rising, Kennedy held a rally in a closed amusement park, where several hundred people were seated on chairs in the roller rink, a many-faceted reflecting ball hanging over them as they waved plastic American flags. It was a bizarre setting, devoid of life, but Kennedy tried to make the best of it. "It's appropriate we're here today," he boomed, "because we have a roller-coaster economy. We have been on a merry-go-around on energy. Our foreign policy is a chamber of horrors." But mostly he complained that Carter still refused to debate him. Kennedy had become almost obsessive about Carter's refusal to debate, although no politician in Carter's winning position would have done differently. Kennedy seemed to want to prove, the failure of his campaign aside, that he could at least best Carter head on head. The Kennedy campaign had come down to that. It was no longer Kennedy in search of the nomination. It was Kennedy, defeated, trying to restore his good name. It was no longer a political exercise, it was a personal trial he felt he must endure. He tolerated the grueling schedule. He tolerated the sometimes awful pain from the back injury he had suffered in a plane crash years earlier. He tolerated the press, which mocked him on his plane. And he tolerated the risks of personal injury he always faced as a campaigner.

Two days later Kennedy was on his way to a meeting of the Jewish community at a temple in Livingston, New Jersey. His motorcade was moving swiftly down a main street when suddenly the candidate's limousine swerved away to the left. Machine guns popped through the windows of the Secret Service "battle wagon," a station wagon loaded with agents and weapons that always follows the candidate's car. Other agents stopped and ran toward a house. There they found a local policeman who had been detailed to guard the Kennedy route with a rifle. An agent had seen the rifle and ordered the defensive action, not knowing it was held by one of their protective detail. Kennedy had almost been harmed by the intensity of his own security force.

At the temple Kennedy was met by the overflow crowd, a crowd that wanted to believe in him. There was a John Kennedy memorial pew in the temple. The memories of John and Bob Kennedy lived on in that place. Three rabbis introduced Kennedy, each more elegantly and movingly than the one before. The last was Rabbi Alexander Schindler, a distinguished leader of American Judaism. "As an American and as a Jew, I endorse Senator Kennedy for these reasons," Schindler said slowly, with a touch of the Old World in his voice. "I would welcome the release from the pain and the anguish and the disaster of the present administration. Our economy is in shambles. Israel is in danger because this administration has decided to scapegoat Israel for the world's energy problem. We have decided to pay the extortionists' price. . . . There is the gratitude to him for seventeen years of exemplary service in the U.S. Senate. Today, we look to Kennedy as we once looked to Humphrey. . . . He feels the pain of others. He feels their suffering.

"And I admire the man within him. I respect his essential qualities. . . . He has been buffeted as few others by cruel fate. And yet he never allowed destiny to defeat him." Schindler paused. The elegance and power of his words held the room spellbound. He continued:

"I do not suggest to you that he is an angel. I do not suggest that he is a saint. He is just a man." Schindler paused again. "But what a man."

Kennedy rose to thunderous applause. He was speaking on the day before what would have been John Kennedy's sixty-third birthday. It had been nearly two decades since his death. Ted Kennedy began slowly, carefully, effectively. "We must not be left with the choice between trivialities and banalities," he said. He condemned Carter for his budgetary policies and for his treatment of Israel. And he was interrupted frequently by applause.

But soon the solemn speech he was delivering, written for an earlier occasion by aide Robert Shrum, was abandoned. Kennedy had turned his performance into a ranting, bellowing attack on Jimmy Carter. His voice was too loud, his attack too personal for

141

the people in the audience to accept. His timing and pace were off as his anger rose with his voice. The audience had difficulty knowing when to applaud. They clapped here and there, only to be interrupted by Kennedy's shouts.

In the end, Kennedy had become a sideshow in the politics of 1980. He carried on, not gallantly, but compulsively, trying to rescue his family name from the ignominy of defeat, a defeat that was as much his fault as it was the freak chance of history, of events outside the nation. Kennedy had become a self-parody. He was too powerful on the stump. He was too patient with his detractors. He was too persevering, too willing to go on when it did not matter to the outcome.

Kennedy managed to win those last primaries in California and New Jersey, losing Ohio and some smaller states. He flew home to Washington proclaiming the greatest day of his campaign. In some ways it was. But it was also the worst. He had only been able to win when it didn't matter, when he was no longer taken seriously. The Democratic party had a nominee. It was Jimmy Carter. But Carter had not won the nomination so much as Kennedy had lost it. Carter had been the beneficiary of Kennedy's failings—and in a perverse way, of American failures abroad. Carter had won by campaigning for exactly one day through the nine-month primary season. He was a victor, but he had won his party's nomination by default. Ted Kennedy had assured Jimmy Carter's victory.

9

The Routes
to Failure

It is not quite true that once Ronald Regan got a grip on his campaign in New Hampshire and began to exploit his natural strengths—to display his affability and to demonstrate his vitality —the campaign for the Republican nomination was over. The Republicans who voted in the primaries and the caucuses were not all wild supporters of Ronald Reagan. They had their doubts. But the doubts were about him personally, about his stamina, his ability to handle the pressures of a campaign, his intellect—and about whether he could win in the fall. The party's voters had long since come to agree with his politics; issues were thus never much at stake in the Republican primaries. That race was not a battle for the minds of Republicans; it was a personal contest. And when Reagan cut loose in New Hampshire, the questions being asked about him personally were, in large measure, answered.

American politics is too fluky a process to say with absolute certainty that Reagan's victory in New Hampshire assured his nomination. But after New Hampshire the race had become Reagan's to lose. No other candidate, after New Hampshire, controlled his own destiny. Reagan, on the other hand, was in a position from which to win easily, barring any critical mistakes of word or deed. He left New Hampshire for the South, where his support was solid and had always been so. He could bank also on the later primaries in the West, especially California, and so the numbers of delegates he stood to win made his nomination a virtual certainty.

Immediately after New Hampshire, Reagan lost the Massachusetts primary to George Bush; but on the same day, he won in Vermont. The Massachusetts loss was hardly surprising and not terribly damaging, since it came in one of the most liberal states in the union. Moreover, George Bush won the state only narrowly, beating Reagan easily, but only barely edging past John Anderson. Massachusetts was Anderson's best showing of the Republican primary season and it created a momentary stir that detracted from Bush's victory. Bush had hoped all along to make the race into a two-man contest with Reagan. Thus, when Anderson's close second added his name, albeit briefly, to the "other than Reagan" category, it took a bit of the luster off Bush's victory.

Anderson's flash was doubly frustrating to Bush because shortly after Massachusetts the one other man who could lay legitimate claim as a challenger to Reagan, Howard Baker, dropped his futile campaign. Baker had served, for a time, as a lightning rod for conservative attacks, thus sparing Bush some of the heat he would soon experience. Back in Washington, Baker retired from the race gracefully, perhaps helped by the notion that he would no longer have to operate outside the political comfort of the U.S. Senate. He spoke without bitterness, only with some disappointment at the outcome. He had found the campaigning itself exhilarating in many ways, but he had found the system by which presidential selections are made flawed in several ways. He later admitted to me to having been dismayed at the differences between legislative and presidential politics. He had plunged from the orderliness of his Senate routine into what he called the "messiness of the campaign trail." It is true that campaigns are necessarily messy, but Baker's was more disorderly than most because he did not focus his full attention on it.

"The lack of this tight control over staff arrangements, telephone calls, letters, and that sort of thing comes as a cultural shock in a campaign," Baker said to me after he dropped out. "We sort of turn loose and let those things take care of themselves and they almost never do take care of themselves. And you always have a bunch of indignant people in your wake in a campaign because they never work very well. . . . It does take a lot of getting used to.

"I just found I had a lot to learn. It doesn't make any difference how well you prepare for it or staff for it. You never know how to run for president until you try to run for president. There is no substitute for it. Nobody knows what a different world that is until you jump into it. . . . It takes a lot of preparation in advance. I am talking about internal preparation. And it takes as much, if not more, to decide to get out too. . . . The most difficult part was telling people who wanted me to stay in that I had decided to get out, including my own family, including my staff and principal supporters. But I had sort of made that promise to myself to begin with, that I wasn't going to hang on until it was ludicrous, but I was going to continue to face reality in the campaign. And if it ever reached the place where I was faced with economic ruination or political embarrassment, then I would stop. And I think I stuck as long as possible. I think the New England set of primaries was the only— I had to prosper there or there was no realistic possibility. And the campaign at that point was costing a million dollars a month. And you can't stand it long. It turned out that we were about a million dollars in debt."

He found campaigning was psychologically different from other personal encounters. Meeting the voters, he felt comfortable and free, explaining, perhaps, his affection for the political life. "Images do blur on you," he said. "Faces and names and places, all sorts of things dissolve into a oneness, but there are images that also come through and stay with you. You know, the smells, the sights, the sounds, the attitudes are different from one town to the next town in a state, and their points of view, their concerns, their ambitions are different from state to state.

"I have a pet theory that every audience thinks there are a

certain number of stock questions they have got to ask in order to appear intelligent. But also in every meeting you also get, oh, a third of them that are slightly different—different emphasis, sometimes new questions—and that is where you pick up the play. . . .

"I guess the first thing that happens to you is you realize it is a big country with almost endless variations, but that there is no innate and inherent hostility except in certain spots and on certain issues. It is an attractive country; it is an attractive people who make up the country. And you can be enthralled by it, fall in love with it. And that is really sort of what happens in a presidential campaign."

There were moments, Baker admitted, when he was less than enthralled. "I am going to tell you one quick story to illustrate it," he said, grinning, "and then I am going to shut up before I get in real trouble. I was in Florida, speaking to a group of lawyers. It was a luncheon meeting. We had questions and answers after my remarks and the first question was from somebody who stood up with a smirk and said, 'Senator Baker, do you have any idea how tired we get of these presidential candidates traipsing through Florida?' Before I could stop myself, I heard myself saying, 'Do you have any idea how tired we presidential candidates get of people like you?' Fortunately there was a huge roar of laughter and that saved me."

Nor was he enamored with the design of the nomination process. "We can't continue with a system that runs this long," Baker said, worrying as he said it that his criticism would sound like sour grapes from a loser. "This many states, under such disparate rules. What is it now? Thirty-six primaries. I'm not even sure about the number. And the rules change in the middle of the game. It has gotten to the place where the straw polls are about as important as the primaries. You never know when the process ends. I think the length of the campaign and the repetitiveness of it is the greatest problem. I saw the Canadian government fall and reconstitute itself with a new election and a new Parliament while I was campaigning in New England. One way or another we have to devise a way to shorten it. . . . I think under the present system you have to spend a couple of years at it in order to make a go. With the present system you've got to get out there and you got to cover precincts and county chairmen and party structure and apparatus for so long and in such an invisible way that you emerge a full-grown candidate someday."

And that is precisely what Howard Baker hadn't done. The game was half over before he began to play. He had started in the Senate, stayed in the Senate while the others were building their organizations and laying the groundwork for their candidacies. It was almost as if he didn't want to force himself on the American people, as if he wanted to be picked but not to take it for himself. After but a handful of primaries and caucuses this thoughtful and experienced man was back in the Senate, oddly happy about the experience of having run for the presidency, but not unhappy either that he was back where he felt he belonged.

There are many routes to failure in presidential politics. Howard Baker's was one, but John Connally traveled another. For thirteen months, he had spread himself and eleven million dollars in campaign money across the country, hoping to create some sort of national boom for his candidacy that would translate into primary or caucus wins. Instead he had won exactly one delegate, Ada Mills from Arkansas. After the New England primaries he was down to his last dollars and his last chance. He was taking that chance in South Carolina, the first state on which he really focused his efforts and, ironically, one of Reagan's most invulnerable strongholds. Connally, however, had some assets there himself. The popular governor, James Edwards, supported him. More important, the state's political giant, Senator Strom Thurmond, had enlisted in the Connally cause and was working hard for the Texan.

The Lear jet was long gone, replaced by a twin-engine Fairchild, cast off from the Bush campaign's Iowa phase. The name *Asterisk One,* derived from Bush's early nonstatus in the opinion polls, had only recently been scratched off the fuselage. We in the press, gathered to watch the Connally campaign end, were packed into the plane with the imperious Texan. A card game was under way ten feet from him. Television gear was crammed into every available cranny of the twenty-seat plane. At airports throughout the state, Bush's chartered 737 jet provided unhappy comparisons to the Connally campaign's condition, a comparison that must

147

have galled Connally, who despised Bush from their Texas days.

In the air Connally drew his privacy around him like a cloak. Despite the proximity of the press, a group which, as a whole, he disdained and distrusted, he fell instantly into deep sleeps, more to be alone than to rest. When we did engage him in conversation, he criticized the media for "spending all your time predicting and not enough reporting." The predictions had hurt Connally ever since it was predictable that he wouldn't win the Republican nomination. At his side, all day and all evening long, was Thurmond, age seventy-six, father of three young children and husband to a pretty young wife. He had the energy of a thirty-year-old running for the state legislature. He had been elected in South Carolina as a Democrat, a Dixiecrat, an Independent, and then as a Republican. Thurmond wore a baggy plaid suit. His hair, transplanted into his bald scalp years ago, was tinted a color close to orange. The hairline high back on his forehead was as straight as an Iowa cornrow. His speech was heavily southern, but with a peculiar accent that rendered "work" as "woik" and made him sound like he had lived some years in Brooklyn. The total effect was that of a carnival barker, not a U.S. senator. But Thurmond was a power in his state, and if any politician could have helped Connally—and rarely anymore is political power transferable from one person to another—it would have been Thurmond.

Together they worked the state, by bus, by plane, and by car. At every opportunity Thurmond worked the phone lines, checking with his wife, calling constituents and friends to urge support for Connally and to remind them he himself was in the state and cared about them. Together they worked plant gates, where Connally, complete with his gray fedora—the last American presidential candidate to wear a hat—slapped backs and urged the workers to "drop one in for me on Saturday." It was a measure of Connally's trouble that he was out tracking down workers that way. Unlike the smoothly run plant gate operations of the Democrats, who make their political living from the laboring folks, Connally's effort was disorganized; no funnel of bodies moved the fleeing workers past the former governor. Rather, Connally and Thurmond had to trot after their targets, clutching them by the arm and patting them on the back. It was not a gesture that Connally made easily.

In Charleston, Connally's eight-car motorcade was the last to arrive at a county Republican convention. Bush and Howard Baker (on the verge of withdrawal) had already arrived, complete with their Secret Service details. Connally, despite his own wound in the JFK assassination and the fact that as Nixon's Treasury secretary he was the boss of the Secret Service, had chosen to campaign without their protection. He had argued when he was Treasury secretary that each candidate should have a pair of bodyguards, not the massive details now assigned to candidates. He felt, correctly, that a determined assassin could easily penetrate the most elaborate arrangements as long as the candidate wanted to meet people and shake their hands. He thus rejected the full protection of the Secret Service and characteristically chose to go his way alone.

Without its own Secret Service detail, Connally's motorcade was asked to wait in the street while Bush left the meeting. James Brady, then Connally's press secretary, left his car to inquire about the delay. A Secret Service agent looked at him warily as he approached, and then asked him whether he or any member of the Connally party was carrying firearms. Brady was incredulous. Connally, tired of waiting, left his car, slapped his fedora on his silver head, and stalked toward the Secret Service agent. Before he had covered half the distance to the agent, his motorcade was waved through.

Connally was still a powerful figure, but during that last week in South Carolina, the hard edge was off the Connally presence. His speeches were still superbly constructed, but the stridency was gone. "What kind of leadership do you want in this country?" he asked his audiences. "Who do you want to lead this country? Who do you think *can* lead this country? That's the question," he said. He still thought, as he had all along, that the answer to those questions was John B. Connally. But he also knew that few people shared his conviction.

"This is where the campaign starts," he said over and over in South Carolina. But on primary day only 43,000 people "dropped one in" for John Connally, slightly more than half the number that voted for Reagan. For Connally, South Carolina was the end. His toughness, his slickness, the wheeler-dealer image was not what the country wanted. He was simply not trusted enough to become president. Connally had known that his personality, his brash and abrasive self-assuredness was a problem, but he had tried to use that weakness to his advantage. As his campaign manager, Eddie Mahe, put it: "That perception was so deep, we couldn't change it. We had no choice but to try to use it." His arrogance hurt in other ways as well. He never fully trusted his campaign organization and advisers. His television advertising was created by committee and lacked quality and focus. His scheduling was haphazard because he wouldn't give up personal control over all decisions. And when things got tough he turned away from his staff even more. "We were all newcomers in his life," Eddie Mahe observed. And when it got tense he turned to the people he knew best from Texas." But even the Texans couldn't help Connally. The Sunday after the South Carolina primary, Connally and his Texas friends, his wife, Nellie, and his oldest son, John B. III, flew the Fairchild home to Houston. For five and a half hours they mulled over his chances. After they arrived, Connally stood up in a hotel room, his wife's arm around his waist, his eyes just a bit moist, and announced that he did not "intend ever to be a candidate again." His withdrawal was his most graceful act of the campaign. He and Nellie then drove to the River Oaks Country Club for a late supper. As they entered the dark grill room, the home folks' heads all turned in recognition. Suddenly, as a group, they all stood at their seats and applauded their fellow Texan.

Just as he swept South Carolina, Ronald Reagan swept Georgia, Florida, and Alabama. The future of the Republican party was clearly in Ronald Reagan's hands and that bothered some elements of his party. Most notably it bothered Gerald Rudolph Ford, the former president whom Reagan had nearly beaten in the nomination battle in 1976. Ford resented the fact that he had lost the presidency, even though he had only been appointed to that job by the falling Nixon. And he resented too that Reagan himself had damaged him in the nomination fight and then, in Ford's view, had stood too quietly aside in the fall of 1976 while Carter won the presidency. Retired in California, earning a fortune on the lecture circuit by commanding fees of us much as ten thousand dollars per speech, Ford had waited through the fall and winter, watching the Republican contest unfold. He had sworn to his friends—especially to his wife, recovered from a bout of alcohol and drug abuse brought on by the years of loneliness while Ford politicked—that he would not run in the primaries. But he had said that if the convention turned to him as an alternative, he would, of course, accept. He was trying to run for president by not running.

Any possibility of the convention "turning" to a noncandidate to break a deadlock or to satisfy the notions of the ruling bosses of the party had vanished after convention delegates began to be chosen almost exclusively by democratic process rather than by the bosses themselves. And so Ford's dream of another chance at the presidency was little more than that, unless he was willing to actually compete in the primaries and to gather delegates to his cause. By mid-March some Republicans were urging Ford to put himself into contention. Most prominent of these was Henry Kissinger, who had served as Ford's secretary of state. It was clear to Kissinger and to everyone else that if Ford somehow became president, Kissinger would return to the State Department. That was something Kissinger very much wanted. And in pursuit of that goal Kissinger went public in March, saying he supported Ford for president. In many ways Kissinger's own campaign to return to government, the Ford endorsement being only a part of it, was as interesting as the political fight being waged for the presidency. Kissinger wouldn't limit his personal campaign to trying to get Ford to run for president.

With Kissinger behind him (for whatever little political benefit that was) and with the specter of a Reagan victory growing, Ford began a week-long tease about his own intentions. A collection of his former administration employees established a group to urge him to run. And Ford himself finally journeyed to Washington on the twelfth of March to make his own assessments. What he was hoping for was a groundswell of public declarations of support from the senior figure in his party. But many Republicans who were privately begging Ford to run refused to come out in public and announce support for a Ford candidacy. "They are hedging their bets," Ford observed correctly. And they were wise to do so. Ford had waited so long that only about one third of the convention delegates remained to be selected. Assuming even the most optimistic scenerio—that Bush would drop out and Ford could quickly achieve a kind of parity with Reagan—Ford could hope to go to the convention with only six hundred or so delegates. The best Ford could expect would be to go to Detroit in a position to bargain, not to win. Most realistically, he would go to Detroit a loser, and worse, as a spoiler who had managed to divide the Republican party. And that was the advice Jerry Ford got from the best Republican minds in Washington.

Still, Ford believed Ronald Reagan could not extend his base beyond the conservative activists of the Republican party, and thus had only a slim chance of winning against Carter. Ford went on to New York the next day and met with members of the party's state central committee. There he heard more encouraging noises but no hard promises of support. "We recommend that he get in so we have that option," the state party chairman said. "But we are not guaranteeing him anything."

It was a game of cat and mouse. Republicans expected a Reagan victory in the nomination fight and, at the same time, feared that he could not beat Carter, no matter what a hash of things the President was making. Some wanted Ford, but they were afraid to say so for fear of a Reagan win. Ford wanted them to endorse him before he announced. And they wanted to wait for an announcement before they considered endorsing him. Ford spent his evening in New York addressing a huge dinner at the Waldorf Astoria, where the "chief executive of the year" was honored. There the most wooden speaker in the higher reaches of American public life thoroughly bored his audience. He told the diners, in his inimitable way, that he had struggled to improve the economy when "the economic clouds were not bright and shiny." He reminded them too that while honored for his interregnum presidency, he had never been an inspirational leader.

In 1968 George McGovern had attempted to stop Hubert Humphrey's nomination by the Democratic party by launching an ill-fated little campaign in August after Bob Kennedy's death. In 1972 Humphrey and his former running mate Edmund Muskie repaid the favor by trying to stop McGovern. In 1976 Humphrey nearly tried again, then held back from an attempt to stop Carter at the eleventh hour. The last-ditch movements had become commonplace. But Jerry Ford, whose strength was not in his brilliance nor his rhetoric, but rather in his good sense, avoided that course in 1980. After his speech in New York, he went home to California and soon announced, sensibly, that he was going to remain on the sidelines. But the near-campaign of March 1980 was not Jerry Ford's last appearance in the presidential burletta.

After New Hampshire, George Bush felt the nomination slipping from his grasp. The manic enthusiasm that followed after Iowa gave way to a shrill intensity after New Hampshire. In the southern primaries in South Carolina, Alabama, Georgia and Florida, Bush, for the first time, began to attack Reagan directly. On a radio advertisement run in Florida, an announcer's voice asked, "Can we afford the same mistakes twice?" suggesting that Reagan, like Carter, "has no real understanding of the dangers we face in the decade of the eighties." In front of the conservative Republican audiences in the South, Bush's voice rose in pitch and decibels as he denied any connection with the Trilateral Commission. He virtually screamed his opposition to abortion. His reasonableness and even temper had given way under the taunts of the right wing.

By April Bush had lost to Reagan, not just in the South but also in Illinois, a northern industrial state that should have presented a better chance for Bush. The Bush organization, like their principal, knew their man was doomed, and at one point they even tried to effect a secret alliance with John Anderson in a stop-Reagan effort. Nothing ever came of the deal, since both sides were too worried about being discovered in the collusion for it to have operated effectively. And as Bush got tighter and tighter, Reagan became looser and looser. Reagan, once the defensive and unsure campaigner of the early winter, began to joke easily about the age question, one of the personal characteristics that might once have threatened his candidacy. At a debate in Illinois, for example, Reagan launched an attack on wage and price controls, saying that they had never worked, not even when the death penalty was used as an enforcement device under the Roman emperor Diocletian. "And I'm one of the few persons here old enough to remember that," he added.

Pennsylvania's primary presented itself as a chance for recovery for Bush, although the arithmetic of delegate counting said that even with Pennsylvania in his column there was not much hope of stopping Reagan. In Pittsburgh, one morning, Bush started out to conquer the Keystone State. He was now willing to go after Reagan and bit more pointedly than before, but the shrillness of his speeches projected not the calm assurance of Reagan, but desperation. "We've got too darn much regulation in this country," Bush told a real estate convention that day, his voice too loud and made louder by a public address system that was overenergized and a huge hall that was too empty. "Why can't we get rid of those McGovern-type regulators Jimmy Carter put in there?

"A thirty percent tax cut?" Bush asked, his eyes closed. "God, that's great politics. People stand up and cheer. But I don't believe you can do it." Bush had felt the political sting of Reagan's adoption of the famous Kemp-Roth tax-cut program, which called for a ten percent across-the-board tax reduction each year for three years. It was a peculiar idea, an idea totally out of the tradition of Republican fiscal prudence. Conventional economic thought dictated that in a highly inflationary economy the last thing that makes any sense is to lower taxes and thus set loose additional demand that will only further overheat the economy. After much debate and over the continuing objections of his more traditional economic advisers, Reagan endorsed the tax-cut idea, and although he waffled a bit now and then, he refused to tie such a reduction directly to a reduction in federal spending. That link, some of his advisers argued, was the only way a large tax reduction would not fuel inflation. Reagan liked the idea, however, not because it made much economic sense, but because it fit with his predisposition to reduce the role of the federal government in American life. He seemed untroubled by the economic implications of the idea.

Bush, on the other hand, with a degree in economics from Yale and a host of traditionally conservative economic advisers, couldn't bring himself to embrace the Kemp-Roth notion. His understanding of economic rules was too sophisticated to permit him to make a promise he thought was damaging. He was stuck with a less flashy program to whip inflation and to re-energize the economy. He said, instead, he would reduce taxation on savings and give businesses a tax break. And so Bush, frustrated by defeat, finally summoned the nerve to attack the Reagan program directly. "Economic madness," he called it in Pittsburgh. Standing in front of a huge coal tipple in Clearfield County later the same day, he called the Reagan program "voodoo economics," a phrase coined by press aide Pete Teeley and the best and most politically effective line of the entire Bush campaign.

The differences between Bush and Reagan on this question of taxation were more important than simply a disagreement about economic policy. They signified a fundamental difference in disposition. Bush, hewing closely to conventional conservative advice, could never embrace a notion like Kemp-Roth. Reagan, on the other hand, took to it rather easily. Reagan was inherently the more radical politician. His purpose in running was to advance his almost single-minded idea of a solution to America's problems— to dismantle much of what the federal government had done over the past thirty years. Bush, and indeed most of the other candidates opposing Reagan, including Jimmy Carter, were more careful, more conservative in the traditional sense of preserving what is good and avoiding reckless change. Reagan years before had found his simple answer to all that ailed America and that was to get the federal government "off the backs" of the creative and energetic American people. Bush and the others were too smart and too sophisticated to think that idea would open the way to the millennium.

By the time they got to Pennsylvania, Bush knew that Reagan's radical appeal and his reassuring personality were a tough political combination to beat. Bush, in contrast, had a public demeanor that suggested from time to time that he was not fully sure of himself. Yet Bush's policy positions were much more reassuringly conventional than were Reagan's. Bush, as a last ditch effort, intended to make Reagan's radical program the issue. And so he stepped up his attacks on the economic program.

On the ninth of April Bush and Reagan shared the platform at a huge Republican dinner in Westmoreland County. Bush was already at the head table in front of a room about an acre in area. He shifted nervously from foot to foot as Reagan and Nancy made their way in. She, dressed in purple, looked soft and radiant. But hours earlier she had read the riot act to *Time* magazine correspondent Walter Isaacson for having written a story about Reagan's penchant for unchecked facts ("factoids," the press called them). She was as tough and single-minded a political wife as there was.

Bush started off uneasily. "I didn't pay for this mike," he joked, trying to diffuse the bad feelings left over from New Hampshire, "but I intend to use it." He proceeded with his usual speech urging a return to traditional conservative principles. It was startling to watch Bush on the same podium as Reagan, who followed later with his one-liners and homilies. Bush, the former head of the CIA, an ambassador, the head of his party in its darkest days, seemed so much less *substantial* than Reagan, who, with the exception of eight years as a governor, had never done anything but make movies and give after-dinner speeches. Bush had spent his entire campaign hoping to bring the race down to where it was then, Bush against Reagan. But, head to head, Bush lost by comparison. Not that he was not brighter, more experienced, more measured, more judicious, more responsible, and more sensible. He was all those things. But, at the core, Bush did not seem to be a man to whom a nation of 220 million people could comfortably trust their future.

That night in Westmoreland County Bush skipped every one of his attack lines against Reagan. There was no mention of "voodoo economics" nor of the "economic madness" of Kemp-Roth. Bush was very nearly deferential with Ronald Reagan standing by. And, in fact, something had changed in the Bush campaign. Bush was the sole survivor among the Reagan opposition. Bush strategists like Jim Baker realized that once Reagan had the nomination in his pocket his next big problem would be the selection of a running mate. And Baker realized as well that Bush could offer some substantial political help to Reagan in the fall election. The problem was to keep Bush politically strong, to perhaps win a few more primaries, like Pennsylvania, but at the same time not to offend terminally Reagan and his supporters. And so Bush was willing to attack Reagan's program, but, when they shared the platform in Westmoreland County, Bush rolled over and was polite to the future Republican nominee.

Bush, by spending more money than Reagan, whose lack of campaign control had permitted early profligacy and thus reduced his budget in the later primaries, won Pennsylvania handily. Bush later also won in Michigan, after that state's governor lent him substantial support. But by the end of May Bush's chances of victory were clearly gone, even in his own excited reckoning. On May 27 Bush, after anguishing about the decision for days, dropped out, calling that decision the toughest of his life, and pledged his support to Reagan. He had only now to sit and wait and hope that Reagan would put him on the ticket.

There were those in the Bush organization who had always seen their candidate as perhaps a future vice-president. They had estimated that Bush could not make the big jump to the presidential nomination in his first attempt, despite his previous experience. In 1980 especially, with a strong Ronald Reagan, some of those closest to Bush had calculated all along that their best hope was to run a campaign that forced their man into the second spot.

Campaign manager Jim Baker explained it best: "When we sat down and decided to do this, we were running for both the presidency and the vice-presidency. If we could survive the others and build up enough strength to represent the other (anti-Reagan) wing of the party, then we would have enough cards to force ourselves as number two on the ticket." And in many ways, that is precisely what they did. Bush had been quite slow to sharpen his attack on Reagan, even after winning in Iowa. In part, that was a result of his own sense of decency and deference, but it was also a desire to avoid offending Reagan and his supporters. When the attacks did come in the end, they were designed to improve Bush's standing, to win him enough delegates to have a voice at the convention, and perhaps to provide Reagan with a political reason to choose Bush as his vice-presidential nominee. (Although Baker certainly never planned it this way, he himself moved onto the Reagan team in the fall. After the election, he became White House chief of staff and wound up with much more power than vice-president Bush would acquire on the Reagan team.)

When it was all over, however, Ronald and Nancy Reagan did not much like George Bush. Many in the Reagan camp shared that view. They still believed what they had believed in New Hampshire, that Bush was the product of privilege, status, money, and the East. They were not comfortable with Bush. But Bush's campaign had succeeded in demonstrating some strength in the Northeast and the industrial Middle West, and, whether they liked him or not, the Reagan people knew they could use some help in those areas when they faced Jimmy Carter in the fall. Bush himself, although he quit the campaign hoping for the vice-presidential spot, had come too close and worked too hard not to be disappointed by defeat. He had given the effort two years of his life. He had raised and spent $16.2 million dollars, and had three hundred delegates in his name going to Detroit. Whatever else he had done, he had worked like hell. He had stuck it out. He had endured in a process that rewards stamina, if nothing else.

After his withdrawal from the race, Bush and his wife, Barbara, went off to their summer home in Maine. One would expect that George Bush would seek solace in the sea, but one would think his escape would be aboard a large yawl, its sails filled as it sliced cleanly through the ocean. George Bush, however, did not have the patience for that. Instead, he hopped aboard his 270-horsepower racing boat, and sped out to sea at forty knots. He was not happy unless he was pushing ahead, as fast as he could afford to go. "It makes me feel like I've been challenged," Bush explained to *Time* magazine's Doug Brew, as the defeated challenger waited grumpily to see if he would be picked to run with the man who had, in Bush's phrase, "worn me down."

10

The Third Man

It was an odd place for a Republican presidential candidate to be. But on the strength of his rather un-Republican performance in the Iowa debates, John Anderson was beginning to catch on with, of all people, the liberals. There he was, on Manhattan's East Side, standing in the elegantly furnished offices of Walter Scheuer, one of that city's liberal Democratic money raisers and money givers, preaching to a crowd that only months before was sending money to Ted Kennedy and hoping for a restoration of the liberal political movement they had supported for years, from Stevenson to McCarthy to McGovern. They were the certified limousine liberals, Manhattan's trendiest, Gucci-est, Vineyard-summering set. And their fascination was riveted on a silver-haired man, a Republican all his life, a midwesterner and avowed fiscal conservative. Drinks in hand that late January evening, seated on soft couches and leaning against the posts of the greenhouse hung out high over Madison Avenue, they listened while the attorney general of the state of New York, Louis Lefkowitz, introduced Anderson. "He is a poyson who is highly qualified," Lefkowitz said in his New York accent. "He doesn't change positions fifteen times you don't know where he stands."

Anderson turned it on for the liberals, marveling at the "quantum leap" his candidacy had taken after Iowa, and recounting how he had been confronted by people praising him for "talking to us like adults." And the message he had for the liberals, whose money he wanted in order to run as a Republican, was that America needed to revitalize itself at home before any sort of foreign policy strength could be projected abroad. Jimmy Carter, stunned at the nakedness of the Soviet march into Afghanistan, had just labeled that act "the most serious foreign policy crisis since World War II." It was a standard piece of Carter hyperbole with which he constantly confused himself and the country and which ignored the Korean War, the Soviet invasion of Czechoslovakia and Hungary, the Berlin blockade, the Cuban missile crisis, and a half dozen other incidents in the postwar period. Anderson correctly described what Carter had done. "He has politicized this problem," Anderson said. But Anderson had other signals to send to his new friends. The MX missile, he observed, was "the looniest idea to come down the pike and out of the Pentagon in twenty years." He made sure he told them that he was in favor of the Equal Rights Amendment. And that he was against Carter's attempt to re-institute a preliminary registration for the draft. No Republican presidential candidate had talked that way since, perhaps, Nelson Rockefeller in 1964, although even Rocky wouldn't have gone that far.

"We are welding a new coalition," he told the Brie and Chablis set. "There are new kinds of political issues that transcend traditional party lines." In some ways, Anderson was right. He was indeed an anomaly, a Republican candidate who could raise money on Manhattan's East Side and in the liberal enclaves of California. His willingness to take liberal positions on some issues (he maintained a fairly orthodox conservative view of fiscal matters) attracted the kind of attention that comes naturally in contemporary politics from simply being different.

The search for someone to believe in, as John Sears had put it, made any candidate who was willing to break rules and defy convention a potentially powerful figure. Perhaps the most endur-

ing and damaging legacy of an era of presidential deceit, an era
that began with Johnson's escalation of the war in Vietnam and
ended with Nixon's attenuated coverup of the Watergate crimes,
was to instill a massive and pervasive disbelief in politics and
politicians of any conventional stripe. As a result, the politics of
being impolitic became an important force as the decade of the
1970s ended. If a politician like Anderson had the nerve to walk
beyond the bounds of his party's orthodoxy, beyond the limits of
what seemed, by the polls, the popular position, then, by implication, that politician must be something special, a man willing to
overthrow the reigning self-interest and self-preservation that
dominated Washington.

Anderson, in Iowa, moved himself into that category by bucking the Republican tide on the issue of the grain embargo. Almost
a year earlier, he had advocated a fifty-cents-a-gallon tax on gasoline (coupled with a fifty percent reduction on social security
taxes). And he did it again in New Hampshire by standing up at
a meeting of a gun club, at which all the other Republican candidates genuflected before that group's prevailing paranoia, and
arguing for gun control. He was hooted at and jeered by the gun
owners, but afterward he was featured prominently on network
television for his act of defiance. Indeed, Anderson's almost perverse tendency to fly in the face of political convention made him
the media darling of the 1980 campaign. The press liked him—
he was bright, articulate, skeptical, well-educated, all traits the
press imagines in itself and values in the people it covers—and his
very difference made a good story. In the Republican primaries
Anderson was a man biting a dog.

After his performance in Iowa attracted the attention of both
the electorate and the media, Anderson got more favorable press
coverage than did any other candidate in 1980. But every story
about what an interesting and unusual politician John Anderson
was ended with a disclaimer from the political analysts noting
that, for all his virtues, Anderson could not be nominated inside
the Republican party. Some have interpreted this regular adden-
dum to the flattering news stories as the product of the guilt
reporters felt in writing such uncritical pieces. In fact, the explanation is simpler: Anderson *could not* have been nominated by the
conservative Republican Party. And he knew it better than any-

one, although he seemed to try to avoid acknowledging that fact to himself. No incident better represented that truth than the sight of John Anderson, after Iowa and New Hampshire, raising money from Manhattan liberals, opposing the MX missile, and, as he often did, calling Ronald Reagan a product of "Eighteenth Century-Fox." The party was Reagan's, or was at least Reaganite, and John Anderson had learned that fact, painfully, in his past congressional campaigns. That coastal liberals, nearly all Democrats and thus unable to vote in the primaries in which Anderson was running, would support him was explained by some as new evidence of the liberal penchant for backing losers. "This way, they're sure they can't win," went the line. But the more serious question in the winter of 1980 was just what did John Anderson himself think he was doing?

Anderson grew up in Rockford, Illinois, where, by his own account, the predominant influence in his young life was the Evangelical church. In his 1970 autobiography, *Between Two Worlds,* he described a conversion experience he had at age nine at a summer tent meeting.

> Seated there beside my parents on the rough planking of a makeshift church pew, I was suddenly gripped as never before in my young life by the message of . . . God. . . . I fell on my knees and beseeched God's mercy."

He was educated at the University of Illinois at Champaign-Urbana and received an advanced law degree from Harvard. He returned to Rockford for a time to practice law, and then joined the foreign service for three years. He and his wife, Keke, whom he met while she was taking passport photos for the State Department, returned to Rockford, where he again took up the practice of law. In 1956 he entered politics by running successfully for state's attorney. Four years later he ran for Congress and went to Washington in time to become part of the conservative bloc in the House of Representatives that opposed much of John Kennedy's New Frontier program and later Lyndon Johnson's Great Society. He served ten terms in the House and his record there is of a migration—or perhaps a conversion—from hardline Republican conservatism to a more balanced and moderate voting pattern that, in the end, reflected the mix of doctrines he brought to his presidential candidacy. In 1961, for example, his rating by the liberal Americans for Democratic Action (ADA) was a flat zero while the conservative Americans for Constitutional Action (ACA) gave him a nearly perfect ninety-five rating. By 1978 his ADA rating had risen to fifty-five and his ACA rating had declined to forty-four.

In 1968 Anderson broke out of the Republican pack by casting the critical vote on the House Rules Committee to send an open housing bill to the floor. He then argued passionately for its passage. He said later that his Christian faith had made him realize that he "had to be willing to give up age-old prejudices, even to the point of subordinating something as fundamental as the right of contract to the even more fundamental principle of human rights." From that watershed experience, he went on to criticize the war in Vietnam, denounce the Watergate coverup, support the Panama Canal treaties and the SALT II agreement, and oppose the B-1 bomber and the neutron bomb. At the same time, he achieved a leadership position among House Republicans, a tribute to his intellect and fiscal conservatism. As a member of the House leadership, he endorsed the Kemp-Roth tax-cut plan, the very one Reagan later embraced and which, as a candidate, Anderson disavowed as inflationary and pie-in-the-sky. He explained his shift by saying economic circumstances had changed. Although most evangelical Christians adhere to arch conservative doctrine, Anderson had become, in both senses of the phrase, a born-again moderate.

That conversion did not occur, however, until after he had joined three times, in the 1960s, in sponsoring a so-called Christian Amendment to the Constitution. It read:

Section 1.   This Nation devoutly recognizes the authority and laws of Jesus Christ, Savior and Ruler of nations, through whom are bestowed the blessings of Almighty God.

Section 2.   This amendment shall not be interpreted so as to result in the establishment of any particular ecclesiastical organization or in the abridgement of the rights of religious freedom or freedom of speech and press or of peaceful assemblage.

Section 3. Congress shall have power, in such cases as it may deem proper, to provide a suitable oath or affirmation for citizens whose religious scruples prevent them from giving unqualified allegiance to the Constitution as herein amended.

It was the kind of thing Christian enthusiasts did in those days (and would try to do again if it weren't so patently offensive to other religious groups). John Anderson went along. But he grew out of that phase of his political life, moderating his policies and his politics. He did not, however, moderate the intensity of his moral feelings and the often self-righteous tone of his pronouncements. So it was ironic that Anderson himself was the target of the self-righteous right wing when he sought re-election to the House in 1978. A Fundamentalist minister named Don Lyon, backed by the right-wing direct-mail specialist Richard Viguerie and a group of conservative single-issue groups, challenged Anderson in the Republican primary. Anderson countered by getting big-name national Republicans, like Jerry Ford, Jack Kemp, Henry Kissinger, and most of the congressional leadership, to campaign for him. He kept his seat, but the resentment he felt against the right never abated. He decided then that the 1978 contest had been his last congressional race and began planning for a run on the presidency. Every respectable opinion he could solicit told him, correctly, that he had no chance. But he went ahead, fashioning his sort of antipolitics campaign, running for president with little money, no hope, and, until Iowa, almost no national attention. After he reached a national constituency in Iowa, Anderson got plenty of press attention. But in early February he nonetheless called political reporters, including me, to try to drum up more coverage. I was surprised to hear his voice, but I was more surprised to hear him say that if he could only get more coverage, he had a real chance at the Republican nomination. There was, however, a perfunctory tone to his voice. I doubted he believed his own words. It sounded as if some hot-shot press aide had talked him into the phone calls.

What John Anderson was doing, then, in the Republican primary race was trying to even up the score, to take his own kind of revenge against the right wing, to go out of national politics, if not in a blaze of glory, then at least having had the satisfaction

164

of traveling the nation, like the tent preachers of his youth, damning the right wing and seeking converts to his views. He had no future in his own party, nor in politics, really. He had planned to retire in 1981 anyway. He was a loose cannon in American politics. That role was a familiar one, since he had always been a loner, even in the House of Representatives. He had never made an effort to cultivate other members, to get their support or their votes by friendship or trading votes. His positions were fashioned according to what he thought was intellectually and morally correct, not what was politic. As Gerald Lipson, a one-time member of Anderson's House staff, explained to me, "He's not afraid to go against the tide. In some respects he is more comfortable when he is bucking the trend." He was respected in the House for his brainpower and integrity, but he was never easy to be with in person.

The Anderson boomlet that began in Iowa helped him finish second in Massachusetts and Vermont, but died its natural death in the spring in the Illinois and Wisconsin primaries, where, despite the ability of Democrats to cross over and vote in the Republican columns, Anderson ran poorly against Reagan and Bush. There were simply never enough moderates and liberals in his party to sustain his candidacy. But the stir he had caused among groups outside the Republican party, in the press, among liberals and students, among suburbanites who admired the intellectual quality of his positions, and even among the nearly extinct Republican moderates, presented him with a new possibility, one that some political experts had sensed for months would be available to him. That was a risky and quixotic attempt to run for president as an independent, outside the boundaries of the Republican and Democratic parties. It was not an idea that immediately appealed to Anderson. Above all else, Anderson was a proud, almost arrogant man and he feared making a fool of himself, especially after having run so weakly as a Republican. As much as he resented the right-wing turn his party had taken, Anderson could not forget that he had made it his home for almost three decades in public life. He had wanted to teach his party a lesson, to bring it around to a less conservative slant, to make it reflect his views, but he did not take easily to the idea of abandoning that party altogether.

On the other hand, an independent candidacy was a logical extension of what he had already been doing in the campaign of

1980. If his party would not bend to his ideas, then why not teach it an even more dramatic lesson and move outside the party boundaries altogether? Certainly it was no more improbable for him to seek the presidency via an independent course in the fall than it had been to seek to capture the Republican nomination itself from the left. The main arguments for launching an independent candidacy were made by Tom Matthews, a direct-mail fund raiser whose list of clients included Ted Kennedy, the Sierra Club, and the American Civil Liberties Union. As the spring wore on and Anderson's chances of winning the Republican nomination didn't improve, the success of his direct mail fund-raising drives under Matthews never flagged. Matthews recognized that Anderson had the potential to reach across and beyond the traditional parties. He solicited a promise of help from David Garth, a New York political consultant with an impressive record of winning campaigns and a demeanor that is a mixture of profanity, abrasiveness, paranoia, and coarse good humor. By mid-April, after a week of thought, Anderson was ready to embark on his new course, with Matthews raising money and Garth more or less managing what for him would be his first national campaign.

On April 24, Anderson, his wife, Keke, and three of their four children, appeared before 150 reporters at Washington's National Press Club to declare that the Anderson Unity Campaign was under way. To some there that day the Anderson effort seemed improbable, but nonetheless potentially unsettling to the politics of 1980. To others it was simply preposterous. "John Fucking Anderson, I can't believe it," grumbled Jack Germond of the Washington *Star,* who has seen more than his share of crusading politicians and who can tell a phony in a pin-striped suit just by the sound of his voice.

Both views were, in their own ways, correct. There was plenty of reason to believe that in 1980, with an unpopular president about to be renominated, almost by default, and a very conservative former movie actor about to be nominated by the Republican party, a third choice might prove attractive to the electorate. On the other hand, there was abundant good sense in doubting that John Anderson was the candidate who could crystalize and capitalize on the discontent over having to choose between Reagan and Carter. Anderson's potential was highest as a force for disruption, as a spoiler who could steal away critical electoral votes from one candidate or another, not enough to win the presidency himself perhaps, but enough to deny the victory to one of the other two candidates. It was even conceivable, although never likely, that Anderson could deny either candidate an electoral vote majority, thus forcing the election into the House of Representatives.

With one exception, the history of third-party or major independent candidacies is one of failure. The exception came at the birth of the Republican party in the mid-nineteenth century when, as a third party, it came on to replace the Whigs as the other major political alliance in American politics. But aside from that success (and Anderson himself, talking with me the week before his announcement, said his candidacy just might drive the Republicans into permanent oblivion) independents and third parties never succeeded, but they were sometimes influential. In only six elections since the mid-1800s did third-party figures win any electoral votes at all. Most important, of course, was Theodore Roosevelt's run as a Progressive in 1912, when, under the banner of the Bull Moose, he won eighty-eight electoral votes by carrying six states and nearly thirty percent of the popular vote. He finished second to Woodrow Wilson and ahead of conservative Republican William Howard Taft.

Others followed Roosevelt. LaFolette in 1924. Strom Thurmond as a Dixiecrat in 1948. Henry Wallace as a Progressive the same year. George Wallace in 1968, who set the record for popular votes gathered by an independent with 9.9 million who followed his platform of racism and reaction. Even in the election of 1976, Eugene McCarthy, never quite recovered from his bitter defeat in his party in 1968 following his success in driving Lyndon Johnson into early retirement, ran as a third-party candidate. He won nothing, but a close analysis of the 1976 results showed that McCarthy had won enough votes to take victory away from Jimmy Carter in four states. McCarthy failed to get on the ballot in New York State that year, but had he managed that, he could have cost Carter the election.

It was at the margin that Anderson figured to play a role in the election of 1980. Handled well by an attractive candidate, his hybrid mix of policy positions had the potential to grab the political middle ground, forcing Reagan off to the right, and Carter, if not to the left, then off into obscurity because of his failed presidency. There was the remote possibility that the Anderson candidacy, driven by media hype and playing to the relative unpopularity of Reagan and Carter, could explode into something larger than the role of a spoiler. The coming of the Anderson candidacy thus caused much anxiety in both the Republican and Democratic camps. The Democrats were most anxious, figuring that Anderson could pick up the disenchanted liberals, the Kennedy voters who were already angry at Carter, and thus hurt the President more than Reagan. But in some states, especially those of the East and Midwest, suburban Republicans who were less conservative than Reagan could also be seen defecting to Anderson. As soon as he announced, the big guns at both party headquarters began firing away. "A fool's errand," Democratic National Chariman John White said. "Dangerous and self-serving," said Republican chairman Bill Brock, who feared that Anderson might actually generate some enthusiasm among young voters, who tend to identify themselves as Democrats but who don't turn out to vote in large numbers. With Anderson to attract them, Brock worried, they might come to the polls to vote for him and then vote for Democrats farther down the ticket. Brock had spent years trying to revitalize his party at the local level, pouring money into training candidates and workers, advertising on television and radio to dispel the negative image the Republican party had built over the years. And now it looked like one wild hare candidate could damage that effort.

The party leaders had good reason to be nervous on other grounds as well. By the spring it was clear that the choice between Jimmy Carter and Ronald Reagan was not a happy one for most Americans. A Yankelovich poll for *Time* magazine found fifty-eight percent of the electorate saying they thought that pair of candidates was unsatisfactory. There was substantial feeling, as measured by the polls, that a third choice would be a good idea. A third of the Republicans surveyed by Yankelovich said they wanted to see Anderson run as an independent. Forty percent of Democrats agreed and forty-four percent of the independents favored an Anderson candidacy outside the party structures. That sentiment existed for such a run was, of course, far different from a promise of firm support for Anderson himself. It was a situation not unlike that Ted Kennedy had faced the previous fall, in which the expectation of his candidacy was more alluring than its fact. But in the same polls, Anderson did respectably when pitted against the two major candidates. One such matchup gave Carter thirty-nine percent, Reagan thirty-two percent, and Anderson twenty percent. In addition, Anderson, at that stage, was not considered unthinkable as president. He rated sixty-five percent "acceptable" as the next president, higher than Reagan's sixty-two percent and only a bit lower than Carter's sixty-nine percent.

By any reasonable calculation, however, Anderson was embarking on a perilous and difficult venture. In many ways the political situation that surrounded his entry as an independent was ripe for disruption. Party loyalty, party-line voting, the control by the parties themselves over their voters, all these had declined dramatically in the decade before. Neither Reagan nor Carter had lit any fires of passion and enthusiasm in the electorate. Yet the parties themselves had written the rules under which presidential elections are held. Those rules naturally were stacked heavily against a third-party or independent candidacy. The first obstacle for Anderson was access to the state ballots. Normally, presidential candidates were placed automatically on the ballot after nomination by their party. For Anderson, who had no party, ballot access meant a massive petition drive in state after state, with thousands and tens of thousands of signatures required before state election commissions would certify him for a place on the ballot. Money too was a problem for an independent candidate. Under the federal election rules, the nominees of both major parties automatically receive nearly thirty million dollars with which to run their fall campaigns. Anderson would get nothing from the federal treasury. All of his funds would have to be raised from the public, and it was highly unlikely that he could ever pull together enough money to match the party candidates.

The twin problems of ballot access and money combined to form a third and potentially even more damaging problem for the Anderson candidacy. To get his name on the ballot in enough states to give him a mathematical chance of actually winning the presidency (he eventually was on the ballot in all fifty states) Anderson needed volunteers to carry petitions. And to raise money he needed to tap the kinds of dedicated, politically aware types who respond to direct-mail pleas. In Anderson's case the temptation was to turn to the young and to the liberal. But to the extent Anderson pleased these groups to get their money and their help, he forfeited his claim on the political center. This was the dilemma of the Anderson campaign from its very beginning. He needed to occupy a place in the political spectrum that was seen as neither conservative nor liberal. But to raise the money and get the workers he needed, he had to play more heavily to the liberals. The problem was more intense for Anderson than it might have been for others, because Anderson was already perceived as something of an intellectual and an elitist. And as George Bush had learned in New Hampshire, there was no profit in the politics of 1980 in being labeled a liberal elitist. In practical terms this problem translated into the necessity for Anderson to appeal to the so-called blue-collar vote, labor, working class, and in the wealthier America of 1980, white-collar and middle-class voters as well. As he began his independent quest for the presidency, John Anderson was bucking long odds and a history of failure by previous third-man candidacies. Yet, given the delicate circumstances of 1980 and the nature of the opponents he faced, he also posed a threat to the balance and stability of the American presidential election system. In a sense, Anderson was like both Reagan and Carter in that he was running *against* the political establishment. Carter had run against his own party's establishment in the 1976 primaries and then against the political elite in Washington in the general election of that year. Reagan finally had come to the threshold of nomination by the Republican party by running against the federal government as an institution. And then came Anderson. He was running against the two political parties that had shared control of Washington and the government for more than a century.

At the National Press Club in April, Anderson, of course, denied that he was challenging the parties themselves. "This is a challenge to the nominating process," he declared, "not an assault on the two-party system. . . . I intend to pursue an independent candidacy because our nation faces a crisis and because we need alternatives. A new national unity is required to recognize the profound problems before us and to face up to the serious new approaches required to overcome those problems.

"It is a time for patriotism, not partisanship.

"It is a time for vision, not nostalgia.

"It is a time for honesty and boldness. . . .

"I believe there is a new willingness to accept sacrifice, to accept discipline, to accept, yes, unpleasant truths. . . ."

The "unpleasant truths"—supporting the embargo in Iowa, favoring gun control in New Hampshire—had got Anderson where he was. But as a full-fledged presidential candidate, Anderson began to see his politics differently. He began to seek out constituencies, to try to line up their support, like bricks in a wall, one by one. And one of his first attempts was to seize the Jewish vote. That group is usually so heavily Democratic that the weakest performance by a Democratic presidential candidate in a postwar election had been McGovern's sixty-five percent support by Jewish voters. But the Jewish electorate was bitterly unhappy with Carter, not just because of the bungled UN vote, but also over a series of other policies, including disapproval of Israeli settlements on the West Bank, former UN ambassador Andrew Young's secret meeting with a representative of the Palestine Liberation Organization, and a widespread fear that if re-elected, Carter would put even more pressure on Israel to settle with the Palestinians. Nor was the Jewish voter comfortable with Reagan's conservatism. It looked like a fat target for John Anderson.

In May Anderson appeared before the Conference of Presidents of Major American Jewish Organizations, an assemblage of the leaders of thirty-four separate Jewish organizations, and the true high command of American Judaism. The group was eager to hear John Anderson. "The American Jewish community is getting more conservative on economic issues," the conference president noted as he introduced Anderson, "while we are staying liberal on most social questions. John Anderson has been getting more liberal on social issues while remaining conservative on most economic issues. So from different starting points, it is possible that we have arrived at the same place."

That was indeed possible, and Anderson quickly let the Jewish leaders know that he shared every one of their positions on the handling of Israel and the Middle East. His was the single most pro-Israel speech of the 1980 campaign, a speech so lacking in nuance and appreciation of the complexities of the Arab-Israeli struggle that it was, in effect, an attempt to pander to the Jewish leaders. It was one of Anderson's first major speeches since his declaration of independence, and it was one of the most crass grabs for votes in the campaign of 1980.

He added that day another, more necessary, message. It was an abject apology for his part in the Christian amendments. "Let me say here and now again," Anderson declared, "so each of you can hear me say it: That resolution was ill-advised. It was wrong. Said in still another way, it was a mistake on my part. Religion has no place in a political state. . . . Without minimizing in any way your concern over that resolution, abandoned fifteen years ago, you must understand that all of us—at one time or another—have held beliefs and positions, or have done something, that we later regretted. . . ."

The Jewish leaders loved the speech and loved the apology. At the back of the room David Garth was chatting with reporters after watching his new client's performance. In other campaigns Garth had salvaged nearly unelectable candidates by having them confess their sins to the electorate. He too loved the Anderson performance. "Look," Garth whispered to *New York* magazine's Michael Kramer, "if it weren't for this damn Christ amendment, we'd have to invent something else for Anderson to confess to." But the fact was that Anderson, the candidate who would be different, who would be above politics, was going to grub votes like any other candidate. And worse, the man who was offering himself as a better leader than Carter or Reagan had to start his campaign with an apology.

They were off on their quest together. Anderson, thin, prim, and preachy, his speeches at times a marvel of rhetoric and locution, spontaneous and changing, as his mind produced new ways of saying the standard thing. And Garth, short, stout, the cursing, shouting, hardball political manager, the master of voter psychology. They were an odd couple, thrown together, along with scores of young and inexperienced staffers and volunteers all over the country, by the opportunity and opportunism presented by Anderson's ambition and the disjointed politics of 1980.

He was far from the perfect candidate for such a venture, and Garth was far from the perfect manager. Anderson was too stiff and proper; Garth too wedded to what had worked for him before in conventional liberal campaigns, too used to campaigns with money and tight organization. In two days, late in May, those failings were evident.

Anderson was the main speaker at the sixtieth annual meeting of the United States Jaycees. They were meeting in the cavernous old Cleveland Coliseum, several thousand strong. Delegates had come from all the states, and each was attired in a symbolic getup. New Hampshirites wore buckskin jackets and tricornered hats. Alaskans sported light-blue parkas trimmed in fur. The crowd was a sea of Indian headdresses and baseball caps, suspenders and sneakers. When a delegate won an award, his entire state delegation sprinted to the stage to help him receive it. They were much given to group chants. The entire convention broke into a deafening "United States. Number One! United States. Number One!" Before Anderson arrived, a delegate from Georgia, carrying a Confederate flag, waved a hand-lettered Reagan sign defiantly at the press corps. Anderson, his voice cracked and strained with overuse, worked through his usual speech, thoughtful and unexciting. The Jaycees, typical of the great middle class Anderson needed to reach, sent him away with only tepid applause. After he was gone, the delegates, sensing the need for higher energy in their meeting, chanted together: "Fire up Jaycees, fire up!" John Anderson was not about to sweep the great body of voters in Middle America into his cause.

"I have to be more than a lightning rod for protest," Anderson noted afterward. I want to project a vision of this country and what it can be like." That night Anderson opened his downtown headquarters in Pittsburgh. One hundred people showed up. Anderson spoke for a half hour, pouring out more words. A young man in a T-shirt listened patiently. The T-shirt was lettered with "Yale Sailing, 1979." Anderson was still the candidate of the young and the elite.

The next morning Anderson turned out for what was advertised as a breakfast with Pittsburgh area labor leaders, in another attempt to extend his political reach. Twenty people had been invited and had accepted. Only three people showed up, a minor Teamster official and two employees of a government job placement agency. The TV cameras recorded John B. Anderson, independent candidate for president of the United States, reading a newspaper at the head of a nearly empty table.

For all that, however, a poll by the Harris organization had Reagan leading the pack with thirty-nine percent, Carter second with thirty-three, and Anderson last with a respectable twenty-three percent. Harris then asked an unusual question, one of doubtful scientific validity. He asked respondents to assume that Anderson actually had a real chance to be elected and then asked again their preferences. That result came in with Reagan at thirty-five percent, Carter at thirty-one, and Anderson at twenty-nine. And, with the assumed viability, Harris found Anderson actually leading in eight of the nation's largest states.

SUMMER
1980

11

Coming Together
in Detroit

Only in the most formal sense do the presidential conventions
actually choose their party's nominee for the nation's highest
office. Candidate's names are still placed in nomination. Votes of
the delegates are still dutifully recorded state by state. The winner
is announced and celebrated. But the actual selection of the presidential nominee has been accomplished elsewhere—in the thirty-
six primaries, in state conventions, and in caucuses where delegates bound to support one candidate or another are picked and
sent off to the national convention. By the end of those primaries
in the first week of June, simple addition indicates who the nominee will be.

But in the third week of July 1980, 20,000 people poured into
Detroit, Michigan, anyway, to attend the Republican National
Convention. They did so at no small personal expense and not

177

inconsiderable inconvenience. They came to occupy 13,000 hotel rooms within a forty-mile radius of the new riverfront convention center there, so choking the Motor City's accommodations that thousands spilled over the border to stay in Canada. The horde included 4,000 delegates and alternates to the convention. But that number was swelled by 15,000 news media personnel, including 3,000 people from the three television networks, which would spend $30 million covering and broadcasting the proceedings. The conventioneers and the press would together use 10,000 specially installed telephones linked together and to the outside world by 25,000 miles of phone cable. They would use enough electrical power running through a million feet of wire to serve a city of 25,000 people.

They came as they had always come since the first full-scale political convention in 1831, but they no longer came to serve the same purpose. They did not come to deliberate and fight and argue and then to make their party's choice, but rather to play bit parts in what had become a carefully scripted drama played for the exclusive benefit of television cameras and the passive audience beyond.

After their disastrous Chicago convention of 1968, in which the party leadership nominated Hubert Humphrey despite the primary success of antiwar candidates McCarthy and Kennedy, turning the convention itself into a brawl and the streets of Chicago into a riot scene, Democrats led the way to changing the process by which presidential nominees are chosen. Instead of leaving control with party leaders, they provided that delegates be chosen not in closed meetings of bosses, but rather in public primaries and caucuses. The result was to make the convention itself a mere formality and a nearly total media event. The Republicans meeting in Miami in 1972 took the convention to the last logical step into the television era, by actually writing a minute-by-minute script for their convention, programming everything from speeches to "spontanenous" demonstrations down to the last detail. In Detroit the official convention program even included the scheduled appearances of the party's leaders on morning and evening television news and talk shows.

In Detroit, as before, the television broadcasters were more the center of attention than the politicians who populated the floor of the Joe Louis Arena. High above the convention floor, Walter Cronkite and John Chancellor and David Brinkley and Frank Reynolds looked down from glass-fronted aeries at the mob below. Occasionally one of them strode from their booths onto little porches to survey the crowds, like a Latin American dictator looking onto his people in the plaza. On the floor the Brokaws and Rathers drew their own crowds. Nattily dressed in starched shirts and collar pins, in expensive suits and running shoes to save their feet, they signed autographs between interviews and commentary. Nor was it just the national television people who roamed the aisles. The enormous profitability of local television news shows brought crews and reporters from small stations all over the country. The blown-dry and powdered hometown Cronkites hovered near their state delegations, pushing Live-Action Eyewitness News cameras into the faces of the delegates.

By 1980 television had captured the conventions totally. But the process is a two-way street, for the parties and the conventions have also captured television, holding it hostage in prime-time for four days, using it as the vehicle to reach the American people. With television the convention has in some ways become more important than in the days when it actually picked the nominee. It has become something more than thousands of people perspiring in the same large room. The convention has become the largest single political event in the election year. And the success of that event, its entertainment value, its drama, its grace, and the quality of the performances by all the players, from nominee to delegate, becomes a critical event in the presidential selection process. It is during the convention that the electorate begins to make critical choices about the parties and the candidates. Indeed, the summer conventions are second only to the last ten days of the fall campaign itself in terms of voter interest and attention to the presidential selection question.

For those attending, the conventions are something more too. They serve the same function for political activists from around the country as do conventions of Jaycees, Lions, and Elks. They are part reunion and part reassurance that others care about the same things in the same way. They become rallies of the party faithful, the workers who sign petitions, canvass for votes, give money, and provide what is left of the old-fashioned hard work of politics. And the conventions, if they are properly handled by the party leadership, provide a chance to heal the often deep wounds that have been opened during the interminable preconvention campaign. If an aura of good feeling can be created for winners and losers alike, the convention becomes a talent pool from which the volunteers for the fall campaign can be recruited. At the least, they can salve the feelings of the losers so that they stay with the party ticket in the fall, so that they don't bolt or stay at home, angry and bitter. It was the failure to accomplish this necessary task in Kansas City in 1976 that hurt Jerry Ford's chances for a term as an elected president.

Conventions take on a personality of their own, a character and mood and demeanor that is nearly always the reflection of the state of health and unity of the party. Parties bitterly divided have bitter and divisive conventions, like the Democrats' Chicago fiasco in 1968. In 1972 the Democrats nominated George McGovern, whose principal political flaws included a nearly pathological inability to organize his staff. His nominating convention was similarly disorganized, forcing McGovern to deliver his acceptance speech, the single message heard by the most voters in any presidential campaign, at 3:00 A.M. Eastern Daylight Time. In the same year, the Republican convention that renominated Nixon was run with Prussian precision, not unlike the way his own White House was organized. As the Republicans flooded into Detroit in 1980 they found a convention that was full of hope and optimism, of good feeling and a sense of purpose. It was a perfect reflection of the state of the Republican party at that moment. And that mood was remarkable for its novelty. Not since the Eisenhower years had the party been drawn together as closely as it was in 1980. The tribal warfare between eastern liberals and western and southern conservatives had raged for decades, with one side or another winning in some years and losing in the next quadrennium. But in 1980 the party belonged to Ronald Reagan and to his supporters of so many years. And in the end the convention was fun, an enjoyable week in Detroit. It was an important foreshadowing of things to come.

No convention, not even the Republican love feast in Detroit, is without its conflicts, however. When either Democratic or Republican party is in the ascendancy, it is because it has formed a broad coalition of interests. And in any coalition there are strains. The test is how those differences of opinion and viewpoint are handled and accommodated, whether the differences are respected and vented, or derided and bottled up. In Detroit the party gave something to everybody.

It began the week before the opening of the convention with the drafting of the party platform. The party platform is just words, of course, a place where the ideologues can struggle over this policy or that phrase. It is a sort of sideshow to the convention that attracts people who imagine that what the party collectively writes in its platform has some enduring meaning, when, in fact, it is what the candidate himself says and does that determines the outcome of the presidential election. In recent years the platform has become the focal point for the extremists of both parties, the ultraconservative Republicans and the extreme liberal Democrats. It is during the drafting of the platform that they try to press their notions on the candidate and the party as a whole. Typically, the candidate and his staff permit the firebrands to have some latitude in the platform hearings. But, frequently, they lose control and the platform becomes in part an embarrassment. So it was in Detroit.

The platform writing sessions there were dominated by South Carolina senator Jesse Helms, a man of enormous parliamentary skill and with an almost monomaniacal devotion to the causes of the New Right. Helms represented the oldest Reagan constituency, the far right wing of Republicanism. So he and they took a large share of the platform spotlight. They used it to full advantage, winning support for some planks that were plainly ridiculous, but which gave the ideological segment of the Republican party a sense that they had won important victories. These planks were an accurate reflection of some of the driving issues that had propelled the Reagan candidacy to success. They were also accurate barometers of the kinds of social resentment that had fueled the growth of the New Right and the so-called Moral Majority, a band of self-righteous followers of television preacher Jerry Falwell. But they did not represent anything near the views of the majority of Americans, nor did they represent the kinds of issues Ronald Reagan himself would press during his coming campaign.

The platform ran to seventy-five densely packed pages, most of it affirmations of patriotic, pro-American views and redundant bemoanings of the ills of America. There were the requisite excoriations of the Democrats and of Jimmy Carter. But larded through the document were the signal flags of the fervent minority.

Among the forty thousand words there was, for example, no support for the Equal Rights Amendment (ERA), an abandonment of the party's long-time commitment to that issue. The ERA, although of questionable constitutional necessity, had become a symbolic issue for both liberals and conservatives. The anti-ERA forces have equated the amendment with a pervasive dissolution of American family life and with changing moral standards throughout the country. They regarded ERA as a direct threat, synonymous with the women's liberation movement, which they felt threatened family stability and old-fashioned values. In a flash, ERA was gone from the Republican platform. (Although 4,500 people staged a march protesting the omission on the convention's first day, parading past the convention hall to the sarcastic strains of "I Want a Girl Just Like the Girl who Married Dear Old Dad.")

Abortion was another issue in which the New Right perceived modernity and liberalism as conspiring to destroy old values. They adopted the anti-abortion cause as one of their own, and it became an issue that was violently debated. The question in point was whether or not the U.S. Constitution should be amended so as to negate a 1973 Supreme Court decision saying abortion was not a matter for governmental decisions, but rather one for individuals and their doctors to make. This classically libertarian decision, one in which the government was taken out of people's private lives, appalled the pro-lifers, of course, but outraged as well the New Right crusaders, who, on other issues, sought less government rule and law making.

"There is no doubt," the platform section read, "that the question of abortion . . . is ultimately concerned with equality of rights under the law. While we recognize differing views on this question among Americans in general—and in our own party—we affirm our support of a Constitutional amendment to restore protection of the rights to life for unborn children. We also support the Congressional efforts to restrict the use of taxpayers' dollars for abortion." To the Republican right wing, it was inconceivable that the more conservative position would have been to oppose both abortions and the writing of federal laws on abortions. Nor was it enough to change the Constitution. "We will work for the appointment of judges at all levels," the platform stated later, "who will respect traditional family values and the sanctity of innocent human life." That meant, of course, they only wanted anti-abortion judges sitting on the nation's courts.

There were other hard lines drawn as well: "We believe that the death penalty serves as an effective deterrent to capital crime and should be applied by the federal government and by states which approve it as an appropriate penalty for certain major crimes," the platform stated.

"We believe the right of citizens to keep and bear arms must be preserved. Accordingly, we oppose federal registration of firearms," the Republicans pronounced. On the death penalty, they were in the majority. Polls showed more than seventy percent of Americans, fed up with violent crime, advocated capital punishment. But on gun control, the party was in a distinct and foolish minority, one that prevents licensing of lethal weapons, weapons useful only for assault on other human beings, in a nation that licenses everything from boat trailers to puppy dogs. But gun control was anathema to the virile Republican right and the platform reflected it. (Public opinion continued to favor registering handguns by margins of sixty percent to thirty-seven percent, and that opinion was only strengthened by the shooting of Reagan and press aide Jim Brady at the end of the new President's second month in office.)

These were all the standard issues that had come to dominate right-wing discourse. But the platform included another protest, one that reflected the party's increasingly southern and western locus. "We believe the federal 55 miles per hour speed limit is counterproductive and contributes to higher costs of goods and services to all communities. . . . The most effective, no-cost federal assistance program available would be for each state to set its own speed limit," the Republicans stated. It was an odd little note in the platform, a striking out, in part, against federal interference, a protest, in part, against the lower highway speeds that made the immense distances in the West seem even more awesome. But it also reflected the Republican belief, as articulated by Ronald Reagan, that America was still a nation of abundance, a nation whose resources had simply been mismanaged by the federal government. Reagan had once stated, inaccurately, that Alaska held more oil than Saudi Arabia. (Alaskan reserves are estimated at about 10 billion barrels; Saudi Arabia's at 167.4 billion.) Reagan and his party believed that America's energy problems could be solved if only the government would get out of the way and let the oil companies explore and drill and produce the oil we have. It was at best a naive notion. At worst it showed that Reagan's sunny optimism about the American future was based on a serious and nearly deliberate misunderstanding of the realities of the late twentieth century.

But if the platform was a sop to the conservatives, the Reagan forces made certain that the televised proceedings of the convention itself would be the picture of harmony and good feeling. They wanted no traces of dispute or rancor, and they made sure they got just that, disciplining the convention to avoid public dissent. The first two days of the convention thus more resembled a Hollywood variety show, complete with Pat Boone and Donny and Marie Osmond, than an old-fashioned political convention.

Henry Kissinger, for example, had been given a speaking slot on the convention's schedule. But Howard Phillips, one of the least temperate leaders of the New Right, began a move to block the former secretary of state's speech. Phillips and the conservatives held Kissinger responsible for all sorts of liberal transgressions, not the least of which was the Nixon era policy of détente toward the Soviet Union. But the Reagan high command stopped Phillips in his tracks, permitted Kissinger to speak, and told its faithful delegates to treat Kissinger politely. Kissinger responded to the favor by delivering a heavily partisan attack on the Carter foreign policy record.

Reagan himself brought together a group of ERA backers to assure them that he was for equal rights, if not the Equal Rights Amendment, and the women left smiling and mollified. Reagan also intervened to permit NAACP director Benjamin Hooks to address the convention. Hooks agreed beforehand not to attack the party. Instead, he delivered a reasoned plea to the GOP to work for full-employment and voting rights. The convention was polite, again on instruction from the Reagan command. It was the kind of gesture that the conservatives had been incapable of for years.

The convention managers also squashed disruption from the left. When Senator Charles Percy of Illinois, one of the endangered species of liberal Republicans, tried to organize a dissent over the platform call for anti-abortion judges, the Reagan apparatus beat him badly inside his own delegation. An attempt by the New York delegation to get the convention to honor the late Nelson Rockefeller was also derailed, out of fear that the mere mention of Rocky's name would incite the convention to the kind of booing and hissing that had been rained on Rockefeller at the Goldwater convention in 1964.

Reagan's men were brooking no nonsense. But Tuesday morning Ronald Reagan himself stirred up the greatest foolishness of the entire campaign by playing out the first act in a melodramatic and ill-considered attempt to get Jerry Ford to run as his vice-president. Coming into the convention Reagan's staff had concluded—on the basis of extensive polling by Richard Wirthlin—that only Jerry Ford, of all the prominent Republicans, could actually add strength to the Reagan ticket. But Ford and Reagan had already discussed that question obliquely, at a meeting before the convention, and Reagan had been left with the impression that Ford was not interested in being number two after having been number one. The next logical choice, the Reagan staff concluded, was George Bush, who, while adding no measurable strength in the polls, would be seen as a bridge to the East and to the political center. The problem was that Reagan, and especially Nancy Reagan, did not much like George Bush. They both remembered his campaign attacks on Reagan and wanted to avoid making him the vice-presidential nominee, if possible. Some of the Reagan staff was pushing for Bush before they ever arrived in Detroit. But Reagan stalled.

On Tuesday morning Reagan met in his suite at the Detroit Plaza Hotel with a group of Republican governors, senators, and members of Congress. He mentioned the idea of getting Ford on the ticket and found agreement that Ford would be ideal if he could be talked into it. Reagan was noncommittal but said he was going to meet Ford later that day. It was clear that Reagan was still trying to avoid the Bush choice.

When Reagan and Ford did meet later in Reagan's seventieth-floor suite, Reagan asked Ford to join him, promising Ford not just the vice-president's job, but perhaps a Cabinet post as well. He suggested that Ford might serve as secretary of defense. Ford did not refuse, but simply said he doubted that the unprecedented idea would work.

From there, the fantasy began to build. Reagan was more than eager to get Ford, but Ford was less than eager to join him. He worried about subjecting his wife to another bout of politics. He worried about an alliance with an old enemy and the fact that it would look like an election ploy. And he worried that there was no way a former president could function comfortably as a vice-president. But he didn't say no. Late into Tuesday night and then throughout the day Wednesday, Henry Kissinger and Alan Greenspan and others close to Ford met with Reagan campaign manager William Casey and Wirthlin and Ed Meese, Reagan's closest aide. All parties tried to work out an arrangement in which Ford would be more than a vice-president. They tried to concoct a function for Ford that would be substantive enough to lure Ford onto the ticket. There was talk of a "co-presidency," of Reagan becoming chairman of the board while Ford served as chief executive officer of the U.S. government. Outside that circle, a group of congressional Republicans and National Chairman Brock had been let in on the idea. They were enthusiastic about what they called the "dream ticket" and tried to pressure Ford into accepting it. Only one of the GOP leaders, House Minority Leader John Rhodes, found the whole idea objectionable and said so. He argued against it, but agreed not to talk Ford out of the vice-presidency. Rhodes was right. The chemistry of the two men on the ticket is always important. Reagan and Ford did not mix well under any circumstances. They were deeply suspicious of each other, and with Ford, the idea of making a former president into a vice-presidential candidate was a kind of reverse alchemy. It was like trying to turn gold back into lead.

By Wednesday night, working under their own deadline to make a decision before the end of that convention session, the Reagan staff began to feel squeezed by Ford's refusal to say yes or no. They were watching the evening television news shows, as was Reagan, when none other than Jerry Ford appeared for an interview by Walter Cronkite. Ford had not known that the story of his negotiations had leaked, but when Cronkite suddenly asked about it he responded just as he had to Reagan. He would not foreclose the possibility of running with Reagan, he said, but he would not go to Washington again just to help Reagan be elected. He wanted substantive responsibility. The tone of his words left the impression at the convention that he would take the job, and across the street at the Pontchartrain Hotel, a crestfallen George Bush figured his chance at national office had just passed him by. Barbara Bush peeked in at her disconsolate husband and asked sarcastically, "How did you like *that?*" Bush left his suite for a scheduled speech at the convention bitterly disappointed, but he brought off his performance without revealing his unhappiness.

Back in the Reagan suite Ford's television appearance struck the Californians as an attempt to take the bargaining into the public arena, to generate excitement and pressure on Reagan from the convention. They resented it deeply, but still waited for Ford's decision. They also resented Kissinger's role in the negotiations, partly because it was Kissinger who kept insisting on more power for his old boss and partly because Ford himself had directly suggested to Reagan that in return for Ford's sacrifice in running, he would like Kissinger to be named secretary of state in the Reagan administration. Reagan had refused, pointing out that Kissinger and his policy of détente toward the Soviet Union still angered the conservatives supporting Reagan.

By 10:00 P.M. the convention floor was wild with rumors of the Reagan-Ford deal. Aides of both men fed stories that the deal had been sealed or that it was about to be consummated. Television reported the arrangement as nearly an accomplished fact. Around the country, early closing newspapers bannered the front pages with a Reagan-Ford ticket. The mood of the delegates approached the hysterical, with some wildly happy about what looked to them to be an unbeatable ticket, while others, the conservatives, were angry at what looked like Reagan's first sellout to the moderate wing of the party. They had wanted Helms or Jack Kemp to form a pure right-wing ticket.

But by 10:30 Jerry Ford's natural good sense took over again. He walked to Reagan's suite and told Reagan he could not accept.

Bush, meanwhile, had returned from his convention speech and

187

changed into a red polo shirt and khaki pants, and had begun drinking a Stroh's beer. He slouched in front of the television set as his anger toward friends like Howard Baker and Bill Brock for pushing the Ford candidacy grew. "This is madness. This is madness," Bush repeated as aides and friends reeled off unkind remarks about Reagan. But as the networks were reporting with ever more certainty that it would be a Reagan-Ford ticket, the phone rang in the Bush suite. At 11:37 P.M. Jim Baker picked up the phone and heard Reagan aide Drew Lewis announce that Reagan wanted to talk to Bush. He told Bush he wanted him on the ticket and Bush, of course, thanked him. The residual distrust still hung in the air, however, and Reagan asked Bush whether he could support the platform "across the board." Bush said he could, with the exception of the abortion amendment, adding that to change his position now would only look phony. Reagan dropped the subject. Bush hung up, pleased at having made it onto the ticket, but with the sour taste of having been the second choice. As he cradled the phone, he shook his head in disbelief at the turn of events.

Reagan, realizing that the convention was nearly out of control with the Reagan-Ford hysteria, broke the precedent that usually reserved the nominee's first convention appearance for the night of his acceptance speech. He hurried to the arena. There, shortly after midnight, he announced that he had selected Bush as his running mate. It was as if the Jerry Ford episode had been no more than a dream.

And it was, indeed, a bad dream. The entire process had proved an embarrassment to both men. Reagan hadn't been able to persuade Ford to join him, and Ford had ended up looking like a power-grabber. It was the kind of idiocy that even the most well-scripted convention can produce. It was the kind of political deal that, had it been made, would likely have damaged Reagan's bid for the presidency seriously, perhaps fatally. In the heat of the moment, in the desire to confect a ticket that seemed unbeatable, Reagan and his aides demonstrated extraordinary shallowness in their political judgment. The overwhelming truth of the matter was that Ford and Reagan stood for widely different ideas about American policy; Ford, the moderate wing willing to accommodate Democratic programs, and Reagan, the resentful right that wanted to undo much of the New Deal. They represented the historic division of the party, and it was inevitable, had they run together, that Ford's presence would have been disruptive and divisive. Ford's experience in the White House would have served as a reminder of Reagan's inexperience. His moderation would have highlighted Reagan's conservatism. Together they would have seemed like two old men trying to win what neither could win on his own. It was a disastrous idea, a silly scheme. It was fortunate for both men that it failed of its own preposterousness.

For George Bush the outcome was as much as he could ever have hoped for. For Reagan, Bush's presence was a positive, if reluctantly taken, step toward moving beyond his very conservative constituency. Reagan's willingness to have him on the ticket, as contrasted with, say, a Jack Kemp or another Republican as conservative as Reagan, signaled the kind of pragmatic and flexible attitude that was reassuring to a nation considering electing a right-wing crusader as its next president.

The selection of Bush was symbolic of the fact that, marching under the banner of an aging movie actor, the Republican party had managed, in Detroit, to reconstitute itself as a major political force in America. They had forged a once unlikely alliance between the eastern and northern Republicans of the traditional Establishment and the often outrageous, populist New Right of the West and South. And by doing so in front of an audience of millions of television viewers, the party put itself in the position to capture the presidency, given good luck and a good performance by its nominee and an assist from the Democrats.

The forces that produced this coalition were varied and remarkable in their coincidence. The appeal of Reagan, the man, blunted anxiety about his often rabid conservatism. The changing national political mood, fostered by events in Iran and Afghanistan, by economic decline and the necessity to abandon the liberal politics of generosity, abetted the migration of the moderate wing of the party toward the more conservative views of their outland brethren. And the chance of actually winning, not just the presidency but other elected offices as well, had muted the old factionalism and internecine struggle that had often made the party its own greatest enemy. History and quirk and luck and good sense had created a party that left Detroit with the potential of constructing a ruling coalition as powerful and pervasive as the New Deal and its offspring, the Fair Deal, the New Frontier, and the Great Society had once been.

In many ways that coalition of the center-right was as improbable as was the old Democratic coalition. A tour of the floor in Joe Louis Arena made that point. The cowboy-hatted, polyester-suited delegates from California, Texas, and Georgia, all sporting "Stop ERA" buttons, and the Alaska delegation, controlled by Moral Majoritarians wearing "Jesus First" buttons, mixed with the rep-tied, Brooks Brothers-suited delegates from Massachusetts, Pennsylvania, and Connecticut. But the contrast in style was no more severe than had been the mixing of the southern, racist, rural delegates in earlier Democratic conventions with the urban, ethnic liberals of the industrial north.

The glue that bound that new Republican coalition together was, of course, the quest for power. But it was also, like the New Deal lash-up, a matter of economics. Westerners and the southerners had long been anti–federal government, as much out of a kind of frontier libertarianism as out of economic self-interest. Easterners had always favored a larger role for free enterprise and tax relief to encourage entrepreneurship, and had disdained unions. There was still strain, to be sure, between the anti-establishmentarians and the old Establishment, but they shared the notion that the federal government needed to step back, make way for business, cut taxes, reduce regulation, balance the budget, and let the business of America once again be business.

Under different historical circumstances the glue might not have held these disparate forces together. Had the country been growing and prosperous, secure in the world with American hegemony still largely intact, then the Republicans would have been reduced to debating their differences instead of papering them over. Had the sitting president been popular and confident, in control and in command, then the Republicans would not have had the immediate prospect of victory to soften their own ideological excesses. Had America not been humiliated by the Iranians and ignored by the Soviets as they marched into Afghanistan, had Carter not authorized a raid to free the hostages that ended in impotent tragedy, then the rabid anticommunism and Americafirstism of the more conservative Republicans would have seemed inappropriate.

Inside the Republican party itself, the balance of power had shifted in a way that made the alliances between populist and old Establishment easier. What had happened was simply that the conservatives had taken control. They understood that they had the power in the party to do what they wanted and thus their usual paranoia was somewhat reduced. The old Establishment had no hope of controlling their party and were thus too weak to fight the Reaganites. They had little choice but to go along or leave the party. Most chose to go along, ignoring as best they could the fervid anti-abortionists, the anti-gun-controllers. They chose to support Reagan for president, knowing that at home in Pennsylvania or New York they could run their own political campaigns in their own ways, soft-pedaling the social issues and emphasizing the economic questions that had suddenly started to play their way.

Most important, however, in the rebirth of the Republican party was not so much what they did in Detroit but what had been happening in the country as a whole. Across the nation attitudes about the party itself had begun to shift, due to the failure of Democratic governance. The Republicans, out of power for decades in the Congress, and out of the White House for four years, were benefiting from the fact that they could not legitimately be blamed for rising unemployment, high inflation, and the decline of American power. Quite logically, public perceptions about the two parties had begun to be more negative about the Democrats and more positive about the Republicans. A few years before, polling results showed that simply having the word *Republican* attached to any candidate's name gave that candidate a nine-point disadvantage against any Democrat. By 1980 that handicap had vanished. A national poll by Market Opinion Research for the Republican National Committee showed the Democratic party at its lowest point in public esteem since the early 1950s when it lost control of the Congress for a short time. On a series of issues of wide national concern, the Republicans were consistently rated as more competent than the Democrats. In their ability to control government spending, control inflation, hold

191

down taxes, and maintain military security, the Republicans were favored by margins of about two to one over the Democrats. Only on the question of "maintaining world peace" did the Republicans not have an advantage, and on that question there seemed a good deal of skepticism that either party knew what it was doing in foreign affairs.

The new strength and unity of the Republican party was to be an important asset in the coming general election campaign. But it would be only one factor in the final outcome. More important than anything else would be the quality of the presidential candidate himself. In the politics of celebrity the star determines the quality of the show. And in the nuclear age the collective judgment made about the character and personality of the would-be president would determine the election result. It would be, then, Reagan's own ability to convince the public, not just that Carter had failed (the public already understood that), but that he, Reagan, could do better. That would be no easy job. Reagan's sincerity and good humor could not mask his inexperience. His ability to use television well could not mask his penchant for the verbal mistake. His smile and his rosy cheeks could not disguise the fact that the level of intellectual sophistication he brought to his politics was unimpressive. It was up to him to make himself appear presidential.

On the last night of the convention in Detroit, Reagan proved in at least one speech in one place at the beginning of the final run toward the presidency, that he could do just that. Delivering the speech with the aid of a teleprompter, Reagan was as smooth and solid as a beach stone. He was critical of Carter and the Democrats without being bitter or unfair. His chief speech writer, Peter Hannafard, had reworked the familiar after-dinner lines into new prose that was softer and more appealing, and Reagan took care to be reassuring about his plans and his party. He promised, at the beginning of his speech, to ask the governors of the states to work at eliminating any discrimination against women and to monitor federal laws, adding more if necessary, to achieve the same goal. He was thus able to divert attention from the party's refusal to endorse ERA.

"More than anything else," Reagan told the hushed convention, "I want my candidacy to unify our country, to renew the American spirit and sense of purpose. I want to carry our message to every American, regardless of party affiliation, who is a member of this community of shared values. . . .

"Together, let us make this a new beginning. Let us make a commitment to care for the needy, to teach our children the values and virtues handed down to us by our families, to have the courage to defend those values and the willingness to sacrifice for them. . . .

"As your nominee, I pledge to restore to the federal government the capacity to do the people's work without dominating their lives. I pledge to you a government that not only works well, but wisely, its ability to act tempered by prudence, and its willingness to do good balanced by the knowledge that government is never more dangerous than when our desire to have it help blinds us to its great power to harm us. . . .

"We must have the clarity of vision to see the difference between what is essential and what is merely desirable, and then the courage to use this insight to bring our government back under control and make it acceptable to the people. . . .

"Thanks to the economic politics of the Democratic party, millions of Americans find themselves out of work. Millions more have never even had a fair chance to learn new skills, hold a decent job, seize the opportunity to climb the ladder and secure for themselves and their families a share in the prosperity of this nation. . . .

"It is time to put Americans back to work, to make our cities and our towns resound with the confident voices of men and women of all races, nationalities, and faith bringing home to their families a decent paycheck they can cash for honest money. . . .

"For those who have abandoned hope, we'll restore hope and we'll welcome them into a great national crusade to make America great again! . . .

"Of all the objectives we seek, first and foremost is the establishment of lasting world peace. We must always stand ready to negotiate in good faith, ready to pursue any reasonable avenue that holds forth the promise of lessening tensions and furthering the prospects for peace. But let our friends and those who may wish us ill take note: The United States had an obligation to its

193

citizens and to the people of the world never to let those who would destroy freedom dictate the future course of human life on this planet. . . ."

The speech was a brilliant performance by a skilled performer. He had blended the conservative populism that had brought him to the nomination with the economic concerns that had held the Democrats together for years. He promised prosperity, not for the big business friends of the old Republican Establishment, but rather for the people who worked at those jobs. The speech represented an historic shift in Republican thinking. It was an expression of a new Republican populism whose rhetorical focus at least was directed at the middle class, not the traditional Republican bastions of big business and those of great wealth. Reagan would campaign against the entrenched interests the way Teddy Roosevelt had campaigned in the early years of the century, only in 1980 the entrenched interests were seen not as the robber barons of corporate America, but rather as the bureaucrats, the congressmen, and the millions who benefited from federal largesse at the expense of the average tax payer. That message was not new, of course, but Reagan had cleansed it of the tinges of racism it carried in the past. He had clothed it in a call for unity and a desire to help everyone. The speech was Reagan and his conservatism grown up, aged past the stage of petulance and resentment and exclusionary politics.

The overriding impression left by the speech was, however, of Reagan's comfortableness, not just with his words and his performance, but with himself. At the end of the speech, Reagan inserted a few paragraphs that he had planned to use only if he still had the full attention of the convention. It was common for him to construct important parts of his own speeches and he often produced more moving and succinct sections than did his speech writers. To some, the added remarks were banal and cloying, a too-theatrical trick to be played on national television. But Reagan, knowing the risk, was secure enough to use the lines anyway.

"I've thought of something that is not part of my speech and I'm worried over whether I should do it," he began.

"Can we doubt that only a Divine Providence placed this land, this island of freedom, here as a refuge for all those people in the world who yearn to breathe freely: Jews and Christians enduring persecution behind the Iron Curtain, the boat people of Southeast Asia, of Cuba and Haiti, the victims of drought in Africa, the freedom fighters in Afghanistan and our own countrymen held in savage captivity?

"I'll confess that I've been a little afraid to suggest what I'm going to suggest—I'm more afraid not to—that we begin our crusade joined together in a moment of silent prayer."

The hall fell silent. Reagan and the delegates to the Republican National Convention of 1980 bowed their heads.

"God bless America," Reagan said.

12

Jimmy and Ted

Between the end of the primaries and the Democratic party's convention in mid-August there was an uneasy ten-week wait. Carter was to be renominated, without a doubt, and that was the problem. The decision had been made, but, Democrats wondered, was it the right one? Could Carter beat Ronald Reagan? Like a live mullet on the end of a tarpon fisherman's line, Democrats were nervous and began skittering wildly back and forth, worried that they were about to be devoured. First-term Democratic congressmen from once-Republican districts, like Maryland's Michael Barnes, liberals who felt no kinship to Carter, like Connecticut's Representative Toby Moffett and New York's Governor Hugh Carey, and old-line moneymen like "Sonny" Dougle of Philadelphia feared that Carter would damage the whole ticket and began urging that the party look for a new nominee.

Their anxiety was only heightened by the antics of Ted Kennedy. He had done well on the final primary round, but his cause was lost and had been lost for months. Kennedy, however, against the advice of his brother-in law Steve Smith and political aides like Paul Kirk, refused to concede his defeat. There had been a long-simmering dispute between the older, veteran Kennedy staff and the younger staff, who had spent the most time on the plane with Kennedy. Young aides Richard Burke, Bob Shrum, and Carey Parker wanted Kennedy to fight on. As if he still couldn't digest after all the months of his political frustration the fact that he had lost, Kennedy vowed to go to the New York convention as an active candidate. There was, of course, no practical point to this endeavor since he did not have the delegate strength to win the nomination and indeed the rules of the convention made it certain that he could not get that strength by converting Carter delegates to his cause. Thus, as part of his plan to contest the nomination up until a vote was taken at the convention, Kennedy demanded a change in the rules, a change, in effect, after the game had been played. Kennedy argued that the Democratic convention be made "open" so that delegates, no matter for whom they were elected to vote, could vote for the presidential nominee of their own, personal choice.

There was no small irony in this position, since it was the liberals and many of Kennedy's own operatives who, after the Chicago debacle of 1968, had changed the party rules to make popular primary voting binding on the votes of the delegates. But in 1980, with their candidate on the losing side, the word "open" meant something different to the liberals than it had before.

At the heart of the controversy was Rule 11-H of the party's delegate selection procedures and its companion, Rule F-3 (c) of the convention rules. They both bound delegates to vote for the candidate they represented on the first ballot at the convention unless released from that vote by a written statement from the candidate himself. Moreover, the convention rules provided that a delegate not faithful to his candidate could be replaced on the convention floor by an alternate chosen by the candidate. These rules, the Kennedy forces argued, had turned the delegates into automatons who simply voted by rote, not by what their consciences told them or by what their judgment dictated. They were, of course, no more automatons under the new system than under the old; the difference was from whom they took their orders. In the old arrangement, the state and local party bosses picked the delegates and then told them how to vote; in the new, the primary and caucus voters held the power.

That it was hypocritical for Kennedy to argue for a rules change did not, however, obviate the fact that there was a certain wisdom in not completely settling the nomination question in the primaries. The new rules eliminated the ability of the party and its convention to arrive at an institutional judgment about their nominee's qualifications and electability and, if necessary, to react to circumstances that might change between the time of primary voting and the actual nomination. Seven months had passed since Carter had swept Iowa. Nearly half a year had gone by since his victory in New Hampshire. Much had occurred in the interim. The hostages were still in Iran and the government there had evolved toward an ever more irrational blend of Islamic radicalism, xenophobia, and brutality. The American economy had begun a plunge into recession that, week after week, tossed laboring people—mostly Democrats—onto the unemployment roles. Inflation had continued to plague the nation. And, as a consequence, Jimmy Carter had taken another of his periodic slides downward in public esteem. And as a final reminder of Carter's problems in office, his brother Billy had got caught up in a minor scandal over his taking of $220,000 (he called it a loan) from the government of Libya in return for representing them in the United States. Billy had for months refused to register, as required, as an agent of a foreign government. Then one day he slipped quietly into the Justice Department and filed the proper papers. Billy, whose resentment of his older brother's ambition and self-righteousness had led him to a public life of beer swilling, wise-cracking irreverence and rudeness, had haunted Jimmy for years, a kind of living reminder of just what the President had struggled so hard to escape. Billy played a parody of the smalltown southern redneck, a pose he was at considerable strain to maintain because of his own sensitivity, intelligence, and bookishness. Reporters who met him out of the public limelight found him bright and polite and an acute judge of his brother's weaknesses. He was terribly concerned about the effects Jimmy's fame had on his own family in Plains and eventually moved away from the town to seclusion. But his exploitation of his brother's fame had been pointedly shameless and tasteless. He gave his name to a cheap beer, he appeared at shopping center openings and carnivals for a large fee, and when the Libyans visited Atlanta, he made an anti-Semitic remark to the effect that Arabs deserved some voice in America since Jews controlled so much of American life. His brother then publicly rebuked him.

His involvement with the Libyans, however, raised some questions about the conduct of Carter's official family and reminded voters of the President's persistent defense of Bert Lance, the fast-buck Georgia banker whom Carter had made head of the Office of Management and Budget. Lance was finally forced to resign when it was clear he would be charged with violations of banking laws. (He was later acquitted.) There were suspicions that the Justice Department had warned Billy of his coming legal problems so that he could register in time to avoid prosecution. There had been meetings with the White House counsel and with the President's assistant for national security. And Carter himself had used Billy to try to get his Libyan patron, the dictator Muammar el-Qaddafi, to intercede with the Iranians on behalf of the hostages. This all came to light after the Republican convention and added to Carter's tumbling public opinion standing. A few weeks before the Democratic convention Carter's job rating had tumbled to twenty-one percent, an historic low for a sitting president, lower even than Richard Nixon's rating during the worst days of the Watergate scandal.

The combination of events, stirred by Kennedy's refusal to bow out, caused a near panic among some Democrats. Most of these politicians had stayed well clear of the Democratic primary fight since its beginning the previous fall. Now, however, at the eleventh hour, they too wanted an "open" convention with the aim of unloading Jimmy Carter. Movements quickly sprang up to nominate Ed Muskie or Henry Jackson, both failed presidential contenders from earlier contests. There were fevered speculations about the President stepping aside to let Walter Mondale run in his place. It was all merely an elaborate fantasy. Only an impeachable offense could have come close to panicking the convention itself, which, after all, consisted of people who had volunteered to run as Carter delegates, who were bound to Carter, who actually liked Carter and felt he could win. Carter himself helped squash the panic when, a week before the convention was to open, he held a press conference in which he defended himself against any impropriety in the Brother Billy affair. It was one of Carter's most impressive performances and, in retrospect, that was not surprising. Carter had sought and won the presidency on the strength of his moral virtue, his contrast with the unconstitutional sleaziness of the Nixon regime. What made him so convincing in 1976 was what made him impressive as he defended himself on his dealing with the Billy problem. Jimmy Carter, as unsure as he was about tax policy or foreign policy or this policy or that, believed in his own rectitude. And when he spoke about that rectitude, he was an impressive man, a man of beliefs and firmly held values. He was presidential, at least at that moment.

The open convention movement was also damaged, ironically, by Ted Kennedy himself. In addition to wanting to change the rules for his own benefit, Kennedy's refusal to take himself out of contention for the nomination meant that any move to dislodge Carter delegates was frozen by their opposition to Kennedy. Some of the young congressmen worried about the Carter slide asked the Kennedy people to pull Kennedy out of the race. "He's killing us," said one. More than that, Kennedy was helping discredit the whole anti-Carter movement by insisting, obsessively, that the only way he would withdraw before the convention was if Carter agreed to debate him. Over the long months of the campaign Kennedy had increasingly focused on the debate issue. Feeling that all his own campaign failings could be overcome if only he could meet and beat Carter in debate, Kennedy was livid over the President's refusal to accept the challenge. He was even angrier because Carter had said before the Iran crisis (when he trailed Kennedy in the polls) that he would meet Kennedy man to man. The debate question crystalized for Kennedy the frustration of campaigning against a president who refused not only to debate, but who would not even campaign. It also symbolized Kennedy's inability ever to get Democratic voters' attention turned on Carter's total record.

Immediately after the June 3 primaries Carter and Kennedy met alone in the White House. Again Kennedy made his demand for a debate. Carter, after trying to be conciliatory, refused, as well he should have. That a winner in the primary process should subject himself to political risk inside his own party before his general election campaign in the fall was political lunacy. Even some of Kennedy's closest advisers were embarrassed by their man's insistent demand. "It made sense before the end of the primaries, but now it doesn't," one of the family's most devoted retainers said that summer.

It was odd about Ted Kennedy. He had won some grudging credit for having stayed the course in the nomination struggle, against the advice of some of his aides who had been counseling quitting ever since Iowa. But when the time came and there was no more left to do, Kennedy bulled ahead, again raising doubts about his maturity and good sense. He was not without both those qualities, although during the campaign he seemed to conspire with himself to hide them.

Shortly before the Democratic convention began, I joined my colleagues at *Time* for a luncheon with Kennedy in New York. In that session he was better than I had ever seen him. In interviews and on the campaign trail, the Kennedy I saw was someone other than the one who was having lunch with us at *Time*. He was more relaxed and less defensive than before, fully at ease and quick with the sort of self-deprecating humor that had taken the aggressive edge off both his brothers. He argued for the open convention as well as it could be argued, leaving the impression that he understood the unfairness of what he was asking and the impossibility of achieving it. "I'm interested now not just in a candidacy, but also in a cause," he said. It seemed to me that he was more comfortable with a liberal crusade than a Kennedy-for-president campaign.

Kennedy explained his devotion to wage and price controls as a cure for inflation. While the case wasn't compelling, it was well argued, sensibly presented, in sharp contrast to his blathering months before on the same question in New Hampshire. And even as he argued for liberal concerns, he showed an awareness of the changing times, a sensitivity that had vanished in public after his Georgetown speech. He spoke clearly and concisely about the need for more industrial investment and for business tax cuts and remarked how even labor, in his experience always antagonistic to business, had come around to the idea that American business needed help.

He was still battling Carter at that time, but he recognized that he would lose. He conceded, finally, that from his point of view Carter's re-election was preferable to a Reagan presidency, but he also noted that any help he could give Carter in the fall would be limited, since his own attacks on the President would be remembered too well. At the same time, he repeated an observation he made before, and which went to the heart of his disdain for Carter. It was Kennedy's theory that Carter's handwringing and wailing about complex and unsolvable problems had legitimized Reagan's attacks on the role of the federal government. Kennedy detested the President's inability to seem in control, to present a positive, clear direction for his administration. This, Kennedy said, made people ready to believe Reagan's theme that the government was part of the problem, not part of the solution. He was right.

Kennedy was still quite heavy, but he took a good dose of bread and butter that day, ordered a beer with his steak, and spoke frequently with his mouth full, as if he were sitting around the dinner table with close friends. Only his speech writer, Bob Shrum, was with him, and Shrum didn't say a word, except to quietly bum a cigarette. Kennedy considered the questions and answered them thoughtfully. He presented a sharp contrast with Reagan, who had lunched with the same group a few weeks before and who had brought along five advisers, several of whom interrupted to answer questions for Reagan. Reagan himself had used each question only as an introduction to repeat his best one-liners from the campaign. Where Kennedy was thoughtful, Reagan performed his usual routine.

The character of the Democratic convention was nearly the direct opposite of the Republican session a month earlier. The divisions between Carter and Kennedy and the President's own weak standing in the polls created a sense of futility and fatigue. It was a convention of a party exhausted by its labor of governing and frustrated by its failures, lately, to govern well. The Democrats, their New Deal agenda long since enacted into law, had no more burning causes to hold them together. The convention had no real agenda, no major reforms to give it the energy of new ideas and new purpose. As Senator Daniel Patrick Moynihan of New York put it, "Somewhere in the 1960s we ceased to be a party of ideas, but we then went on to become a party rather opposed to ideas, which is a different matter. This had to do with embracing, simultaneously or in sequence, so many incompatible positions that it became necessary *not* to think too much."

The problem, however, was even worse than intellectual bankruptcy and deliberate avoidance of contradiction. The Republican party in 1980 was able to embrace many contradictions, the most important of which was its libertarian desire for less government coupled uneasily with its desire to write new laws controlling the life of the nation. They could overlook this contradiction, however, because the Republicans wanted more than anything else to seize control and to change the pattern of policy. The Democrats wanted little more than to cling to power. They had become the party of government, the party of the status quo. Unfortunately for them, the status quo was not a happy one, and so they were in a defensive position, reduced to arguing that they who had caused the trouble should be left alone to fix it. Some Democrats understood that a time in which national wealth was not expanding as explosively as it had in the 1960s, was not a time for a whole new list of federal spending ideas. They understood that they could not convince the heavily taxed and inflation-plagued middle class to endorse more plans for income redistribution when, it seemed, the size of the pie was shrinking for everyone. But they had no clear idea of how to increase national prosperity once again.

The Democratic party was left to rely on the clientele it had created with federal dollars. Throughout its years of reform the party had striven to make sure that the delegates to its convention were "representative" of the public at large. And in New York the party was proud that 15 percent of the 3,381 delegates were black and that 49 percent were women (the rules of the convention required that balance of sex) and that 30 percent of the delegates were under thirty years of age. But the convention was wildly unrepresentative in other, crucial ways. A tenth of the delegates were members of the two great teachers unions, the National Education Association and the American Federation of Teachers. They had been primed by their unions to go to caucuses, to run as delegates (mostly for Carter, whom the NEA had endorsed in 1976 and who had delivered on a promise to create a new federal bureaucracy for them, the Department of Education). Even more

telling, however, was a fact discovered by *Time* magazine colum-
nist Hugh Sidey. At the request of Sidey's researcher, Cassie
Furgurson, CBS News ran through its computerized information
on the delegates and found that 40.3 percent were public offi-
ceholders or government employees of one sort or another. Only
sixty-nine members of Congress and governors were among them,
largely because they wanted to avoid declared primary preferences, leaving government employees at all levels to make up
almost half the convention. The Democrats and their convention
had become a party interested in holding on to its own perquisites,
as much as it was interested in helping the poor and the forgotten.

There were other contrasts with the Republican convention. In
Detroit, most delegates arrived happy and eager for celebration.
In August, however, the Kennedy delegates arrived in New York
bitter and anticipating defeat. The Carter delegates arrived nervous about their man's future. Even the two cities that hosted the
conventions reflected those differences. Detroit had been bright
and dressed up, eager to prove that it was recovering and rebuilding from blight and economic depression. New York, as always,
was blasé, indifferent to the struggles in Madison Square Garden
and preoccupied with its own life, as if what the Democrats did
could make no difference whatsoever.

Predictably, Carter held tight to his delegates that first night in
New York, and the rules change proposed by Kennedy died. But
on Tuesday the place belonged to Ted Kennedy. The floor was a
sea of blue, as even many of the Carterites waved the senator's
posters back and forth. Kennedy had come to concede, to have his
last word in the 1980 campaign. He came with a speech that was
written by Shrum and was the purest distillation of the liberal
message. As was often the case when he was well prepared with
a well-written speech, Ted Kennedy was magnificent. His great
resonant voice rumbled from the podium and through the Garden,
capturing the full attention of the Democrats below him. His curly
graying head bobbed in acknowledgment of the cheers that en-
veloped him. His strange uncertainty had vanished. He had, at
that moment, the force to move a multitude's emotions.

"The commitment I seek," Kennedy boomed, "is not to out-
worn views, but to old values that will never wear out. Programs
may sometimes become obsolete, but the ideal of fairness always

endures. Circumstances may change, but the work of compassion must continue. It is surely correct that we cannot solve problems by throwing money at them; but it is also correct that we dare not throw our national problems onto a scrap heap of inattention and indifference. The poor may be out of political fashion, but they are not without human needs. The middle class may be angry, but they have not lost the dream that all Americans can advance together. . . .

"The task of leadership in 1980 is not to parade scapegoats or to seek refuge in reaction but to match our power to the possibilities of progress."

It was, perhaps, the last great liberal speech and it marked the end of an era in American life. In that respect, it was a sad occasion for Democrats of all stripes. Their last great hope had lost; the Kennedy myth had been shattered. The New Deal coalition had fallen apart. Tough times would follow, as Kennedy and the rest of his party set off to find new answers and new approaches and new ideas.

"There were hard hours on our journey and often we sailed against the wind," Kennedy concluded, "but we always kept our rudder true. And there were so many of you who stayed the course and shared our hope. You gave your help; but even more, you gave your hearts. When I think back on all the miles and all the months and all the memories, I think of you. I recall the poet's words, and I say: "What golden friends I had. . . .

"And someday, long after this convention, long after the signs come down, and the crowds stop cheering, and the bands stop playing, may it be said of our campaign that we kept the faith. May it be said of our party in 1980 that we found the faith again. May it be said of us, both in dark passages and in bright days, in the words of Tennyson that my brothers quoted and loved—and that have special meaning for me now:

> I am part of all that I have met . . .
> Tho' much is taken, much abides . . .
> That which we are, we are—
> One equal temper of heroic hearts . . .
>   strong in will
> To strive, to seek, to find and not to yield.

"For me, a few hours ago, this campaign came to an end. For all those whose cares have been our concern, the work goes on, the cause endures, the hope still lives, and the dream shall never die."

That Kennedy had many years of political life left was beyond doubt. But his performance in 1980 was so meager as to suggest that either some part of him didn't want the presidency and that he would thus continue to contrive not to get it. His campaign—especially his perseverance beyond the point of his having had any chance of winning—was a campaign of atonement and it did have the effect, in part, of washing away the haunting specter of his performance at Chappaquiddick. Redemption is a recurrent theme in American politics, as Richard Nixon demonstrated in his eight-year comeback from his loss to Ted Kennedy's brother in 1960. Kennedy may choose to run again for the presidency, but if he does it will be as a changed man—and a different politician. The lines from Tennyson that he quoted were from "Ulysses," but as he spoke those words, my colleague at *Time,* Neil MacNeil, realized that Kennedy had excised the lines in which the aging wanderer admits his weakness and lost strength:

> Tho' much is taken, much abides; and tho'
> We are not now that strength which in old days
> Moved earth and heaven, that which we are, we are—
> One equal temper of heroic hearts,
> Made weak by time and fate, but strong in will
> To strive, to seek, to find and not to yield.

From a trailer parked in the concrete corridor behind the convention floor, the Carter high command watched and heard the delegates go wild as Ted Kennedy finished his speech. In charge, along with Hamilton Jordan, was Robert Strauss, one of the great Texas bullshitters in national politics, a man who had served as Democratic National Committee chairman during Carter's 1976 campaign. Then he had little but disdain for the Georgians, but his ability and savvy soon led Carter to recruit him, first for a variety of jobs in the administration, and then to be the front man and fund raiser for the campaign. The pair were managing the floor fight over the party platform in which Kennedy was insisting on planks calling for wage and price controls, a twelve-billion-dollar jobs program and a declaration that unemployment was a higher priority for federal action than inflation. The President, in touch with his lieutenants by phone from Camp David, where he was preparing his acceptance speech, was resisting all three because they were directly counter to his economic program. But when the convention spun into delirium following Kennedy's speech, Strauss and Jordan finally accepted a proffered deal from the Kennedy forces. Kennedy would concede on wage and price controls in return for the other two planks. Convention chairman Thomas P. "Tip" O'Neill, the Speaker of the House of Representatives, was given the word. Even as the delegates stomped and shouted in continued approval of Kennedy's speech, O'Neill gaveled through the two planks on jobs and unemployment, and gaveled down the wage and price controls plank, all by announcing the results of voice votes that bore little relationship to his ruling. The reformed, more "democratic" convention had, *in extremis,* reverted to its oldest form.

By the time Carter himself spoke Thursday night, the vast blue sea of Kennedy placards had been replaced by green Carter-Mondale posters. The party, reluctantly and without much enthusiasm, belonged again to Jimmy Carter. Throughout the week Carter's closest aides had been predicting a speech filled with "vision," which would finally supply the sense of direction his administration had lacked and which his nearly nonexistent campaign had never hinted at. It was a tough order, not just because Jimmy Carter, in three and a half years as president, had failed to communicate such a vision, but also because Reagan, the month before, had done so well at just that task. In a sense Reagan had stolen Carter's theme, at least the theme that Carter had played so well in 1976, and that was to pledge to clean up Washington and to make the government work better. In Reagan's case that pledge was also to make the government work less. But Carter had the unenviable problem of not being able to run against his own administration, which stripped him of the rhetoric of resentment and reform that had been so powerful in his own first campaign. The problem for Carter was made worse by the stirring

207

Kennedy speech, no matter that much of the Kennedy rhetoric was outmoded. Kennedy had said his piece superbly. Carter had a tough act to follow.

When he finally took the podium Carter was disappointing. He simply lacked Kennedy's rhetorical gift (although Carter could be superb in smaller groups, answering questions, thinking on his feet, just the opposite of Kennedy's weak performance in that sort of forum). Carter's voice was reedy, unsure, tense. He understood the importance of the moment. The tension seemed to have grabbed him by the throat. Unfortunately for Carter, what will be remembered most about that speech in New York was a slip of the tongue that occurred only moments into his presentation. It was the kind of mistake any politician could make, but it seemed so symptomatic of Carter's entire political problem that when he committed the error the entire convention hall was for an instant shocked with embarrassment.

Carter was working his way through the pantheon of great Democrats: Roosevelt, Truman, Kennedy, and Johnson. "And [we're] the party of a great man," Carter continued, "who should have been president and would have been one of the greatest presidents in history—Hubert Horatio Hornblower . . . er . . Humphrey." Hubert Humphrey: the greatest liberal figure in the party since the 1948 convention, Mondale's mentor, the party's nominee in 1968, for a time a devil in the eyes of the antiwar left for his support of Johnson's policies. But finally, as he aged and edged toward death, honored and revered. That Carter would stumble over that name reminded the convention that Carter had come from nowhere in the party to be its nominee in 1976. It reminded that he had come to Washington loathing and ignoring the Democratic majority in the Congress. It reminded that he had been trying to edge the party away from the programs and the ideas Humphrey stood for. It reminded that Jimmy Carter was little more than an interloper in the post–World War II history of the Democratic party.

Carter plunged on: "I'd like to say a personal word to Senator Kennedy. Ted, you're a tough competitor and a superb campaigner and I can attest to that. Your speech before this convention was a magnificent statement of what the Democratic party is and what it means to the people of this country—and why a

Democratic victory is so important this year. I reach out to you tonight and I reach out to all those who have supported you in your valiant and passionate campaign.

"Ted, your party needs—and I need—you and your idealism and dedication working for us. There is no doubt that even greater service lies ahead of you—and we are grateful to you to have your strong partnership now in the larger cause to which your own life has been dedicated."

In Carter's mouth the words sounded pleading and for a sitting president, demeaning. He went on to deliver a mild apologia for the failures of his first term.

"I've learned that only the most complex and difficult tasks come to the Oval Office. No easy answers are found there, because no easy questions come there.

"I've learned that for a president, experience is the best guide to the right decisions. I'm wiser tonight than I was four years ago."

That passage was also the beginning of a theme that Carter would expand and exaggerate through the fall. He may have failed in this area or that, he was saying, but the fact was that he had been *the President,* the United States had survived his steward-ship, and thus there was no concern for the national safety in another four years.

"This election," Carter said, "is a stark choice between two men, two parties, two sharply different pictures of what America is and what the world is. But it is more than that.

"It is a choice between two futures. . . ."

The future that Carter saw was naturally one marked by secu-rity and peace, economic well-being, justice, more jobs, equal opportunity, and "confidence and hope and a good life." Just how he would produce the very results that had eluded him for three and one-half years, he did not say.

His opponent, however, offered "despair" and "surrender of our energy future to the merchants of oil, the surrender of our economic future to a bizarre program of massive tax cuts for the rich, service cuts for the poor, and massive inflation for everyone.

"And," Carter went on, "I see risk—the risk of international confrontation; the risk of an uncontrollable, unaffordable, and unwinnable nuclear arms race."

His world, he said, was the real world. The Republican's world of the future was a "world of tinsel and make-believe."

It was not an ill-directed attack. Reagan in fact had raised questions about his judgment and his intelligence through most of his political life. He was often too quick to suggest U.S. military intervention. He and his party had urged not parity with the Soviets in strategic arms, but superiority, a trigger word for an arms race. The Kemp-Roth program did not make much sense in an inflated economy, and Reagan's energy solution was to free the oil companies of government restraint. If Carter was to win re-election, his speech suggested, it would not be as a reward for his first-term record. Nor would it be because he instilled great hope and confidence in his own plans for the next four years. Rather, it would come only if a kind of anti-Reagan panic could be fanned into existence, a massive fear that Reagan's inexperience and often intemperate rhetoric threatened the security and stability of the United States. For Carter to win, public opinion would have to seize on those anxieties more than it was already focused on rising prices, rising unemployment, the Soviet incursion in Afghanistan, the Iranian hostages, and Carter's own uninspiring presence. It was to be a campaign of competing and conflicting anxieties.

It was clear that Carter would need all the help he could get in that campaign. He would need help to reassure the country about his own abilities and to help fan the doubts that already existed about Ronald Reagan's capacities. First, he would need the help of Ted Kennedy.

As Carter finished his speech, his delegates began a demonstration that was tepid by comparison to the one that had rocked the Garden after Kennedy's appearance. All eyes focused on the podium, waiting for the expected and planned arrival of Ted Kennedy. All Democrats hoped that, for all that had gone before between Carter and Kennedy, there would be at least that one ritualistic gesture, the raising of their joined hands in unity. Time passed and the demonstration lost energy and pitch. "Where's Ted?" Carter asked through his toothy smile as he and Fritz Mondale waved to the crowd. Carter and Mondale family members joined the pair on the podium. Democrats of high rank joined the crowd. The demonstration strained harder to keep going.

Carter's aides later said they had asked Kennedy to wait in a holding area behind the podium during the speech. Kennedy's people explained their man had been asked to wait at his hotel. Only after the Carter speech did Kennedy move by motorcade through the snarled traffic of New York toward Madison Square Garden. The President of the United States, now surrounded by every conceivable relative and party functionary, waited, looking for the absent senator. The band played on.

Finally, Kennedy appeared. The delay appeared to be a snub, intended or not. He shook Carter's hand and the President patted his back. The roar of the crowd increased with Kennedy's appearance. But Kennedy was clearly more interested in smiling, rather grimly, down at the crowd. Carter waited awkwardly for Kennedy's hand to raise in unity, but Kennedy virtually ignored him. Carter looked hurt. And then Kennedy left. There was to be no picture signifying a truce. Kennedy had done the minimum; he had come to the platform, but that was all. His reluctant appearance was more of a reproach than a rapprochement. It was a shabby gesture by Kennedy, a last campaign snub by a politician who oscillated between the inspirational and the adolescent. I found Kennedy infuriating that way. The flashes of brilliance, of the old Kennedy panache, raising the hope of leadership. But then the inexplicable bouts of inarticulateness, the roaring, incomprehensible flood of words and emotion, left me finally bewildered about this politician and this man. The poetry he chose to leave out of his speech described him best: ". . . made weak by time and fate, but strong in will."

FALL
1980

13

The Least of
Three Evils

In the days before the presidential selection process had become an ordeal in which politicians, press, and public were locked together in a three-year embrace, Labor Day was the beginning of the serious business of selecting a president. It was the right time, too, for such an endeavor. The parching heat of the summer was breaking, and most of the country was moving toward the crisp glory of autumn, when clearheaded decisions could be made. In the fall of 1980, however, the country was already exhausted by the presidential endurance contest. It had seen and heard the candidates without relief. It knew, in large measure, where they stood and who they were. What remained was to make a final choice among the three remaining contenders.

That was not to be an easy task, nor one undertaken with much joy or enthusiasm. No candidate, not the President nor Ronald

Reagan nor John Anderson, had captured the imagination of the country. As it had been the year before when Carter had flayed the nation and himself for selfishness and loss of purpose, the country was still unsettled about where it wanted to go and who it wanted to take it there. It was tired of Carter and embarrassed by his failures. It feared Reagan for his lack of experience and his quick-draw pronouncements on matters of great sensitivity. And by late August the rising star of John Anderson had begun to sink quickly. Reagan's huge lead in the polls over the summer had nearly vanished. The presidential campaign of 1980 had sunk into a slough of public indecision and dissatisfaction.

A public opinion survey by the Yankelovich organization described that state of political inertia. Carter and Reagan each pulled support from thirty-nine percent of the electorate as Labor Day approached. Anderson, once at twenty-three percent in the same poll, had sunk to fifteen percent and looked to be heading farther down, the victim in part of a public belief that he simply couldn't win. The poll showed that no particular issue was helping or hurting one candidate or another. Rather, the choice seemed to come down to a question of personality and character, a decision based on the man himself rather than a program or party or political philosophy. Only seven percent in the poll said that they had actually not decided among the candidates, a low number for that time in the campaign. At first glance the undecideds suggested a race in which the public mind had been made up early, which was not surprising considering that Carter was a sitting president and Reagan was a more-than-familiar face on the political scene. But a closer look at the opinion survey showed that the depth of commitment to all the candidates by their supporters was extraordinarily shallow and negative, suggesting that given the right circumstances the standing of one or the other could change dramatically. Other opinion polls taken at the time reflected the same loose attachment to the candidates.

The candidates' strength by region, however, seemed to foretell trouble for Carter. Reagan was still in command in the West, where no Democrat had run well since the Johnson landslide of 1964. The Midwest was effectively tied, not surprisingly. More important was the South, where Carter held only a one-point lead over Reagan. Given Reagan's conservatism, that was perhaps not surprising either, but in 1976 Carter's ability to bring the South back from an increasingly Republican presidential voting pattern had insured his election. In 1980, however, Reagan looked to have a good chance of at least penetrating that Carter base, while Carter seemed to have little hope of snatching off much of Reagan's natural western support. Carter had never been either popular or comfortable in the West. The region's very openness and space was the antithesis of Carter's controlled and precise personality. One of his first official acts as President was a necessary but ham-handed attempt to cut back on western water projects. What remaining support John Anderson commanded was located most heavily in two regions. The northeast, in which Carter needed to do well to offset possible erosion in the South, still registered twenty percent support for Anderson, suggesting that if he could maintain that level he would hurt Carter's chances against Reagan in states like New York, Connecticut, and Massachusetts. Anderson also pulled twenty percent of the sampled vote in the Far West —California, Oregon, and Washington—in early September. Reagan's strongest western support lay in the Mountain States and in the Southwest. With Anderson still a factor in the coastal states, Carter stood even less chance of picking up one or two states from the Reagan base.

Even more descriptive of public attitudes toward the candidates were findings in the Yankelovich survey about the firmness of support each commanded. Among those who said they were for Carter, more than half expressed doubts and reservations about their choice. Fifty-seven percent of Reagan's potential voters had the same feelings about him, and a similar percentage said they weren't that certain about their support for Anderson. This was hardly a pattern of deep and unchangeable commitment. Moreover, large proportions of the vote for each candidate seemed to be motivated not by a positive attitude toward that man's virtues, but rather was described by those surveyed as being really a vote against the other candidates. Forty-three percent of the Reagan voters said they were "really voting against Carter." More than a third of Carter's supporters said they were really anti-Reagan. And sixty-one percent of the Anderson vote was frankly described as a vote against both Carter and Reagan. Another measure of public sourness about the choices offered in 1980 was the response to a question asking which candidate the voter was "personally interested in or excited about." Reagan led that category with only eleven percent. Carter got nine percent and Anderson six percent. In 1980 the quest for the presidency had become, in the mind of the American public, an exercise in picking the least of three evils. The campaigns of the three men seeking the highest office in the land were, in fact, tailored to just that attitude. The campaign strategists had read their own polls showing the same unhappiness. Each campaign was thus designed to make the opponents look unsuited for the office. It was, all around, a negative campaign designed more to diminish the opposition than to elevate the principals. In 1976 Jimmy Carter wrote his own campaign biography, *Why Not the Best?* "Our theme in 1980 is different from 1976," cracked one Carter operative. "This year it's 'At least not the worst.' "

John Anderson's independent candidacy had arisen out of dissatisfaction with the choice between Reagan and Carter. But after a summer of constant campaigning, including a trip to Israel which he used to pander again to the Jewish vote back home, Anderson had by Labor Day lost any chance of upsetting the balance of two-party politics. His major problem was a simple one, one that has plagued all modern third-party and independent candidates. It was that to most voters he didn't seem to have a chance of winning. In primary elections voters are more willing to cast a simple protest ballot for an apparent loser, to "send them a message," as George Wallace had urged during his days as a third-party candidate in 1968. But when the general election comes around, voting behavior changes. Voters want to make a meaningful choice; they are eager to have their vote matter in the final outcome. So when John Anderson's public opinion poll standing began to sink, partly as a natural result of the huge attention paid to the Democratic and Republican conventions during the summer, he was caught in the classic Catch-22 of modern politics. He couldn't win if he didn't seem to have a chance of winning. Each decline in the polls fed a later decline, and John Anderson's candidacy, the one that earlier frightened some into thinking the election might be thrown into the House of Representatives, simply and quietly went downhill.

Without bosses and without the strength of party organization, Anderson became a case study in reverse momentum. George Bush had ridden his "big mo" up in the polls after Iowa. John Anderson's case was the opposite. Failure begat failure. A summer of active courting of unhappy, big-name Democrats, like Governor Hugh Carey of New York, failed to produce one willing to take the risks of bolting his party to join Anderson as a vice-presidential candidate on a sort of fusion ticket. In late August Anderson was left with Patrick J. Lucey as his running mate. Lucey was virtually unknown, despite having served as governor of Wisconsin and then as Carter's ambassador to Mexico. Lucey quit his diplomatic post to join Kennedy's campaign as one of several managers. After the collapse of that candidacy, Lucey had nothing better to do with his time than to join Anderson. That Lucey was the best Anderson could attract was a further public sign that Anderson was not taken seriously by political pros, which, of course, led to his being taken even less seriously by the public.

Anderson's decline was an interesting example of the role of the press and of public opinion surveys in presidential campaigns. To some immeasurable extent, press predictions and polls are self-fulfilling. The press and the pollsters are not powerful enough by themselves to reverse the great tides of political feeling. But at the margin they are important influences indeed. Anderson's early success was partly a result of very favorable press and television attention, some of it generated by his own interesting and bold words, some by the media's perception, as measured by their polls, that the Carter-Reagan choice was not being well-received by the public. Given the state of American politics generally, some in the press concluded, not unreasonably, that a third-force candidacy was not necessarily doomed. This fed the initial public interest in this novel candidate. The polls then measured and documented that interest, a fact the press then reported. But after the two conventions the serious vote syndrome began to plague Anderson. His polls declined and the press reported that as well. The conventional wisdom that had greeted Anderson's announcement—that third-party candidates fade in the fall—was being proved true.

In mid-autumn I visited a series of voters in Pennsylvania.* One voter there, an executive with the Westinghouse Corporation in Pittsburgh, summed up Anderson's situation this way: "I have great admiration for him. They said on *Sixty Minutes* that he is the best candidate with no chance to win. I guess he still is. He is refreshing and outspoken. If I thought he really could win, I'd vote for him. But I don't think he can win and so I won't vote for him. If I lived in a vacuum, if I didn't know about what the polls are saying, I'd go ahead and vote for Anderson."

Anderson's decline wasn't simply situational, however. He and his campaign organization contributed heavily to his demise. Anderson, on the advice of his campaign manager, David Garth, spent the summer making as few waves as possible on issues and policies. The plan was to devote July and August to ballot-access drives across the country, which were, after great amounts of money and time were spent, successful in placing Anderson's name on the ballots in all fifty states. They really had no alternative but to finish the ballot-access process, but by taking a deliberately low-key approach, Anderson vanished from the front pages.

This approach had been advocated by Garth, over the objections of some of the younger members of the Anderson staff who felt that Anderson needed to continue the outspoken style of campaigning that had put him in the national spotlight in the first place. Inside the Anderson organization, the younger staffers felt that Garth had captured their man and, by muting Anderson's high-profile statements, had turned him into just another politician. Garth, on the other hand, felt the younger staff members were too inexperienced in politics. Finally, in the late summer, Garth, who had tried to run the campaign from his New York headquarters, moved to Washington to take command of the failing Anderson operation.

The fact was that both the Young Turks and Garth were right

---

*The Pennsylvanians were selected from the Yankelovich telephone sample for *Time* magazine's polls. They were picked for personal interviewing because they lived in a state that was, at the time, neither heavily for Carter nor for Reagan. These voters had also expressed a great deal of conflict over their choice of candidate and therefore represented just the kind of difficulty many Americans were having making up their minds. Members of this group will be quoted in this chapter.

in their criticisms of each other. Anderson had become more conventional the closer one looked at him and the more he campaigned. He felt the need to avoid offending key constituencies, and thus toned down some of his less politic remarks. On an early summer trip to North Carolina, for example, he was asked whether he favored a continuation of the subsidy for tobacco growers. Anderson began to say no, but quickly caught himself and feathered his answer to say he would have to study the matter. Garth, despite his successes with statewide campaigns in the past, was involved in his first national campaign, and thus had a good deal to learn himself. His biggest problem was that he was in charge of an almost impossible mission. His solution was to do what he did best and that was to organize television advertising campaigns. But with more than five million dollars being pumped into ballot-access drives across the country, Garth had little money for a large-scale television blitz. Instead, the Anderson campaign needed the free attention from the network news operations and the print media. Garth tried his best to talk reporters into believing that Anderson had a chance, but he was usually unconvincing. He was given to fits of temper when unfavorable stories were written about him or his candidate. When a story appeared in late August in *Time* citing the disaffected younger staff's criticism of Garth's tactics, Garth vowed never to talk to anyone from the magazine ever again. Through a mutual friend I convinced Garth to speak to me on the phone. Garth spent twenty minutes slandering the correspondent who had reported the offending story. He then spent another twenty minutes in perfectly rational discussion of the campaign. The interview ended, but Garth had not forgotten his wrath. "Thanks a lot," I said. "Fuck ya," snarled Garth and hung up.

David Garth was more than a little embarrassed to have his first national campaign turning into a failure, especially given his reputation for turning losers into winners which he had won in this political consulting business. But Garth did not destroy the Anderson campaign. Anderson himself, stiff and unsure, intense and self-righteous, did not wear well with voters. His promises of new solutions and new answers was never fulfilled. Although he and his staff produced a platform of more than three hundred pages, there was little novelty in it. His positions amounted to a sensible progressive platform, not too distant from Carter and the Democrats'. Ultimately Anderson was unable to distinguish himself intellectually from the field.

Rather than become a true fusion candidate, melding the best of the left and the right in American politics, Anderson fell into the very trap he needed to avoid. He became too identified with the liberals. His candidacy was seen as another protest from the left, with forty-three percent of the country saying they thought he was "too liberal." In the end Anderson was left only with voters who could simply not reconcile themselves to Carter or Reagan. In most cases those voters were liberals of the old Adlai Stevenson variety. A retired philosophy professor in suburban Philadelphia put it this way:

"The fact that Jerry Ford, by comparison to Carter, has now been elevated to the rank of elder statesman is sufficient reason to oppose Carter. I find Carter condescendingly insincere and self-righteous. And Reagan. His economics are incomprehensible. His urgings that we have to be number one in military strength means only an arms race. He's shallow and frightening in that respect. Anderson, from a personal point of view, gives the appearance of having grown. His early views were certainly abhorrent to me. But I like the fact that he is not brandishing the military club. I think he's a man willing to buck the tide. I think he might even be willing to take a risk for peace."

When he began the race as an independent in April, Anderson's candidacy was more than a pipe dream and an ego trip. It was the expression of serious discontent operating in a fragmented and fractured political system. But his campaign was hurriedly assembled and starved for money, at least compared to the $29.4 million doled out by the federal treasury to the Republican and Democratic parties. He lacked a sure sense of how to capitalize on that discontent and produce the money and the political positions that could have carried him beyond the realm of the hopeless and quixotic.

Anderson's one great hope in the fall was to be included in the presidential debates with Carter and Reagan. The League of Women Voters, under pressure from the White House which announced a categorical refusal to have Carter appear in any debate forum with Anderson so as to avoid giving Anderson any additional standing, finally decided that if Anderson was getting fifteen percent support in the polls, they would invite him to join the league's debates. By mid-September, after checking all the public polls and agonizing a great deal, the league invited Anderson to join the first debate in Baltimore. Carter promptly refused his invitation, but Reagan, eager to show up Carter for not appearing, agreed.

On the twenty-first of September, Anderson and Reagan met in a debate (more properly a joint press conference with selected reporters asking them both questions). Both men did what they always had done. Anderson cited Harvard and Princeton studies to buttress his points. Reagan smiled, cocked his head, and was pleasant as he chided Carter for not showing up. But without the President the debate was dismissed as second-string stuff. Reagan managed to keep his facts in order. Anderson managed to sound erudite, although he was too intense for television, a medium made for the cool, quiet friendliness of Ronald Reagan. David Garth had predicted a five-point rise in his candidate's poll standings after the debate. But when America saw John Anderson that night it remained unimpressed. His standings continued to decline with no hope of reversal. Free of the burden of being a serious candidate, John Anderson began to relax as the campaign wound down. He relaxed on the stump, told jokes, even on himself. Like Ted Kennedy, he was doing better when it didn't matter. He had been worried about being thought a fool and an opportunist. But in 1980 John Anderson was neither. He had been bold enough to take a chance with an unconventional campaign for the presidency. To some his failure is proof that an independent or a third-party candidate can't upset the two-party hegemony in American politics. But Anderson's failures were personal and circumstantial. Although, starting in April 1980, it was clear Anderson couldn't win, his experience also suggests that with luck, another candidacy, well planned and carefully financed, begun earlier and conducted by another sort of politician, just might have been able to upset the existing order—and an independent could indeed win the American presidency. Anderson raised more than $12 million in six months. More could be raised with an earlier start. Access to television can be bought and created by careful tactics, thus obviating the need for party structures and

endorsements. With the two parties' nominating process dominated by their ideological activists, both Republicans and Democrats are hard-pressed to select true moderates. By the way he
tried and failed, Anderson showed how an independent might try
and succeed. That is no small lesson.

Four years earlier, Jimmy Carter had been campaigning promising a new decency in American government, new prosperity for
its people, and, most of all, a return of government that would
again, after the shocks of the 1960s and the 1970s, command the
respect of the American people. In the fall of 1980 Jimmy Carter
was again dashing about the country, but this time he was not full
of new promises and prospects. He could not promise easier and
better times. He could only scramble desperately to hold onto the
office he had narrowly won in 1976. He could only hope that,
given another four years, he could live up to the expectations he
had raised in his first campaign and fulfill the dreams of greatness
he held for himself. It was, in its way, a sad sight. Carter had
visibly aged during his presidency. He had had to confront his own
failures and shortcomings. He had had to recognize the huge gap
between his nearly unlimited demands on himself and his personal
and political limits. Months earlier he had provided the perfect
paradigm for his presidency when he tried to run a twenty-six-mile
marathon race along the mountain roads near the presidential
retreat at Camp David. Less than halfway through the race he had
nearly collapsed from exhaustion. Ashen-faced and gasping, his
legs buckling under him, Carter was escorted off the raceway by
his doctor and the Secret Service.

Carter had had the misfortune to govern in a restless and unsure
time, and in a public atmosphere of impatience. To compound his
problems he had chosen to govern essentially alone, shunning the
friendship and advice that was easily available to him in Washington. When trouble struck, he preferred to go it alone, relying
almost exclusively on the young men from Georgia who had
helped him win the presidency. Outsiders came and went at the
White House and in the Cabinet, but they were rarely fully trusted
or listened to. It was as if the Georgians, including the President,
needed to prove they could govern by themselves. The wisdom
and experience of old hands like lawyer Clark Clifford, journalist

Hedley Donovan, even Cabinet members like Joe Califano, were sought but never relied upon.

Carter was not without accomplishments in office. He had won approval of the Panama Canal treaties. His own negotiating skill and patience had produced the first significant progress in the Middle East in decades, in the form of the Camp David accords between Israel and Egypt. He had begun to move the nation toward a sensible (and unpopular, among Democrats) course on energy, in which oil for domestic consumption would be priced in keeping with world prices. This forced conservation and a major reconfiguration of American industrial plants to accommodate those higher prices. He had fulfilled his major promise and had returned a standard of truthfulness and honesty to the office he held. But Carter had also failed in that while he was trusted he was not respected. Unlike most incumbents in that office, Carter seemed not to have grown in the office; rather he seemed diminished by it.

At the Democratic convention in New York, Carter's pollster Patrick Caddell looked ahead to the fall campaign. In many ways Caddell was often more realistic than other Carter aides in measuring the President's problems. He had a professional reputation to defend and had to deal as well with the hard truths his polls told him. "The amazing thing," Caddell confided then, "is that Carter can have [poll] ratings like this and that we would even be discussing the fact that he could get re-elected. There is no way that I could begin to overestimate Jimmy Carter's problems politically in the country."

The fact was, however, that in August and through most of the fall, Jimmy Carter did have a chance of being re-elected despite it all. The reason was simple: his opponent. Caddell had found the American people harboring enormous doubts about Ronald Reagan, about his wisdom and about his ideological stripe. In 1980, Caddell argued, the level of public skepticism about all politicians made this a particularly potent advantage for Carter. "No matter how troublesome his own performance has been to the electorate," Caddell said, "he at least has the advantage of having been there. He has the advantage of having at least gotten you through." In the pollster's mind, that was a special advantage in the nuclear era when an irrational president could produce not just disaster, but

The Disaster. It was also a special advantage against a candidate like Ronald Reagan, who was already perceived by some voters as too prone to suggest American military involvement abroad.

Throughout the spring and summer, the Carter camp had struggled to find a theme for the fall campaign. Some argued for a campaign based on their record. Others, like Caddell, argued that that was too defensive. Besides, it was impossible to correct what the Carter forces felt were public misapprehensions about their record in the few weeks left in the campaign. Instead, the aim of the Carter campaign became precisely what Caddell had suggested: scare the hell out of the American people about Ronald Wilson Reagan. Historically, negative campaigning soon winds up being called mudslinging, and the perpetrator loses out in public esteem. But with a public predisposed to distrust all politicians anyway, Caddell felt there was little risk. "The success of negative campaigns in American politics since 1978 has been almost unabated," he advised. "There has been almost no level of backfire."

Jimmy Carter was never as high-minded as he wanted the nation to think. Under all the moralism and religiosity, Carter was, like most politicians, a tough, ambitious, and determined man. His campaigns in Georgia had frequently been marked by personal and unfair attacks on his opponents. Winning was not just a chance to serve the public, it was also for Carter self-affirmation and ego support. It was vindication and proof of virtue. To attack Ronald Reagan was then an easy thing for Jimmy Carter. It flowed naturally out of his sense of his own goodness. It came as second nature to a man who thought he was doing the best that could be done.

In mid-September I joined the White House press corps for a campaign tour with Carter. We flew to Corpus Christi, Texas, for another town meeting. Then on to Houston for party rallies at which Carter was greeted with only restrained enthusiasm. The road show moved on to Atlanta, Carter's home turf, for a speech to southern black political leaders at the Ebenezer Baptist Church, the home church of the Reverend Martin Luther King, Sr., one of Carter's most powerful supporters in 1976. It was an important and emotional occasion for Jimmy Carter. For the black leaders too it was an important event. The black community in the South had been instrumental in sending Carter to Washington, allowing him to build an electoral base in his home region that would have been impossible without their support. It would have been impossible too two decades earlier, before the civil rights revolution.

Ebenezer Baptist Church is an unpretentious building, but its history as a locus and inspiration for the civil rights struggle of the 1960s is awesome. It was a moving experience sitting there, remembering the importance of the place. The all-black audience was dressed as for Sunday services, a sharp contrast to the mostly white and mostly bedraggled national press contingent dressed in khaki pants and tennis shoes. Middle-aged black women in white gloves moved people to their seats in the church. The all-male choir of Morehouse College performed one stately piece after another, making the church seem the site of a High Episcopal mass. When Carter finally entered, he was greeted and then introduced by the southern black civil rights Establishment: "Daddy" King, Coretta Scott King, Andrew Young, Mayor Maynard Jackson of Atlanta. Carter knew where he was and why he was there.

"I was going to describe to you in my opening remarks how far we've come," Carter began, "but I think Maynard Jackson did it better than anyone that I know when he, as a black mayor, referred to me, a white president, as a 'Georgia boy.' " The church was filled with laughter and applause.

"If it hadn't been for Daddy King and his beloved wife, I would not be President," Carter continued. "Had they not had their son, Martin Luther King, Jr., I would not be President. . . . And had it not been for the people in this audience . . . I would not be President. You all had confidence in me in 1976, when very few people knew who I was and there was an actual stigma attached to southern white politicians . . . that you helped to remove.

"I have had continual need for you. Once during the campaign [of 1976] I made a remark about ethnic purity and it almost crippled me fatally. I didn't know what to do. I got a call from Andy and I got a call from Daddy King and I got a call from many of you and I decided to come home to Atlanta and had a rally in the downtown square. Four or five thousand people came. There I was in front of the TV cameras and Daddy King grabbed my hand and the people all over the nation saw it and it healed the wound that I had done to myself. So I'm very aware of the importance of this meeting.

227

"This meeting this morning could very well decide the outcome of this election and, more importantly, the future of this country. When my presidency has not always satisfied every one of you, I acknowledge that fact. My phone has been open to you and others that are not here this morning and you have never failed to use it. . . . But if my opponent should be elected, you're going to have a hard time getting a telephone answered at the White House."

The message was simple and heartfelt. Carter had been helped by black voters and he had tried to help them. And no matter how tough things had been, they would doubtless get worse under Ronald Reagan. It was an obvious point to make to the black Americans, an obvious appeal for more help, for a chance at a second term. Without a heavy black vote in the South, Carter's chances of holding that region were slim indeed. Nationwide, Carter was sure to attract most of the black vote. But the question was just how much black vote there would be.

There can be no doubt that Carter felt close to those black leaders in Atlanta. He cared about their problems and their causes, about their people and their needs. He had appointed more blacks and minorities to federal office than all the presidents before him. His claim on them was legitimate. But he went just slightly beyond that claim. He tried to scare them about the prospect of Ronald Reagan:

"You've seen in this campaign the stirrings of hate and the rebirth of code words like 'states rights' in a speech in Mississippi, in a campaign reference to the Ku Klux Klan relating to the South. That is a message that creates a cloud on the political horizon. Hatred has no place in this country. Racism has no place in this country."

The implication was, obviously, that Reagan's presidency would see a return of those evils in race relations. That Reagan was not popular with blacks was no secret; nor was it a secret that Reagan's idea of federal austerity would threaten much of the special help blacks had received in recent years, both economic and legal help through federal jobs programs, welfare payments, food stamps, affirmative action, busing, and the like. But the notion that Reagan himself would condone racism and hate were out of bounds. Shortly after the speech, Press Secretary Jody Powell circulated among the press corps, trying to soften Carter's words, saying Carter had not meant Reagan himself was a racist, only that there were legitimate interests that minority groups had in retaining Carter as president.

So it went through September and early October. Carter attacked; Jody Powell clarified. In other speeches Carter suggested Reagan's foreign policy proclivities amounted to warmongering. He said Reagan would divide the nation along racial, religious, and regional lines. He pounded away at Reagan. And, in part, it worked. The doubts that existed about Reagan were reinforced. Reagan was, after all, the challenger. Carter was the incumbent and thus better known. It was the devil you knew versus the one you didn't.

The press that covered Carter did not much like him and he returned the sentiment. They found him brittle and suspicious and unpredictable, all behind a facade of smiles and warmth and earnest goals grandly enunciated. The tough campaign against Reagan confirmed those feelings and soon the dominant theme in the presidential campaign of 1980 was the "mean Jimmy" issue. Editorial pages were filled with charges that Carter had always been a mean-spirited little man and that his campaign was unworthy of a president of the United States. More important, however, was the fact that by allowing himself the luxury of simply blasting away at Reagan, Carter forfeited the opportunity to justify his own claim to another term. Carter undermined the public perception that he was honest and decent and well intentioned. More damaging still was the fact that his attacks made him, not Reagan, the leading issue of the campaign for five crucial weeks. He attempted to make Reagan the issue, but contrary to Caddell's August prediction, the tactic backfired.

The Carter strategy was plainly not working. Inside the President's official family that perception was growing, and there were repeated attempts to get Carter to tone down his attacks. They pointed out to Carter that he could raise questions about Reagan without assaulting him personally. On Reagan's lack of appeal to black groups, for example, it was suggested that he should simply ask the question, "How many civil rights leaders support Reagan? The answer: None. Why is that?" Or on foreign policy, a recital of the times Reagan has urged military intervention abroad would serve better than labeling Reagan a warmonger. The point was not that Reagan should not be made the issue, but rather that Carter had done it artlessly, making himself the subject of public doubt. No one in the Carter organization was more frustrated with this than Vice-President Walter Mondale, a direct descendent of the politics of joy practiced by Hubert Humphrey. "I don't like feeling dirty," Mondale confided in the midst of the Carter mean streak. "And I don't mind losing fair and square. But I hate to lose for stupid reasons."

Finally, in an interview on ABC television on October 8, Carter publicly acknowledged that he had been "carried away on a couple of occasions" and that his attacks on Reagan were "probably ill-advised." Thereafter, Carter was more subdued. But he had lost valuable time and suffered serious political damage. His supporters from 1976 were fed up and disappointed. He had given them little reason to vote for him again. About the only sentiment he could still tap was that of forgiveness and the hope that he had learned from his mistakes. An unemployed truck driver from the suburbs of Pittsburgh provided about as much of an endorsement as could be found for Jimmy Carter in the fall of 1980:

"I voted for Carter in 1976. I'm not a pro–Jimmy Carter person, yet I think I feel Carter can do a better job than Reagan, even though Carter has loused up the economy. Some of that was caused by previous administrations and it's not all his fault. The presidency is overrated anyway. It's like a quarterback on a football team. He gets all the glory but without the rest of the team he couldn't do it. And I think Carter's finally waking up on foreign policy. He's learned by trial and error."

For those who didn't expect much from either Carter or Reagan, it seemed easier to leave Carter in office, less risky somehow than breaking in a new man, who, like the others, couldn't really control the nation's destiny anyway. That was meager support indeed for an incumbent president seeking re-election. For the man who had promised new hope and change and reform and a fresh start only four years before, it had been a long fall. He was left with the skeptics and the pessimists and the fatalists. That wasn't enough.

The Republican party constituted a distinct minority in American politics in 1980. Only between twenty and twenty-five percent of the national electorate said they were Republicans. Moreover, the attitudes the party members and its leadership hold were distinctly more conservative than are those held by a majority of Americans. Although it is undeniably true that the country has edged a bit toward more conservative political attitudes in the last decade, Republicans were still stuck by and large over on the right wing of American politics.

For a Republican to be elected president, then, he must be able to perform a certain legerdemain. First he must be nominated by an ideological minority and then he must convince the broad center of the electorate that he isn't as faithful to the ideas and policies of his party as he seemed to be during the nomination process. For Ronald Reagan this required exploiting the central paradox of his personality: his smiling, sunny, optimistic manner and the ability to articulate the angry, resentful politics of antigovernment conservatism. What Reagan needed to do in the fall of 1980 was to emphasize his pleasant, reasonable side. He needed to diminish the notion that he was a dangerous ideologue intent upon ripping up the roots of the New Deal and its social programs.

In the electorate as a whole there existed a nearly clinical schizophrenia about the role of the federal government. It wanted the benefits of Big Government, but didn't want the rules and regulations and strictures that often came with those benefits. It wanted reduced federal spending and taxes, but it also wanted social services. The same malady existed in foreign policy. The public wanted a tougher stand against the world, but it did not want the threat of war and did not want the draft. For Reagan the job was to play to one side of the schizoid American personality while not stirring up the anxieties on the other side.

In essence, his job was to confuse the American voter about who Ronald Reagan was. The country knew him as a preacher of the right-wing dogma. He wanted them now to know him as a nice man, a former governor of the nation's largest state, who, while in that office, was considerably more practical and pragmatic than his after-dinner speech rhetoric would suggest. In more conventional political terms, Reagan needed to reach beyond the Republican activists who had nominated him and broaden his constituency. Campaign strategist and pollster Richard Wirthlin also saw this broadening effort as the prelude to what all the campaign managers around Reagan felt was to be the climax and key to the Reagan campaign: a frontal attack on Jimmy Carter and his record as president. Wirthlin felt that Reagan first needed to establish his own credibility and then go after Carter.

Day after day, from the late summer through the fall, Reagan did not stop talking about his record as governor of California. In fact, that record was commendable, if not as commendable as he described it. The state was run in an orderly way, with fiscal prudence, and without much evidence of extreme conservatism having dominated decision making. Reagan, the "communicator," was more than happy to delegate the detail work to subordinates. In California he surrounded himself with competent, careful aides and then listened to their advice and followed it. As he campaigned across America Reagan was a bit free with his claims of success in fiscal management, claiming that his new "supply side" economics had actually been tried when he was governor. His claims for welfare reform and tax reduction were overblown, but the essential point was accurate. He had been a good and reasonable governor.

Ronald Reagan is at his best when he has good direction. And like the thespian he is, Reagan takes direction well. He can deliver a well-written speech as effectively as any politician, and has his own wording and sense of pace to contribute. But he gets into trouble when he goes off on his own, extemporizing when he should be reading his lines. Reagan's instinct, honed from too many years on stage, is to please his audience. He is given to saying what an audience wants to hear, rather than what he should be saying. Before the fall campaign was a month old, Reagan's old penchant for the alarming claim, the inaccurate fact, the impolitic remark had raised a storm. The press called it the "gaffe game," and was eager to catch Reagan in as many as possible. They made nice little stories on television and in the papers. The gaffes did Ronald Reagan, the challenger who needed to prove, quickly, that he was smart enough and responsible enough to be president, a great deal of damage.

In late August Reagan and Bush were forced to appear together in Los Angeles while Reagan explained just what his policy toward mainland China was going to be. Earlier, Reagan had said that he favored restoring "official" relations with Taiwan, ending the "unofficial" relationship that had been constructed as a way of keeping some ties with the island nation while opening a full diplomatic relationship with the Communist Chinese. Much of conservative political dialogue on foreign affairs in the postwar era had been dominated by recriminations over "who lost China" to the Communists. Reagan, playing to his core constituency, had urged bringing Taiwan back up to full prominence. The problem was, of course, that such a step would have imperiled the new and strategically important relationship with the Mainland. Indeed, George Bush, who had served as the first envoy to the Communists when the Nixon administration had re-opened diplomatic channels, had just been in Peking explaining that a future Reagan administration would continue the policy of normalization. The two candidates looked sour and uncomfortable as Reagan claimed a "misstatement" about Taiwan and assured the world he would not disturb the new relationship with Red China. Bush, trying hard to be a loyal number two, looked as if his worst fears about Reagan's inexperience had been confirmed.

Appearing later at a Fundamentalist rally in Texas, Reagan wandered into the thicket of controversy generated by new efforts to argue against the scientific basis of human evolution. Reagan, pleasing his crowd once again, said that "creationism" should also be taught in the public schools. It was as if Reagan's own nostalgic vision of the good old days had run amok and the nation was caught in a time warp. The Scopes "monkey trial" seemed about to be relived. (In 1981 two states enacted laws requiring the teaching of "creationism" as well as evolution.) For a moment Reagan looked hopelessly out of date, captive not just of his own nostalgia but also of the evangelical right.

Reagan went on later in September to dredge up the Vietnam war. Speaking before veterans, he let himself go by describing that war as a "noble cause." While some in America may believe that our motives were "noble," the conduct and conclusion of the war and the politics of the war at home were anything but noble. It was the kind of statement that most politicians avoid like a case of strep throat. It was too easily misunderstood. Reagan never mentioned it again.

When Jimmy Carter opened his campaign after Labor Day in Tuscumbia, Alabama, Reagan criticized the President for beginning his quest in the "the birthplace of the Ku Klux Klan." The statement was wrong, and from across the South prideful public officials of both parties lambasted Reagan for implying that the South and the Klan stood for the same thing. (Reagan was also forced to disclaim an endorsement of his candidacy by the Klan, but was later able to assault Carter and his administration officials who kept pointing out that endorsement to their own audiences.)

A less important flap was caused by Reagan's use of the word *depression* to describe the state of the American economy. Technically he was wrong, and even nontechnically the term bore little relationship to economic reality. Again the question of Reagan's depth and intelligence and experience was raised. But throughout his political life Reagan had often managed to be forgiven his transgressions against fact and wisdom. From the moment of that comment on, Reagan converted it into a campaign joke that pleased his audiences. "I'm told I can't use the word *depression,*" Reagan would say. "Well, I'll tell you the definition. A recession is when your neighbor loses his job and a depression is when you lose your job. Recovery is when Jimmy Carter loses his."

The cure for the gaffe plague was simple enough, and before the end of September the Reagan campaign moved to end the problem. They simply put their candidate under tighter control. He was more careful to work from texts and to stick to the prepared and rehearsed material. But Reagan, being a nice chap, had a constitutional inability to ignore the calling of his name. At its sound he would turn and smile almost involuntarily, and then begin to answer whatever question was shouted. After the gaffes began to mount up, Reagan was restricted to a few curbside remarks each day and then only after premeditation.

It became a game for the press. It was hard to get interviews with Reagan. He gave only a few press conferences. And in the dizzy and ridiculous world of television news, the charge-counter-charge format of a campaign is the surest ticket to a spot on the evening news. If Carter said X, Reagan saying Y made a story. Thus there evolved a ritual between Reagan and the press. One day in Cleveland, when I was traveling with Reagan, it went like this:

(Reagan stepped off an elevator in City Hall after a private visit with the mayor. The press was "penned" into an area near the elevators by police and Secret Service. They spotted Reagan. CBS correspondent Bill Plante, one of the best of the shouters, opened up.)

"Governor Reagan, tell us what you think about Carter's refusal to debate."

Reagan turned, smiled, cocked his head, but was kept moving.

"We are preparing a statement. We will have a full statement for all of you," he shouted back.

"When?"

"Very shortly."

"Are you going to give it [in person, before cameras]?"

"I think they're just going to hand it out to you."

"We'd love to hear what you think about it. Come on, Governor."

Reagan, still smiling, departed.

Reagan was finally under control. The point was to reduce his message to the barest essentials and to avoid obscuring that message with verbal gaffes and the consequent alarms raised by the press. And the essential Reagan message was perfectly shaped for the politics of 1980. His first point was the one he had always made: that things are no longer what they were and the present condition of America is much, much worse than it once was. The second point flowed from the first, namely that given the sad state of affairs, it was time to try something new in the form of a new economic approach along with a reduction of the role of the federal government. Finally, Reagan wanted to convey the notion that despite an adult lifetime in ultraconservative politics, he was not a captive of the right wing; that he could be trusted with the presidency because he had been governor of California. To supplement that message, Reagan trimmed back on some of his earlier pronouncements, deciding as the campaign wore on that he was no longer opposed to federal aid to New York City. He decided he no longer opposed the federal bailout for the Chrysler Corporation. He announced that while, as in 1976, he still thought that state and local governments might administer some federal programs more efficiently, he was not proposing transfer of any specific powers away from Washington. He promised and then promised again that Social Security would not be tampered with, despite his repeated suggestions in the past that perhaps the system should be made voluntary.

The Reagan campaign had targeted their efforts wisely, spending very little time in the safe western states, spending a good deal of time in the South, where Carter appeared vulnerable to some erosion of his base, and spending huge amounts of time in the industrial Northeast and Midwest. A typical four-day swing had Reagan in Chicago reading a carefully prepared speech on his economic program, in Milwaukee wooing ethnic voters, in Cleveland, in Buffalo, and in Erie. Everywhere it was the smooth, reassuring Reagan, well prepared, controlled, easygoing. It was Reagan reaching out to the blue-collar, traditionally Democratic voter. It was Reagan, assured of votes from the Republicans and conservatives, trying to broaden his appeal.

The Chicago economic speech, delivered in September, was designed to convince his audience there and on television via the evening news that his version of supply-side economics would cure the conflicting trends of recession and inflation in the American economy. As usual, Reagan delivered the speech well. The act was perfectly played. As they left the hall, one of his audience turned to a friend and remarked: "He didn't even look at his notes. And that was a long speech to memorize." He apparently didn't know that the pair of transparent glass stands to the left and right of Reagan's podium were teleprompters.

In Milwaukee Reagan appeared out of doors in the heart of a Polish neighborhood. A crowd of several hundred stood in the street to hear him and the inevitable accordion and banjo music. As he began, Reagan was confronted by a large sign proclaiming: UAW Supports Carter. It was the perfect provocation. "I'm the first union president to stand on a platform and say I'm now a candidate for president of the United States," said Reagan, reminding his audience of his days as president of the Screen Actors Guild. The rest of his speech was the string of anecdotes and homilies he had given for years. "It is time to get *gummint* off our backs and get back to business," Reagan said. He brought up his misuse of the word *depression* again, and said that the average unemployment level in the United States was eight percent. "That's like a man who drowns in a river whose average depth is three feet," he quipped.

Partway through his little talk, an elderly person fell uncon-
scious just below the platform from which Reagan spoke. The
press, standing on a flatbed truck at the rear of the crowd, quickly
joked that the victim had suffered a case of terminal boredom.
Reagan stopped speaking as a group of paramedics from a nearby
firehouse rushed to the scene. "Now that's the kind of *gummint*
service that we need and which belongs," Reagan observed. He
paused again and then said: "Let's say a little prayer that this will
be a minor problem." The crowd fell silent with him for a moment.

As he began again, a woman in the crowd began shouting,
"What about ERA? What about ERA?" Reagan ignored her, but
on the third repetition a burly man with a creased face turned on
the woman and shouted, "Be quiet, woman." She obeyed. In that
neighborhood, at least, the old order seemed to prevail.

Cute little girls in Polish costumes then trooped to the stage to
hand Reagan roses, a scene he had played a thousand, ten thousand times before. He selected the prettiest little blonde and swept
her up in his arms. "You know what this election is really about?"
he asked as he had so many times before. "It's so little children
like this one can grow up enjoying the freedoms we have lost." As
the press scrambled back to its bus and Reagan was swept away
in his limousine, I looked down the streets that converged in the
square where Reagan had appeared. The porches were filled with
people. They had not stirred themselves to walk one hundred
yards to see the man who might be the next president of the United
States. Reagan was hardly lighting fires of political passion across
America. Who could in 1980? If they cared to, the folks on the
porches in Milwaukee could see Reagan on television. Why bother
with the crowds?

In Cleveland Reagan appeared at a black community health
clinic. The message was the same, except that he added his view
that welfare was a form of bondage "under the benevolent hand
of the social caseworker." A group of scouts in black and red
berets trooped past. Reagan repeated that his campaign was to
restore their freedoms.

A large public rally was set for noon in Cleveland's Center City,
in time to make the evening network news. The candidate emerged
from his hotel within a phalanx of Secret Service. He shook hands
along a path cleared for his passage. A Secret Service agent with

his hand on Reagan's shoulder followed along with him, holding a slim, bulletproof briefcase in front of Reagan's stomach to protect him from a point-blank shot. As Reagan took his place on the stage, Nancy joined him. It was a perfect fall day, crisp and bright. Throughout the crowd of a thousand or so were signs proclaiming Croatians for Reagan; Serbians for Reagan; Bulgarians for Reagan. He had reached for the captive nations vote.

Again it was the same. Homily followed homily. "Family, neighborhood, work, peace, and freedom, that's what this campaign is all about," he said. Next, a little slap at the Carter record on energy, on the economy. Economic recovery would be when Carter loses his job. A little slap at Carter's unctiousness: "Ralph Waldo Emerson wrote that 'the louder he talked of his honor, the faster we counted our spoons.' " And then a quote from John F. Kennedy: " 'We, in this country, in this generation, by destiny rather than by choice, are the watchmen on the walls of world freedom.' Yes we are, and let's meet our destiny."

Reagan did it as if by rote. He played the chords: moderation, resentment of government, unhappiness at the economic situation, disappointment at Carter, experience in California. Over and over again. The point was to remain standing as the opponents fell away. In his own party they had dropped quickly: Crane, Baker, Connally, Dole, Anderson, and finally Bush. In the autumn Anderson was falling fast. Reagan simply had to wait for Carter to crash, and to provide a little shove if necessary.

In a year of presidential politicking, a legion of candidates had come and gone. Millions of dollars had been raised and spent. But nothing much had really changed. Carter's greatest political strength was that he was not Reagan. And Reagan's advantage was that he wasn't Carter.

A young and unemployed industrial safety inspector in Butler, Pennsylvania, had this to say about the choices in mid-October:

"What turned me off Carter was his saying that he wished the hostages a 'safe and speedy' return. If they came home tomorrow, it wouldn't be 'speedy.' We're talking big and not doing anything abroad. We're losing credibility around the world. We're becoming a joke. And that just typifies Carter's ineffectiveness. The only reason people will vote for Carter is that they know what they're in for. They can predict what he'll do. I think I'll vote for Reagan, although it's still not clear. For a while I backed Anderson, but you can't back somebody you know is going to lose. I can't go for a loser, and Carter's been a loser all around, even though I don't agree with Reagan on everything and I don't know where he comes up with his facts. But I think he'll act with more strength. He's not as namby-pamby as Carter. I worry though that he engages his mouth before his brain is in gear. I worry about that in a delicate foreign situation. What I'd really like is to have, along with the lines for the candidates, a 'no preference' line on the ballot. We have to pick somebody because we need a president. This is sad. We really need a *leader* right now."

14

The November Surprise

In mid-October Vincent Breglio, an assistant to Reagan's pollster Richard Wirthlin, was in Texas, sitting in a meeting with the campaign's state managers. He was telling them happily that according to their polls Reagan was comfortably ahead in their state and, indeed, had moved to about a six-point lead over Carter nationwide. In the middle of the meeting, word came that *The New York Times*-CBS poll had just found quite a different result. According to that poll, Breglio was told, the Carter-Reagan race was dead even. Every other major public poll was reporting the same result: a race that was even. Even the private polling that Pat Caddell was doing for the Carter campaign showed Reagan and Carter nearly tied. Anecdotal evidence collected by politicians and reporters around the country, however, showed that on a state-by-state basis, Reagan seemed to have the upper hand in probable electoral votes. Nonetheless, the polling seemed to dictate that with two months to go in the race for the presidency, the race was too close to call.

The conflict between Wirthlin's private polls and the public polling set off alarms inside the Reagan organization. Although Wirthlin's numbers were respected and his analysis of the dynamics of the election had been accurate all along, the Reagan team began a careful re-examination of its polling techniques and data to make sure they had not committed some methodological error that was skewing their results toward their candidates. No errors were found, but Wirthlin's numbers still didn't jibe with what every other important poll was finding. Nor did the Reagan staff traveling with the candidate share Wirthlin's optimism. A certain nervousness, if not quite a panic, began to pervade the Reagan camp. The concern was that the critical last two weeks of the campaign needed to be plotted carefully if a victory was to be secured. Most important of the final strategic decisions was whether or not to join Jimmy Carter in a televised debate, a confrontation that Reagan had long ago agreed to but which had been avoided because of Carter's refusal to appear with John Anderson. Carter had said repeatedly that he would debate Reagan alone, but the presence of Anderson had given him an excuse to duck the confrontation.

To both camps a debate looked like one great roll of the political dice, a gamble that could either successfully crown two years of campaigning or could finally destroy a candidacy. A debate was not something either side was eager to join. But it was something that, under the circumstances, neither could avoid. As reassuring as Wirthlin's figures were, to duck the debate would risk for Reagan the same fallout he had suffered earlier in the year when he avoided the Iowa Republican debates. Besides, if Wirthlin's figures were too optimistic, to miss the debate might mean missing a chance at being president. The dilemma for Carter was similar. The once prevalent notion that the fact-crammed President would destroy the fuzzy-facted Reagan in a debate had vanished from the Carter camp in the face of Reagan's success in debates against his Republican opponents. The debates were not really debates in the classic sense, but rather chances to judge two men, their demeanors, and their characters through the television tube. Carter had a year-long history of avoiding debates. He had escaped from a promised meeting with Kennedy, pleading the pressing business of the Iran hostage problem. He had ducked Reagan and Anderson in Baltimore, claiming Anderson was just another Republican. The risks of canceling an appearance with Reagan, after having said he wanted to meet Reagan one-on-one, were too high. Carter, more than Reagan, also seemed more in need of an equalizing event, a performance on national television that would lift his candidacy. In the end, neither campaign could chance missing the debate. With Anderson now eliminated by the League of Women Voters' arbitrary fifteen percent poll figure (he had plunged toward single digits), the great confrontation of the 1980 campaign was set for October 28 in Cleveland.

The preparations for the confrontation took both men days. They were quizzed and briefed and requizzed by aides. They were told precisely what points they were to make, never mind the questions. Reagan's team set up a complete stage at his rented house outside Washington, D.C., where he had moved to make the fall campaign easier. There, with future budget director David Stockman, whose command of facts was not unlike the President's, playing the role of Jimmy Carter, Reagan played through a full dress rehearsal for the debate. On both sides the point was the same as it had been from the beginning of the campaign: Keep the spotlight on the opponent's weaknesses in order to avoid attention to your own. For Carter that meant an effort to highlight the awesome responsibilities of peace and war and his own success in having avoided armed conflict. For Reagan the point was to pound away on the economy and Carter's dismal record. For each a defense also had to be mounted against those weaknesses.

When the evening of the debate finally came, both Carter and Reagan were tense and nervous. But Reagan had the presence of mind to stride easily across the stage to shake Jimmy Carter's hand. Carter had been looking elsewhere. When he turned and saw Reagan it was as if a specter had appeared before him. He recovered quickly from his shock and the debate began. Watching the debate on television, there seemed little to choose between these two men. The President of the United States was somber and controlled, uncomfortable and self-conscious. Reagan, a bit looser and more comfortable, seemed less well prepared, armed with fewer facts, and less confident about his information. Both played out the roles they had been given by their advisers well enough, making the requisite points over and over:

CARTER. I think habitually Governor Reagan has advocated the injection of military forces into troubled areas when I and my predecessors, both Democrats and Republicans, have advocated resolving those troubles . . . peacefully, diplomatically, and through negotiation.

REAGAN. I have seen four wars in my lifetime. I'm a father of sons, I have a grandson. I don't ever want to see another generation of Americans bleed their lives into sandy beachheads in the Pacific or rice paddies and jungles in Asia, or the muddy, bloody battlefields of Europe.

CARTER. Every president who has served in the Oval Office since Harry Truman has been dedicated to the proposition of controlling nuclear weapons. . . . There is a disturbing pattern in the attitude of Governor Reagan. He has never supported any of those arms-control agreements.

REAGAN. If I have been critical of some of the previous agreements it's because we've been out-negotiated for quite a long time.

REAGAN. When Mr. Carter became President inflation was 4.8 percent. . . . It is now running at 12.7 percent. . . . There are eight million men and women out of work in America today and two million of those who lost their jobs in just the last few months.

CARTER. Governor Reagan's proposal—the Reagan-Kemp-Roth proposal—is one of the most highly inflationary ideas that ever has been presented to the American public. He would actually have to cut government spending by 130 billion dollars in order to balance the budget under this ridiculous proposal.

REAGAN. I think it's evident in most of the answers that Mr. Carter's given tonight that he seeks solutions to anything as another opportunity for a federal government program. I happen to believe that the federal government has usurped powers and autonomy and authority that belongs back at the state and local levels. . . .

CARTER. This is a contest between a Democrat from the mainstream of my party as exemplified by the actions that I've taken in the Oval Office in the last four years, as contrasted with Governor Reagan, who, in most cases, does typify his party, but in some

243

cases there is a radical departure by him from the heritage of Eisenhower and others . . .

They had said it all before and would repeat it as many times as possible in the few days after the debate and before the election. But underneath the words an important point had been made to the 100 million Americans who watched the debate (twenty million more, incidentally, than would eventually vote in the election). The point was that the challenger, Ronald Reagan, had stood his ground with the President of the United States. He had been less than impressive, but he had not been alarming. He seemed reasonable enough, articulate enough, calm enough to defy the image of irresponsibility Carter had tried to paint. He addressed Carter politely, but not deferentially. At one point, when he felt Carter had misrepresented his position on national health insurance, Reagan chided him like a slightly exasperated uncle. "There you go again," said Reagan, shaking his head. Carter, on the other hand, had cloyingly mentioned that his daughter, Amy, had told him control of nuclear arms was the most important election issue, a ploy both to highlight Reagan's opposition to SALT and to point up Carter's younger years.

As the candidates summed up their positions at the debate's end, Carter rambled through a pledge of social justice, peace, and moderation. He urged voters to consider the "stark differences that exist" between him and Reagan. But Reagan brought the entire election campaign back to its most fundamental and basic point. He cut away the gauze of words and claims, of promises and advertisements that had covered the presidential election campaign for more than a year.

"Next Tuesday is Election Day. Next Tuesday all of you will go to the polls. You'll stand there in the polling place and make a decision. I think when you make that decision it might be well if you would ask yourself: Are you better off than you were four years ago? Is it easier for you to go and buy things in the stores than it was four years ago? Is there more or less unemployment in the country than there was four years ago? Is America as respected throughout the world as it was? Do you feel that our security is as safe? That we're as strong as we were four years ago?" Reagan concluded.

It was a devastating point. It brought the election back to where it had begun a year before, with a president with a record that was simply not satisfactory, with a country in economic trouble, with a country seemingly threatened and pushed around abroad.

After the debate Wirthlin's polls showed a steady divergence between Reagan and Carter, with Carter slowly falling and Reagan slowly rising. The debate had settled the question. The country had been looking for more than a year for a replacement for Jimmy Carter. Reagan had become the alternative. In the debate he proved that he was an acceptable alternative. In Wirthlin's view the election was just about settled. Pat Caddell saw something different in his daily poll results. He still saw a rather even match, with Carter rising and falling daily, but not losing significant ground. By Saturday Caddell still saw an even contest on a nationwide basis. Public pollsters, however, were now beginning to find what Wirthlin saw for some time: a growing spread in Reagan's favor. The weekend before the election, no matter whose polls one believes, Jimmy Carter was in deep trouble.

There remained for him, however, one hope. For a year the hostages had been held in Iran. The hostage taking had prompted a national rallying around Carter, enough in the early months of the crisis to finish Ted Kennedy. But the continuation of their captivity, and the sad frustration of the desert raid, had steadily eroded Carter's popularity. In the last days of the 1980 campaign there appeared to be some hopeful signs that the government in Iran was ready to make some arrangement for the release of the hostages. Negotiations had been going on for weeks. And early Sunday morning, two days before Election Day, the word came from Tehran that a set of conditions had been announced for the hostages' freedom. Should they miraculously be freed before the voting, Carter and his aides believed, there might just be enough lift to save the Carter presidency.

The Reaganites had feared just such a development ever since the summer. They did not believe Carter was cynical enough to delay the hostage release until the last possible moment, but they did not dismiss the possibility that a deal could be made in time to influence the election. "The October Surprise" the Reagan people called it, and from the beginning of the fall until Election Day not an opportunity was missed to remind reporters and the public that such an event might damage their chances. It was a clever tactic indeed. Although the October Surprise was always mentioned as one of their chief concerns, the very phrase and its repetition planted the idea that Carter might manipulate the crisis to his own advantage. The effect was thus to feed public cynicism and, the Reagan forces hoped, to negate any credit Carter might get from the hostage release.

In the predawn hours of November 2, Carter was asleep in a hotel room in Chicago when he was awakened to be told the announcement of Iran's new conditions for the hostages' release. He immediately flew back to Washington to meet with his national security team. That evening he asked for network television time and carefully warned the nation not to get its hopes up. The conditions announced by Tehran, while showing movement and providing a bit of encouragement, still required further negotiation. Carter did not want to be accused, as he had been the April morning of the Wisconsin primary, of feeding public expectations in order to gain votes. Still, he hoped the slightly better news would help.

On Sunday Pat Caddell's polls registered a remarkable change that dashed whatever faint hope still existed inside the Carter White House. He found a sudden five-point decline in Carter's poll standings. On Monday another five points fell out of the President's column. By Monday night Caddell, Jordan, and Strauss knew the end of Jimmy Carter's reign was about to come. They phoned Powell, who was with Carter in the Pacific Northwest where the President was making one last desperate plea for votes. The presidential entourage left Seattle for an overnight flight back to Plains, Georgia, where Jimmy was to meet Rosalynn and then vote, before heading back to the White House to await the results. On the flight Powell told Carter Caddell's bad news as the president finished off a double martini. In Plains Carter broke the news to Rosalynn, who switched on her icy self-control to get her through the morning.

Tuesday morning the First Couple voted. Carter then addressed the home folks in Plains. He talked aimlessly for ten minutes about his record as president. "Many people from Plains, from Americus, from Richland, from around this area, have gone all over the nation to speak for me, to shake hands with people in other states to tell them that you have confidence in me and that I would not disappoint them if I became president," he said at the end, his face pale and quivering. "I've tried to honor your commitment to those other people. In the process I've tried . . ." His voice cracked. Tears welled up in his eyes. He had spent his life escaping the confines of this dusty, sweaty, charmless little town in south Georgia. And on his way up and out he had portrayed himself as a man of that town, a man of its people, a man who shared their smalltown concerns. At the convention I had asked Rosalynn Carter whether she had in any way disliked the burdens of public office and whether any part of her longed for the privacy and comfort of being home in Plains. Typically, she answered the question by repeating what Jimmy felt. A few weeks before the end of his term as governor of Georgia, she said, they were home in Plains for a long weekend. The first day they payed the required visits to Jimmy's mother, Lillian, to her mother, and to other relatives. That night she was fixing dinner in the kitchen of their modest ranch-style house. Jimmy was watching television. "This is nice," she remembered him saying to her, "but what will we do the second day I'm out of office?"

Election Day in Plains, Jimmy and Rosalynn Carter saw something vanish from their lives, something they both needed badly to fill up their lives, to prop up their self-esteem, to set them apart from the run of south Georgia life they both proudly hailed as their roots and their origins, but from which they had both run with all their might—to the navy, to the state legislature, to the governor's mansion, and to Washington. Throughout his presidency, there had been a terrible self-consciousness about Jimmy Carter's performance. He was never free to swing away, to take a chance, to risk his political capital to gain a victory. He was always so careful and earnest. He worked hard, first at looking casual, a man of the people. Later in his presidency he worked hard at looking "presidential." His cardigan sweaters gave way to white shirts with collar pins. Without explanation, he suddenly moved the part in his hair from the right side to the left. One of the most powerful men in the White House through those four years later compared him to Nixon and to Lyndon Johnson. These were men, this administration official said to me after the election, who needed the presidency to think of themselves as whole men. Their ambition and lust for power was not an act of sacrifice and generosity to serve the people. Rather it was an act of personal need.

Speaking to his neighbors, many of whom would privately tell reporters that they never much liked the priggish Jimmy Carter, the President of the United States regained his composure that Election Day. He hid what he knew about his own fate. Rosalynn stood by, her face looking as if there had been a death in the family. "Don't forget to vote everybody," he said and was gone. On the flight in Air Force One back to Washington, they sat together in the plane and cried.

Ronald Reagan bounced through his last campaign day, riding the wave of optimism being supplied by Wirthlin's final pollings. In San Diego Reagan was interrupted by hecklers screaming, "ERA, ERA." Years of self-control gave way as he turned on them and said without anger but with great relish, "Aw, shut up." The crowd roared its approval. At the end of the rally he and Nancy led the crowd in singing "God Bless America." For Reagan the campaign ended happily, like his movies. His relentless corniness was cloying and often seemed, because of its play to the simpler emotions of his crowds, contrived. But it was not contrived in the least. Like his moment of prayer at the convention, it was something he felt. That he seemed a throwback in an age of skepticism was, in the end, his strength. He knew himself and was comfortable with himself. And as the confusing decades of the 1960s and the 1970s ended, that in itself was mildly reassuring.

It was less than a massive vote cast on November 4. Hardly more than half the electorate bothered to turn out, even less than in 1976, and less in percentage terms than in any presidential election since 1948. But by early in the afternoon the result was clear. The network news organizations, fielding huge staffs and spending millions to interview voters as they emerged from the polling booths, knew quickly that Reagan had won. By late afternoon reporters from the newspapers and magazines, hearing of those exit polling results, knew too. Across the nation the news media cranked up to report a landslide for Ronald Reagan long before any polls had closed anywhere in the United States. For a couple of hours the networks held themselves in check, waiting for confirmation of the exit polling by real vote counts. At 8:15 P.M. Eastern Standard Time, NBC could wait no longer and announced that Reagan would win—big. Jimmy Carter could wait no longer either and he phoned Reagan in California with his concession, catching the President-elect coming out of the shower draped in a towel. At 10:00 P.M. Carter appeared at a rally of his supporters in Washington and publicly conceded defeat, ignoring the fact that on the West Coast the polls still hadn't closed and that his concession might easily prevent late voters from bothering at all, thus damaging others on his party's ticket. He had never cared much for his party apparatus anyway.

Eighty-three million Americans voted on November 4. Reagan won 43.2 million votes, Carter 34.9 million, and John Anderson only 5.5 million. Reagan's plurality was 8.3 million votes, ten percent of the total. And that margin was spread across the country. Carter won Georgia and carried Vice-President Mondale's native Minnesota. West Virginia, Rhode Island, and Hawaii went for Carter, as did the District of Columbia. Carter won 49 electoral votes. Reagan won 489. What had for months looked like a close election turned into the most stunning defeat for an incumbent president since Franklin Roosevelt had tossed Depression president Herbert Hoover out of office in 1932, to begin his four-term reign and to set the direction for America for nearly the next half century.

At the time the Reagan landslide was a shock to the political industry. Elections that had been close so long had, in the past, stayed close until the end. Kennedy's victory over Nixon in 1960, Nixon's victory over Humphrey in 1968, Carter's victory over Ford in 1976. Rarely since accurate measurement of voter preference became possible had an election broken loose so quickly and suddenly in its last days.

But looking back now, what was more amazing than the size of Reagan's win was the length of time, beginning in the fall of 1979, that Jimmy Carter had been able to hold political disaster at bay. Ronald Reagan's victory was first and foremost a result of the failure of his opponents, principally James Earl Carter. When voters were asked as they left the polls why they had voted for Reagan, more (forty percent) told the questioners that it was "time for a change" than cited any positive virtue of Reagan himself. Carter, to be sure, had been caught in a historical crack. He had become president in reaction to the low moral standing to which the presidency had fallen under Nixon and, before him, under the torment of Vietnam. He was, in a sense, an aberration, a reaction to a very specific problem with the institution and the men who had occupied the highest office in the land. To take advantage of that moment in history, Carter needed to be an outsider, above the politics and clubiness of Washington. He had to be, and was, a loner, aloof from the men and the processes he needed to join in order to govern in his time. He had captured the nomination of his party, an essentially liberal party, and had tried to move that institution toward a more conservative philosophy. Instead, he lost the party's loyalty and the respect of the nation. But the failure of the Carter presidency did not have to be. It was not destined by history. A different man could have governed successfully. With more luck in foreign affairs and more skill in Washington, a Democrat could have bridged the yawning gap between the party's history of New Deal liberalism and the realities of the 1980s. Carter and his men were not up to that job.

Reagan too came to office on the failures of his Republican opponents: Bush's lack of substance and authority, Connally's lack of humility and truthfulness, Baker's lack of strategic skill and a legislative personality that made one wonder just what he believed, and the obscurity and manifest ill-suitedness of the rest of the Republican field. It is too much to say of any presidential candidate in these times that his genius and nearly extrasensory perception of the mood of America produced his victory. Too many other forces have to conspire, and important among them is the weakness and bad luck of the others in the field.

This is not to say, however, that Ronald Reagan and his organization do not deserve credit. He and they are not simply the beneficiaries of monumental good luck, although to deny the role of good fortune would require a rationalist's outlook of such an exaggerated nature as to suggest dementia. Reagan, by and large, conducted himself with dignity and grace. Again, his inner comfort with who he is and what he does was reassuring and helped him past his mistakes of judgment and of pronouncement that might have finished a less appealing man. His campaign staff was good, but no campaign staff can make much more of their candidate's chances than already exists by force of history and circumstance. What they can do is recognize the forces at work and avoid squandering their opportunity. This they did well. Perhaps the most intelligent man in working politics, John Sears, was fired by Reagan because there was staff conflict and because Reagan was more loyal to his older, if less impressive, friends. But it didn't hurt Reagan. Man for man, George Bush had a better staff than Reagan. Carter's political crew was as good as Reagan's. Reagan's was thus not a victory of political mechanics. It was a victory of a man who survived the incredible ordeal of an American presidential campaign and was still around, his humor and purpose still intact, when the electorate decided to replace Jimmy Carter. Those closest to Reagan—Mike Deaver, Edwin Meese, Lyn Nofziger, Richard Wirthlin—had faith in him and in his appeal to voters. They understood his political virtues better than anyone. They did not try to alter what he was. They were content to take their chances with their candidate. And that was enough.

Ronald Reagan came to the presidential campaign unburdened by the weight of incumbency and without the advantage of experience in Washington. He could not be blamed for what was wrong in America. In a time of unhappiness that was an enormous asset. He came to his candidacy unburdened by the hard experiences of governing a fractious nation. He came unscarred by the disillusioning experiences in the world abroad. There was little in his political life to modify his sunny view of the possibilities for the success of his ideas. He was not saddled with an intellectual complexity and experience that would have suggested the possible flaws of his rather radical economic program of spending cuts and tax reductions, which, by the past standards of economic performance and theory, should not work to produce the prosperity and lowered inflation he promised. Yet his willingness to adopt this notion separated him from the history of his party's conventional economics and gave his candidacy the allure of trying something new. With voters willing to experiment as a way of changing an unsatisfactory economic situation, the Reagan program seemed to offer hope of at least being different from the muddled temporizing of Carter. Reagan was unburdened too with the sophistication of the academy, of the intellectual gamesmen in Washington and in the East, unburdened by the cynicism of an age and almost a whole nation. By some bizarre accident of his own insularity, Reagan had lived through the same national traumas as had his compatriots, yet he could lead them in prayer or in patriotic song without self-conciousness. In an age of confusion he seemed sure, sure that what was old and good in the spirit of America was still appropriate and possible. Those in power, those with the hard experiences of failure in Washington, both envied and resented the innocence that gave him political strength. "Reagan's as simple as I used to be," Walter Mondale said to me bitterly and wistfully one afternoon during the campaign.

The failures of his opponents and his own virtues did not alone elect Ronald Reagan. Another considerable force was at work as well. Since 1968, and probably before, the struggle for a readjustment of the American political concensus had been going on. Goldwater was its harbinger. Nixon, in his first term, worked around its edges. But by 1980 it had long since been time for the federal government to readjust its direction. The New Deal had accomplished its main goals. It had provided a decent economic security for the nation. It had brought the most rapacious forces of private enterprise under control, evening the scale between capital and labor. The extensions of the New Deal had done their work too. Civil rights was an established and practiced (although imperfect) fact. The legal barriers for blacks had been struck and what remained was the more deeply rooted economic inequalities that would have to work their way out of the system. Beyond that, the more questionable attempts at social engineering, at curing all the ills of society, had been tried and had been found to be often ineffective and outrageously expensive. The smaller the group being helped, the less universal the affliction or inequity being cured, the more unsatisfying the result of the governmental action. Not that the problems weren't real or the motives good, but as the nation moved from extravagant economic growth to a relatively less prosperous time, the great unafflicted middle class, the tax payers and workers, came more to resent the money and attention being showered on the less fortunate. It was indeed time for a change. And Reagan had become the instrument of that change.

By electing Ronald Reagan the nation did not embrace all that he stood for. It did not share his views on prohibiting all abortions by constitutional amendment. It wanted government's role trimmed and adjusted, not destroyed. The national memory reached back to the time when government was needed to offset the overriding power of private economic institutions and it did not want to dismantle the federal Establishment. It did not share the nearly religious faith of some of the more extreme economic theorists in the beauty and purity of entrepreneurship. The country remained practical and sensible, much less ideological than Reagan himself and than those around the President. Yet the Reagan election was indisputably a watershed, perhaps of the dimensions of Roosevelt's revolution in American government.

In the first few months of his presidency, Reagan and the Republican-controlled Senate he had brought to Washington quickly dominated the vestiges of the Democratic party that nominally controlled the House of Representatives. Reagan's bold proposals to cut back federal spending and taxes by significant amounts sailed through the Congress. Democrats, frightened by Reagan's victory and the victory of large numbers of senators and representatives of his party, were in a state of collapse. They had no arguments of consequence to make against the reduction of the scale of the federal enterprise. They had no record of recent economic success with which to confront his radical plan of spending and tax reduction. Reagan had broken a half-century trend of the federal government's taking an ever larger share of the national wealth and taking an ever larger share of the responsibility for the life of the nation. Within a hundred days a new tone had been set in Washington. And it would not soon change. The great age of social engineering had ended in America. A government that under the Democrats—and even under the Republicans elected in phases throughout the fifty years since the coming of the New Deal—had been expansive and expanding, interventionist and even meddling, was set off on a new course. The country finally recognized that it could not have everything at once, especially in a time of slow economic growth. It finally understood that progress and prosperity may have to be gained more slowly than in the recent past. A becoming modesty, in the person of a modest man, had taken hold in Washington.

There has been and will be considerable debate about the meaning of the election of 1980 and its importance to the nation. Some argue that before this election can be judged a watershed in

American politics a permanent political realignment must take place. Democrats must shrink back from their dominance among the electorate. Republican control of the Congress must be cemented. Reagan or his heir must govern for eight years. I would argue, however, that those events are unnecessary to judge the political events of 1980. That the argument about the size and role of government has been won already is undeniable. It is not important which party carries that argument forward. Indeed, there is ample reason to believe that the new, younger Democrats who will assume national leadership of their party once the shock of 1980 recedes will do so with full understanding that Ronald Reagan and the election of 1980 have fundamentally changed the political premises in America. Promises of programs, spending, entitlements, and expansion of the federal role will not soon again elect a president. That era is past. The watershed event has already occurred.

Whether or not Reagan and the Republican party preside over the next eight or fifteen or fifty years of our national political life is less important than what directions those who do preside will follow. (In fact, Republicans and Democrats shared nearly equally time in the White House in the past era.) They will follow, in one way or another, the path Reagan and the Republicans have now set. Whether it is Reagan and the Republicans who reign through the era they have helped create is a matter of circumstance and chance and their own wisdom and sense of proportion in governing.

Of primary importance to future Republican success will be the performance of the economy. It is easy to forecast failure for the Reagan economic program. It is easy to see the circumstances in which his prescription leads only to more inflation. It is then possible to see a Democratic resurgence, not one powered by the ideas of old liberalism but rather one driven by new economic prescriptions aimed, in different and more sophisticated ways, at the same goals Reagan seeks, that is, the rebuilding of the American economic machine. It is also easy to see resentment and protest over the unfairness of cuts in federal spending as administered by Reagan. It is not hard to imagine a Democratic restoration powered not by promises of overall increases in the federal budget but by a more equitable approach to reduction and paring, and also by a sensible argument that not all short-term reductions amount to long-term savings. Cuts in mass transit, education, and job training, for example, are not cost-effective in that they only require more public spending later.

Ronald Reagan as president must live with and accommodate to some extent those on the far right of the Republican party who were his first and truest believers. In one important way, however, they threaten the very revolution he seeks to effect. The heart of Reagan's approach to government is to reduce its reach. Among his most ardent supporters, however, there is a burning desire to have the federal government reach back into the lives of Americans to control their behavior. The right wing understands and sympathizes with a small business man burdened by federal regulation and paperwork. But it ignores that complaint when it comes from an individual who does not want his own personal choices on difficult questions like abortion regulated by the federal government. The moralistic right wing that supported Reagan wants more regulation of the lives of Americans. It wants controls on difficult and personal decisions. It wants regulations and restrictions on what people read and what they see in movie theaters and on television. It wants the government to subsidize private, religious education through the tax system. It is willing to attack members of either party for deviations from what it believes is correct. The far right is authoritarian and intolerant. It still does not understand, despite the election of a man close to its policies, that successful American politics is more open, tolerant, and compromising than it will ever be. The New Right is about as popular in America as was the New Left a decade ago. The country does not like busybody moralists of either stripe, although there will always be substantial followings for these thought-policemen in times of turmoil and rapid social change. In his early days as president, Reagan held these forces at bay while he set about the important business of his presidency. He may not be able to hold them off forever. If he and his party cannot control their own zealots, they risk losing what they won in 1980.

15

Too Much
Democracy

It is not an accident that a movie actor has become the President of the United States. It was almost necessary. We have so altered the way we choose our presidents that political theater has overwhelmed the more traditional aspects of our system of leadership selection. Legislation written, favors done, political debts accumulated, friends made in party and government circles, faithful service and devotion to the political party, these were all once the keys to advancement up the ladder of American politics. They are no more.

Now the key is television. That has been said so often by so many students of American politics that it has become a tiresome observation. But we still have not fully comprehended what that change entails. Most obviously, it means that the presidency is quite attainable from almost any station of national life rather than through careful progression and service in elective office. It means that one day soon, a television news commentator, a sports hero, or a mere celebrity, famous for heaven-knows-what exploit, will be president of a rich and powerful nation of more than 200 million people. That result may not be catastrophic. It may not bring results worse than those wrought by the men of often surpassing mediocrity who were thrust into the highest office in the land by the old system of political ascension. I, however, am inclined to worry about such an outcome. My bias is toward experience, toward practice, toward an apprenticeship in politics and government as a necessary precondition for a term in the White House.

It is not surprising that in an era of legitimate discontent with the government in Washington, those candidates from outside Washington, those with the least experience and thus the least taint of failure, have succeeded in our presidential system. This may be only a temporary and needed reaction to the failure of government to perform adequately. On the other hand, it may now be a permanent characteristic of our political system. It may be that with access to money and to television, only the inexperienced, only those free of the weight of decision and responsibility, can succeed to the presidency. With television, those who can blame the others in power for whatever failures the nation has experienced have a decided advantage. With television being the main vehicle of leadership, our presidency is under such close and constant scrutiny that no incumbent can escape a term in office or a life in the Congress without seeming somehow to have failed. With computers tracking individual votes on every issue, with direct mail ready to tell computer-selected audiences that candidate X or Y has voted against *your* interest on this bill or that, can anyone long survive in public life without offending an activist, dedicated single-issue group, which will then "target" that official for defeat?

There is nothing clean, simple, or elegant about the process by which we select our presidents. The arrangement is disorderly, complicated, arcane, and in some ways even unseemly. If it were at least a system handed down from generation to generation, embedded in the Constitution, used and worn but tried and familiar, the presidential selection system might have the attraction of the baroque: too ornate, but quaint and peculiarly interesting, a sort of period piece worthy of historic preservation and respect. In fact, the presidential selection system is all modern and plastic, manufactured hurriedly and without much sense of history. It is not the product of craftsmen and patient artists of statecraft. Rather, it was thrown together by "reformers" caught up in the frenzy of the participatory democracy and social change in the late 1960s. The present system in both political parties is another of the uncounted legacies of popular revulsion against an unpopular war in Southeast Asia, a war prosecuted through a deceit so massive that it has distorted our politics for a decade. Quite naturally, our politics sought to correct itself. If the leadership of the nation could not be trusted, then its people would have to be. Systematically and deliberately, leaders were cut out of the presidential selection system. The popular will would work not just in the general election, where a direct vote for president would be cast, but also in the primaries, where in more than sixty percent of the states, direct, popular votes would decide the makeup of national convention delegations and thus the choice of the political party's presidential nominee. Leaders of the party, of the Congress, of the state legislatures, and in the state houses would not be permitted to influence the choice of the nominee. The people would decide. This, it was hoped, would produce presidents "responsive" to the national will. It has.

So responsive, in fact, that the American president is now a revolving door. Since 1960 no president has served two full terms in office. Dwight Eisenhower was the last to do so. Other circumstances conspired to produce this phenomenon, but those circumstances were not unrelated to the central problem. Jack Kennedy was shot because he was the predominant media personality of his time. His killer wanted the fame that went with killing someone famous—and the pattern has been sickeningly repetitious since. Nixon was ousted from office in large measure because he lied on television to the entire American people. Reagan is the sixth president within twenty years. The average term of office since 1960 has been 3.5 years. Although it could be that Reagan, the movie actor-president, is uniquely equipped to survive or, indeed, to thrive under this system that personalizes every political act and every political occurrence, our recent political history suggests that it will be difficult.

Since 1972 our presidential selection system has lurched toward an ever more "open" system of direct, rather than representative, democracy. The undiluted will of the people is the force that produces presidents. It is not blasphemous to note that the political attention span of the American public, taken as a whole, is not long or particularly deep; it is healthy that the country wants basically to go about its own business. In elections, however, it has a tendency to seize upon single notions, to react to perceived failure, and then to try, understandably, to compensate. Carter came to power as the public tried to correct the illegalities and immoralities of Nixon. Reagan came to power as the public tried to compensate for Carter's directionlessness and his paralyzing inability to rise above contradictory advice and information. The first test of the new "open" system was used by the Democrats in 1972. The party chose George McGovern, a maverick senator with deep convictions about the stupidity of the war in Vietnam. He would never have been the choice of his party's elders. They knew how little he knew and understood about the broad range of public policy questions. But in 1972 the so-called Democratic party, that is, registered Democrats who chose to vote in the presidential primaries, were trying to compensate for the last failure—the war in Vietnam. McGovern was the logical vehicle for that correction; he had stood clearly in opposition to that conflict.

The current presidential selection system has become a swinging pendulum of overcorrection. There is no stability to it. By its nature it will produce selections who are seen (sometimes inaccurately) as the antithesis to the most recent political failure. We may be destined, if the existing presidential selection system is not changed, to zigzag along, finding not real leaders but only antidotes to our most recent ailments. The system needs to regain its balance. It needs to be less democratic.

Until very recently the system of American politics and government has been a mix of direct and representative democracy. At the very beginning it relied very little upon direct elections and very heavily upon representative institutions to choose national leaders. Only the members of the House of Representatives were elected directly; the Senate and the President were picked by legislators and electors. The political parties, not even mentioned in the Constitution, had to be invented to bring some institutional order to national politics. Before the 1972 presidential selection reforms it was not the primaries that determined who the presidential nominees would be; it was the party leaders and elected officials from the parties who made that choice. These people were called bosses. They were just that, and they often abused their power. They often made poor selections. They often profited unconscionably from their nearly invisible power. There is no arguing the point that a democracy cannot be operated undemocratically. The direction of reform in 1972 was surely necessary, but it went too far, ignoring some of the unappreciated strengths of the old system.

In a large and complex society, direct democracy can only be the most irrational of processes, especially when the means of gathering information about candidates and issues is controlled by private sector institutions (the press), the first concern of which is profitability and its own continued success in the marketplace, and only secondarily the quality of national leadership. The low arts of deal making, favor trading, and patronage once practiced by bosses have been replaced by the low arts of advertising manipulation, ninety-second news spots on television, and political reporting in print that more closely resembles sports writing than it does serious political analysis. The old order had the virtue of putting the burden of choosing the presidential nominees on a group of people who had an institutional interest in the outcome. Their interest was in winning, holding power, and winning again. By reducing the role of these people gathered together in the form of political parties, the nomination process is now vulnerable to single-issue fanatics, ideologues of the left and right, and thus beyond the influence of the very people who should best know the candidates—those who have worked with them over years in public life. Control instead is left with voters who must rely on information provided by the media.

Under the present nominating process, just what is it about the candidates that is tested and weighed? Endurance, certainly. But an endurance of the wrong kind. The pursuit of the presidency is now a four-year endeavor that clearly favors those without gainful employment of any kind, save after-dinner speaking or honorific law practices. Years of successful and distinguished service in public life was once a clear advantage in seeking the presidency. Now such a record has become a burden. The more that is known about a candidate's positions, the more vulnerable he is. Carter's rise from obscurity was, for example, made easier because few outside his home state knew much about him. He was able to fashion a new persona, suitable to the political moment. Moreover, his record as a one-term governor of Georgia was ambiguous. Reagan too was helped by having been out of office for six years before his candidacy began; the details of his record were half forgotten. Time had washed away many of the sharp edges of his past rhetoric, allowing him to change important parts of his political persona to make him suitable for election. George Bush did rather well in the nominating process, partly because his public life had been confined mostly to low-profile appointed jobs. He had no voting record to attack. What is tested, then, is the extent of a candidate's desire for the presidency. Under the present system, the man must seek the job. It cannot find him.

Most of the qualities that would make a good president—experience, judgment under pressure, dedication, the ability to build and direct political concensus, knowledge of the complicated machinery of government and of the nuances and subtleties of foreign affairs, familiarity with world leaders—none of these have much place in our selection process.

Rather, our politics is the politics of celebrity, of novelty and entertainment, instead of experience and intellect. That is lamentable, but also understandable. Since the political parties are being steadily destroyed, their role in selecting candidates has been thrown to the press and to television, who purvey information and impressions about the candidates to the public voting in primaries.

The press is not, of course, a public institution. It is a private one that performs vital public functions. The rising chorus of criticism of the way the press performs its public functions, especially during presidential elections, is not unfounded. There is much more that the press could do to better inform the public about political choices and issues. At some indefinite point, however, more and better political coverage would impinge on the media's other function, entertainment, and thus eventually on its profitability. If anything, the press today behaves more responsibly, covers politics more fairly and throughly than ever before in the nation's history. But the press cannot be expected to carry alone the burden of screening candidates. What makes the performance of the press in politics now more critical to the outcome is the decline of any other institution upon which voters can rely when making their own choice. Now, rather than a record of long and distinguished public service, a candidate needs and seeks "name recognition." He needs to be famous, to be something of a celebrity. And it is often easier and more rewarding to seek celebrity than to earn recognition through hard work.

Political celebrity is easily gained in the television age. The increasingly common device is simply to run for office over and over again, to win and then quickly move on to higher office. This tactic has now spread even to the presidential level, as evidenced by the inane candidacy of Senator Pressler, the eight-month veteran of the U.S. Senate. Outrageous behavior and sheer brashness works too. Jerry Brown always verged on the bizarre, but his very unorthodoxy gave him the requisite celebrity to at least start out on the presidential campaign trail.

The necessity for celebrity naturally militates against thoughtful, thorough, often moderate and unentertaining politicians who are necessarily less attractive to television and personality journalism. As in show business, the entertaining, different, glitzy politician can rise rapidly to national fame. But, in the same manner as movie and television stars, the media and the public can quickly tire of their act and begin looking for something new and different and thus more entertaining. This quick-rise–quick-fall syndrome can happen even within the space of a single presidential election —witness the candidacy of John Anderson. This leads to the complaint that the press malevolently builds candidates up and then destroys them as a kind of sport. This certainly happens, but not because the press is vicious. It happens because there is so little of enduring substance and interest to the celebrity politician in the first place. In a fragmented and star-burst political system, a new face headed for a victory has to be paid attention. But when the decline sets in, the attention wanes more quickly than it grew. Consider how fresh and appropriate to the moment Jimmy Carter seemed in 1976 and how tired and worn he seemed by 1980. He had ridden to power on that freshness. When it vanished he, as a media politician, had little left to peddle.

The politics of celebrity also explains why the primary process is loaded so heavily toward the results in the early primary contests in Iowa and New Hampshire. The "big mo" is not just a preppy expression invented by George Bush, but a real and powerful force, because the press has such a singular role in the selection process. The press, like everyone else, is attracted to a winner and fascinated by the political horserace. Politics is a big-stakes human contest, and thus the press cannot resist writing about and televising the winners. Nor should we try to deny the sporting nature of politics. It is one of the underrated pleasures of democratic government. Perhaps the most unhappy consequence of the early call of the 1980 election by the networks was that it denied the American public a good night at the races, an important point of contact between the public and its electoral process.

In the presidential selection system, winning in the early primary states should not be everything. The answer isn't to eliminate the sporting quality of our politics, but to balance it. Nor is the point to eliminate the celebrity aspect to our politics, since it is a means by which the public does discover information about the candidates as human beings. But the public knows both too much and too little about its presidential candidates. It knows too much about the little personal characteristics of the candidates, but it doesn't know enough about their character and their ability to govern. No matter how many lines of print and hours of broadcast time the media devote, the public cannot know enough about the politician it finally elects. Only those who work with him, who observe him during his terms in office, can supply that information, albeit imperfectly.

It is time to begin the difficult job of rebuilding America's political parties to a status and power closer to what they were two decades ago. The parties will never again occupy the position they once did, and that is fine. The answer to the problems of a system tilted too far toward direct democracy isn't to revert to a completely closed system. It is one of balance. The system needs a rudder and a keel to keep it from wallowing about, reacting violently to every change of wind and tide. Only the party system offers a chance for that balance and direction. Strengthening the parties would not ensure better presidential nominees or better presidents; nothing would provide such a guarantee. But it might reduce the pendulum swing of our presidential politics. It might increase the importance of previous and distinguished public service for a presidential candidate. It might provide a buffer between the sitting president and the fits and whims of single-interest constituencies, which, in some cases, have a near blackmail power over certain policies, both in the executive and in the legislative branches.

The first step toward rebuilding the parties is to restore their role in the selection of their own presidential nominees. At the moment, the Democratic and Republican parties are little more than names under which candidates compete for the nomination. They are almost like the American and National leagues, convenient groupings designed to produce a World Series playoff. Rather than permitting the nominating conventions to be composed only of delegates picked in the primaries and pledged to one candidate or another, the parties should change their rules to preserve delegate roles for their own national, state, and local leaders and for the elected officials from their party at all levels. These party delegates would be appointed by the state party leadership and would be free to come to the convention supporting one or another candidate or to remain uncommitted. Delegate spots would become a reward for party and elected service. It would give party officials real power in their states and would also give the institutional party real power in the convention. Between a third and a half of the convention should be made up of party-selected delegates; the rest would still be chosen by voters in the primaries.

Such a change would immediately reduce the power of celebrity and media politics. The new and flashy candidate about which not much is known might win primaries but he would still have to impress his peers in order to obtain his party's nomination. The importance of the primaries themselves would be reduced, especially the exaggerated importance of the early contests, because until the actual voting at the convention there could still be an important power block with which to reckon. A mixed convention of this sort would not risk the kind of wrongheadedness the Democratic bosses displayed in 1968. They could not totally control the process. And with as many primaries as now exist to measure popularity, only a fool of a boss would stand in the way of a genuinely popular candidate who was able to dominate the primary elections. Still, under this mixed convention system, a candidate whose early primary season strength faded as the public came to know more about him would still have to face the judgment of his party's leadership at the convention. Such a convention would surely have nominated Ronald Reagan in 1980. It is not certain that Jimmy Carter could have managed renomination. A party fearful of defeat with a candidate like Carter, whose primary success was circumstantial as well as the result of his chief challenger's flaws, might more easily be replaced by the convention. In such a system other challengers could also enter the race at later stages, knowing that a substantial body of delegate strength would remain after the primary process was over.

Another benefit would also accrue from this system. Once the nominee was selected, party leaders and elected officials from that party would have more stake in helping to win the general election and, then, in helping that president govern. As it is now, everyone is on his own. The presidential campaign organizations don't have much to do with the national party organizations (although former GOP chairman Bill Brock did much to correct that in his party in the last few years). The congressional, senatorial, and local political candidates likewise try to stay fairly clear of the national ticket, unless it is overwhelmingly clear that the top man is heading for victory. There is thus a reduced tendency for them all to pull together once in office.

There are other, more mechanical problems with the presidential selection system as well, although they are not unrelated to the decline of the parties and the rise of the press as a chief political broker. The interminable length of the selection process is a necessity for an unknown candidate like Jimmy Carter was in 1976. It takes a lot of months and a lot of miles to get name recognition. A shorter process naturally favors the existing political Establishment. But it is time that the country should favor its established leadership and the expertise and stability it should produce. The selection process has always been long, but in the past it was more private. Jack Kennedy began his quest for the presidency by first seeking the vice-presidential nomination in 1956 and then working the back rooms of his party's power structure for the four years leading to 1960. Under the present system the public is afflicted with the preliminary bouts too soon. It leads to boredom, disinterest, and fatigue.

Although the number of primaries should not be reduced—indeed, every state should have a presidential primary run under uniform rules—they should be compressed to occur over fewer months. The primaries should be held in groups either within geographical divisions or within time zones. They should all be held within three or four months. The order in which they are run should be rotated every four years to avoid permanently favoring candidates from any one region. The Northeast, say, or the Eastern Time Zone, would be first in 1984, second in 1988, and so on. This would tend to ease the frenzy of travel, reduce costs, reduce fatigue, and permit candidates more rational planning of their personal, organizational, and advertising time and money. No regional primary would, of course, be decisive, since the results of the primaries as a whole would not finally determine the winner.

The wearisome length of the selection process has been exacerbated by the campaign finance law that permits only relatively small gifts by individuals ($1,000) or groups ($5,000) and allows for federal matching funds for only those gifts under $250. This rule has forced candidates into a pre-election plebiscite to raise money from a lot of little donors, demanding a lot of time and travel and direct mail. This is the sort of retail politics that should be reserved for vote-getting, not fund raising. The answer to this problem is quite simple: raise the limits on gifts and matching gifts up to, say, $5,000. There is, in fact, little reason (other than the vestigial anxieties about Richard Nixon's extortionate fund-raising techniques) why there should be *any* limit on gifts by individuals to the candidates. What is important is that every gift be reported to the public. Thus, if one man wanted to give one candidate $5 million, there would be no prohibition other than full disclosure. It would remain for the public to decide whether the candidate is a kept person, unduly beholden to that financial angel.

Full federal funding should be retained in the general election, if for no other reason than to relieve the candidates of the burden of hustling money when they should be explaining what they think about SALT or school aid. The total of funds given, however, is much too low in this inflationary age. More money should be given, but not necessarily to the candidate's personal campaign organization. Rather, the political parties should be given federal funds to help their nominees, preferably by spending money at the state and local levels. This would further restore the power of the national party. Republicans would argue that federal grants to the parties would spoil the advantage they have established by a superb fund-raising effort of their own. But federal grants to the parties would only supplement, not replace, their own private fund raising.

All this, and more, needs to be done to alter and improve our presidential selection system. But none of the changes suggested here would likely have changed the outcome in the 1980 campaign. The present system is not so flawed as to prevent the success or to insure the failure of our president. The selection and election of the president is only the first step. It only presents the opportunity to govern well. No system can adequately judge what a man like Ronald Reagan will bring to his presidency. There is no way to predict how the man and his times will fit together. We cannot know, *a priori,* whether a president can shape the period in which he governs or whether he will be crushed and destroyed by history. In 1980 the American people gave their presidency to Ronald Reagan. As always, it was a risky act of faith and hope. Now, he will do with it what he can.

Index

INDEX

INDEX

Matthews, Tom, 166
Meese, Edwin, 186, 251
Michigan primary, 156-57
Middle East conflict, 225
　Connally's policy for, 56, 60-61, 62, 63
Miller, Robert, 105
Miller, Warren, 18
Mondale, Walter F. (Fritz), 10, 19, 199, 208, 210, 230, 249, 252
　campaigning of, 103-4
　as political protégé, 103
Morrow, Lance, 40
Mosbacher, Robert, 93
Moynihan, Daniel Patrick, 23, 202-3
Mudd, Roger, Kennedy interviewed by, 81-85
Muskie, Edmund, 31, 52, 79, 152, 199

Nashua *Telegraph*, 120
Neoconservatives, 23
New Deal, 252
New Hampshire primary, 90, 112-23
　class resentment and, 116-18
　Democratic campaigns in, 129, 130-31, 135-36
　outcome of, 121-23, 135-36
　Republican campaigns in, 112-23, 143-44
　Republican debates before, 119-21
New Jersey primary, 138, 140-42
New York primary, 136-37, 138
1960s:
　American myths destroyed in, 21-22
　values and attitudes changed in, 23-24
1970s:
　as decade of crises, 21, 22, 24
　societal revolution in, 22-23
Nixon, Richard, 16, 49, 54, 62
　Carter compared with, 11, 12-13, 14
　in presidential elections, 31, 50, 180
Nofziger, Lyn, 121-22, 251
Nuclear energy, 57, 113

Ohio primary, 138, 139-40, 142
Oliphant, Tom, 135
O'Neill, Thomas P. ("Tip"), 207

Panama Canal treaties, 111, 225
Parker, Carey, 197
Party system:
　diminished power of, 29-30, 259-60
　need for strengthening of, 263-64
Pennsylvania primary, 138, 153-56
Percy, Charles, 185
Phillips, Howard, 184
Plante, Bill, 235
Powell, Jody, 137, 228-29, 246
Presidential selection system, 256-67
　celebrity as necessity in, 261-62, 263
　direct vs. representational democracy in, 259-60, 263-65

disorderliness of, 257-58
federal funding of, 266-67
information about candidates and issues in, 260-63
interminable length of, 265-66
openness of, 29-31
revolving-door phenomenon and, 258-59
television as key to, 256-57
　See also Conventions; Primary system
Pressler, Larry, 65-68, 262
　candidacy declared by, 65-66
Primary system, 51, 263
　Baker's views on, 144-47
　conventions reduced to mere formalities by, 177-78
　proposal for reform of, 264-65
　See also specific primaries
Public Opinion, 17-18

Qaddafi, Muammar el-, 199

Rafshoon, Gerald, 78, 138
Range, Peter Ross, 134
Ray, Robert, 106
Reagan, Nancy Davis, 47-48, 122, 157, 185, 238, 248
　press relations of, 155-56
Reagan, Ronald W., 20, 45-52, 57, 62, 64, 76, 90, 95, 111, 152, 181, 222, 231-39, 258-59, 261, 267
　acceptance speech of, at Republican convention, 192-95, 207
　age and vitality of, 114, 116, 153
　analysis of victory of, 249-53
　Anderson's independent candidacy and, 166-69, 174
　anti-Soviet stance of, 49
　assumptions underlying candidacy of, 21, 24, 235
　attempted assassination of, 3-4, 183
　big government attacked by, 48-49, 52, 154, 155, 202, 235, 236
　candidacy declared by (1980), 50-51
　Carter attacked by, 232, 233-34, 238
　Carter's attacks on, 225-26, 228-30
　class resentment issue and, 116-18
　conflict within staff of, 121-23
　economic program of, 154-55, 210, 232, 236, 253, 254-55
　energy policy of, 183-84, 210
　enthusiastic supporters lacked by, 215-18, 238-39
　ethnic joke told by, 119
　full-time campaign undertaken by, 115-16
　as governor of California, 37, 232
　image generated by, 45-46, 47-48, 94, 116, 244
　irresponsibility ascribed to, 143, 210, 216, 225-26, 229, 244

273